Comparative Political Finance
Among the Democracies

Comparative Political Finance Among the Democracies

EDITED BY

Herbert E. Alexander
and Rei Shiratori

Westview Press

BOULDER • SAN FRANCISCO • OXFORD

Dedicated to the memory of Jacek Tarkowski,
a respected and beloved student of political corruption,
and a dedicated member of the Research Committee
on Political Finance and Political Corruption

Copyright © 1994 by Westview Press, Inc.

Published in 1994 in the United States of America by Westview Press, Inc., 5500 Central Avenue, Boulder, Colorado 80301-2877, and in the United Kingdom by Westview Press, 36 Lonsdale Road, Summertown, Oxford OX2 7EW

Library of Congress Cataloging-in-Publication Data
Alexander, Herbert E.
  Comparative political finance among the democracies / edited by
Herbert E. Alexander and Rei Shiratori
    p. cm.
  Includes bibliographical references and index.
  ISBN 0-8133-8852-X
  1. Campaign funds—Cross-cultural studies. 2. Political parties—
Cross-cultural studies. I. Shiratori, Rei, 1937– . II. Title.
JF2112.C28A44 1994
324.7'8—dc20   94-29257
                                                                        CIP

Printed and bound in the United States of America

The paper used in this publication meets the requirements
of the American National Standard for Permanence of Paper
for Printed Library Materials Z39.48-1984.

10   9   8   7   6   5   4   3   2   1

Contents

Preface and Acknowledgments

This book is the second in a comparative politics series initiated by the Citizens' Research Foundation on behalf of the Research Committee on Political Finance and Political Corruption, an affiliate of the International Political Science Association. This collection of articles on aspects of the financing of politics and regulatory systems in thirteen countries took root at a conference organized by Rei Shiratori and held in Tokyo, Japan in September, 1989. The Tokyo Roundtable, entitled "Theories and Practices of Political Finance and Election Administration," was jointly sponsored by the Institute for Political Studies in Japan and the Research Committee. The book includes updated chapters selected from among the Tokyo conference papers; chapters on Brazil, France, Korea, and Germany were added subsequently, as were the introductory chapter by Herbert E. Alexander and Rei Shiratori, and the chapter on Canada and the United States by Karl-Heinz Nassmacher.

In recent years, there has been an increase in the number of scandals related to political financing, even leading to governmental crises in countries such as Italy and Japan. Governments have sought to respond by enacting new laws to regulate or to alter their national systems of political finance. Among the reforms are laws governing disclosure or transparency, expenditure and contribution limitations, as well as direct and indirect forms of public subsidies to political parties, candidates, and related organizations, such as party foundations; some of these topics were the subject of recommendations made in a Tokyo Declaration proposed at the Tokyo Roundtable, as noted in the introductory chapter.

This collection of essays not only consists of case studies of various countries, but presents several country-by-country comparisons and a conceptual framework that enables the reader to understand the context and implications of funding sources, campaign expenditures, and regulatory systems. Among the specific themes discussed are: the effects of public money on political systems, the roles of public funding in comparative perspective, the relative merits of direct and indirect public funding, the effects of national election regulation on encouraging or discouraging public participation, partisan alignments on the issue of public financing, campaign costs, the unanticipated consequences of legislative responses to campaign funding abuses and calls for political finance reform, the ambiguous interrelationships of local and national political financing, and the relationships of viable and stable (or lack thereof) political systems to political financing and public funding.

While political finance in its widest application is its prevailing theme, this book emphasizes the particular roles of forms of public assistance as an underlying issue. Of the thirteen countries studied, the roles of each nation's system of public assistance is dealt with by the analysts. The book embraces countries with presidential as well as parliamentary systems, and with both strong and weak party systems. Particularly important in this regard are the chapters dealing with the Asian countries of Japan, India, and Korea, where the questions of political financing as well as public assistance have heretofore been only rudimentarily examined.

Scholarship regarding political finance and election reform in individual countries, and on a comparative basis, has been nurtured by the Research Committee, chaired by Herbert E. Alexander.

As recently as thirty years ago, only a handful of scholars had turned their attention to the study of political funding, of how election campaigns were financed and what the influence of money meant. The activities of these few academics stirred scholarly awareness, but often it was events and actions outside academic halls that brought the matter into public view, as suggested in the introductory chapter.

In recent years, popular interest in political finance has grown exponentially among academics, legislators, the media, and the general public. A sizable number of political scientists now turn their attention to the role of money in politics; organizations have been established to monitor, from various perspectives, the questions of political financing; newsletters have developed, devoted entirely to the subject; and the regulation of political money is now among the most important items on the legislative agenda in many countries.

The interrelations of money and politics have gained attention, not only in the popular sphere, but within the academic community as well. This book highlights sophisticated analytical and expository treatment of the subject among scholars. As a collection of essays by pre-eminent political scientists in the United States, the United Kingdom, Europe, and Asia, it is an in-depth exploration of political finances in and among mature and developing democracies of the world. In addition, the essays in this book project the problems of political financing into the twenty-first century.

The literature on comparative political finance is relatively thin. There are currently a limited number of comparative political finance volumes published in the English language: *Comparative Political Finance: A Sym-*

posium, edited by Richard Rose and Arnold J. Heidenheimer as a special issue of the *Journal of Politics* (Gainsville, Florida: University of Florida, 1963); Arnold J. Heidenheimer, (ed.), *Comparative Political Finance: The Financing of Party Organizations and Election Campaigns* (Lexington, Massachusetts: D. C. Heath and Company, 1970); Herbert E. Alexander (ed.), *Comparative Political Finance in the 1980s* (Cambridge: Cambridge University Press, 1989); Matti Wiberg (ed.), *The Public Purse and Political Parties: Public Financing of Political Parties in Nordic Countries* (Jyvaskyla, Finland: The Finnish Political Science Association, 1991); and Arthur B. Gunlicks (ed.), *Campaign and Party Finance in North America and Western Europe* (Boulder, Colorado: Westview Press, 1992). The Congressional Research Service of the Library of Congress, Law Library, has published a series of country-by-country analyses, the latest being *Campaign Financing of National Elections in Foreign Countries* (Washington, D.C.: Library of Congress, 1991); various publications of the Canadian Royal Commission on Electoral Reform and Party Financing have articles with references to other countries, see especially F. Leslie Seidle, *Comparative Issues in Party and Election Finance*, Vol. 4 of the Research Studies (Toronto: Dundurn Press, 1991); a compendium of brief overviews of regulatory patterns in twenty countries is contained in *The World of Campaign Finance: A Reader's Guide to the Funding of International Elections*, published by the Center for a Democracy and the Center for Responsive Politics (Washington, D.C.: 1993). The present volume seeks to address political finance matters in certain countries included in the above-mentioned books, but adding a dimension by including chapters on Brazil, India, Japan, and South Korea.

The Introduction requires special acknowledgement to Kassem Nabulsi, research assistant at the Citizens' Research Foundation and a graduate student in the Department of Political Science at the University of Southern California. Kassem contributed greatly to the research and organization of the chapter, making an invaluable contribution to its entirety.

Gloria Cornette, CRF's assistant director, coordinated the copying of text onto computer files, transferred the text to new computer programs to provide camera-ready copy for the publisher, and provided technical expertise and moral support at every stage of the manuscript's development. For all who worked on the project, Gloria's encouragement has been especially appreciated.

Isabelle Gros, a graduate student in the French Department at USC, helped with the translation of the Avril chapter. Yaffa Draznin provided editorial assistance on the first draft; and Tiffany Rousculp, a graduate student in the English Department at USC, did the final editing of the volume.

In Tokyo, Izumi Ogata, secretary of the Institute for Political Studies in Japan (IPSJ), provided the secretarial work, both in editing manuscripts and in organizing the Tokyo Roundtable.

None of those who were so helpful is responsible for errors of omission or commission; for those, as for the interpretations, the editors bear sole responsibility.

This volume could not have been completed without the financial assistance and encouragement of the Board of Trustees of the Citizens' Research Foundation and the Institute for Political Studies in Japan.

Herbert E. Alexander
Rei Shiratori

About the Contributors

Herbert E. Alexander is professor of political science at the University of Southern California and director of the Citizens' Research Foundation. In 1961-1962, he was executive director of the President's Commission on Campaign Costs and has been a consultant to various levels of government in the United States. He has written extensively on American and comparative political finance and election reform.

Roberto Oliveira de Aguiar is associate professor of sociology at Federal University of Pernambuco, Brazil. He is the author of *Recife's Front and Populism in Pernambuco, Brazil* and *Political Ideologies in Pernambuco, Brazil*, and of "Electoral Costs in Brazil," published in *Cadernos de Estudos Socias*.

Pierre Avril is professor of public law and political science at Universite' Pantheon-Assas, Paris. He is the author of *Essais sur les Partis Politiques*.

Ernest Chaples is senior lecturer in government at the University of Sydney. He is co-author of *The Wran Model, Case Studies in New South Wales Electoral Politics*, and a wide variety of articles concerning Australian, American and Scandinavian politics. He is a regular commentator on Australian network radio.

Pilar del Castillo is associate professor of political science at Universidad Nacional de Educacion a Distancia in Madrid. She is the author of *La Financiación de Partidos y Candidatos en las Democracies Occidentales*, as well as several articles on Spanish political party finance and voting behavior.

Gullan Gidlund is professor of political science at Umea University in Sweden. She has written on political finance in Sweden and in the Nordic states.

Randhir B. Jain is professor of political science at University of Delhi. He has been a visiting professor at several universities in the United States, Canada and Europe. He is the author of a score of books in the field of comparative politics and public administration and has contributed articles on electoral administration and electoral reform in academic journals in India and abroad.

Ruth S. Jones is professor of political science at Arizona State University. She has written and consulted extensively on general issues of state-level political campaign finance reform with particular emphasis on state-level public funding programs.

Ruud A. Koole is associate professsor of political science at Leiden University (The Netherlands). He has published various articles on party organization and party finance. He was the secretary of the Royal Commission on State Subvention to Political Parties, which made its report in 1992.

Christine Landfried is professor of comparative government at Hamburg University. She has written *Bundesverfassungsgericht und Gesetzheber, Parteifinanzen und politische Macht*, second edition; and *Constitutional Review and Legislation* (ed).

Karl-Heinz Nassmacher is professor of political science at the Institute of Comparative Politics (ICP) at the Carl-von-Ossietzky University in Oldenburg, Germany. He has published books on Austria, the European Community, German local government, political parties and campaign finance. Based on field research in Austria, Canada, Italy, Sweden and the United States, he has authored several articles on comparative political finance.

Chan Wook Park is associate professor of political science at Seoul National University. He has published numerous articles in Korean and American journals on Korean elections, political parties and the national legislature.

Michael Pinto-Duschinsky is senior lecturer in government at Brunel University. He is the author (with David Butler) of *The British General Election of 1970* and of *British Political Finance: 1830-1980*. He contributed to *Britain at the Polls, 1974*, and *Britain at the Polls, 1979*.

Rei Shiratori is professor of political science at Tokai University and chairman of the board of the Institute for Political Studies in Japan. He was professor and director of the Japan Center at University of Essex, United Kingdom, 1984-1989, and a fellow of Woodrow Wilson International Center at Smithsonian Institution in Washington, D.C., 1979-1980.

Introduction

Herbert E. Alexander and
Rei Shiratori

Although democracies ideally provide their citizens with free, fair, periodic, and competitive elections, they must do so while tempering the effects of economic inequalities which enable wealthy persons to translate their economic power into political power. Economic resources are brought to bear upon the political process in many ways, one of which is monetary contributions. In virtually all democratic societies, political donations serve as a significant medium through which command over both energies and resources can be achieved. Money enables individuals as well as groups to develop means of influence and power, competing within the arena of existing political structures, institutions, and processes established by the community for its governance.

The Role of Money

Money's distinguishing characteristic is its ability to be transferred without revealing its original source. In this sense, the importance of money lies in the ways it is used to gain influence by converting it into other resources, or by using it in combination with other resources, to achieve political power. In politics, the convertibility of money is of special advantage; money can buy goods, skills, and services that may not, or cannot, be volunteered. Other resources in turn can be converted into political money, an option which is implicit, for example, in an incumbent's use of public office to award contracts and jobs, control the flow of information, and make appropriate decisions.

Thus, efforts to reconcile the conflict between real inequalities in economic resources and idealized equalities in political resources—and to prevent undue influences generated by monetary donations—become embodied in the goals which election reforms are designed to achieve.

By their nature, electoral reforms are not neutral. They are designed to minimize economic inequalities by restricting the use of resources for political purposes and to maximize political equalities by expanding resources to increase electoral competition. In addition, election laws are used as instruments to achieve certain political goals, influence, power, and control of policy and its implementation. As such, these laws tend to give the "party-in-power" the most advantages; the "party-in-opposition" may accept the changes hoping that when it is in power it will reap the same benefits. In democracies with multiparty systems, parties form coalitions and forge alliances in anticipation of, and as a response to, election law changes.

In every election, the candidates, the electoral process, and the political system are faced with two major issues of concern. The first is rising election costs which trigger the candidates' and the parties' ever-increasing desire to acquire the money to meet these costs. The second concern, which is a corollary of the first, is corruption or the perception thereof. A mixture of "needy candidates/needy parties" and "greedy contributors" may lead the latter to put pressure on the former, possibly creating undue influence. This, in turn, undermines the legitimacy of the political system, the fairness of the electoral process, and the participation of the electorate.

These two concerns are often considered a sufficient reason for a legislature to attempt to reform, regulate, and monitor the flow of money in elections. Not every political culture, however, is a fertile ground for the implementation of election reforms. In addition, there is always the chance that reforms may produce unintended or unforeseen consequences for which no foolproof safeguards can be found.

Notwithstanding these difficulties, attempts to minimize the influence of economic power and prevent electoral corruption are worth trying. To make reforms in accord with its national history and culture, compatible with its government structure (parliamentary, presidential, or a mixture of both), and relevant to its other natio-centric variables, (party-oriented or candidate-centered politics), each country may inject various modifications to legal frameworks of regulations and methods of implementation.

In countries where election reforms achieve their intended goals, reforms should be regarded not as an ultimate end, but as a step in a process. Nor should election reforms be deemed a panacea for all of a democracy's shortcomings, but rather an attempt to limit the number and minimize the effects of these shortcomings.

Although the intended forms of regulation depend on the proposed goals of reform, public financing has been a favorite "practical" political reform in many democracies. Public funding has been an instrument through which legislatures have attempted to minimize opportunities for undue influence on officeholders by private contributors. Public money provides alternatives to special interest money and also enables candidates to present themselves and their ideas to the electorate.

Despite its widespread practice in one form or another, public financing has not been as effective at curbing influence-peddling and corruption as its advocates claim. Nor has public funding necessarily been a recipe for effective governing. In fact, Italy's political impasse and its institutionalized corruption have moved the Italian electorate to vote for the abolishment of public subsidies for political parties.

Scandal and Reform

To be sure, incredibly large monetary contributions and flagrant briberies have permeated the world of politics in most continents: Japan and South Korea in Asia; Brazil in South America; Mexico and the United States in North America; and Italy, Germany, and Spain in Europe. Whatever their stage of democratization (developing or developed), their form of government (parliamentary or presidential), or their level of public funding (partial or substantial), these countries have witnessed the proliferation of scandals stemming from monetary contributions to gain political favors. The size, scope, and intensity of corruption differ from country to country, with Italy's political system being affected the most and Spain's the least.

Italy. Since 1974, Italy has provided its political parties with public subsidies to defray the costs they bear during elections—regional elections, elections to the Chamber of Deputies, elections to the Senate and to the European Parliament. Public funding also consisted of state contributions to cover the costs of the parties' "routine work and activities."[1] On April 19, 1993, however, the Italian electorate voted overwhelmingly (90 percent) in a referendum to end public financing of political parties. The Italian political system appears unable to respond effectively because it has been embroiled in "the largest public-corruption scandal in modern European history,"[2] a scandal that prompted the voters' reaction.

The investigation into kickbacks to political parties in return for public-works contracts has revealed widespread corruption. The inquiry, called "Operation Clean Hands," has claimed the lives of seven high ranking officials, including a former minister who committed suicide after being formally notified that they were under investigation for violating laws on party financing.[3] So far, 1,500 politicians—including two former prime ministers—and businessmen have been imprisoned or interrogated, and six Government ministers and four heads of major political parties have resigned their posts.[4] The money value of projects involved in kick-backs and bribes has been estimated to be some $193 billion.[5] The cost to the taxpayers in the last decade is estimated at $20 billion, the amount by which state contracts were inflated to cover bribes.[6] In a move to protect Italy, its President, Oscar Luigi Scalfaro, said the scandals threatened the state.[7]

Italy's scandals epitomize the abuse of money in politics. However, the convertibility of money into political power and the close relation-ships between the business community and the political establishment is not a phenomenon unique to Italy's political system.

Japan. Japan has been embroiled in political scandals involving influ-ence-peddling and briberies for the last two decades. Ever since the dis-closures of improper payoffs to members of Parliament (Diet) forced Prime Minister Noboru Takeshita to resign in 1989, a string of Cabinet ministers and other top politicians, both in and out of government, have been im-plicated in cases of unreported contributions.[8] Some have been indicted, particularly Shin Kanemaru, who has been "credited for the appointment of three of the last four prime ministers."[9]

Although Kanemaru was charged with evading millions of dollars in taxes, his arrest was accompanied by the discovery of hundreds of pounds of gold bars and roughly $50 million in cash hidden in his home and offices.[10] Investigators also discovered a safe filled with approximately $34 million in cash in Kanemaru's son's house.[11] These staggering amounts of money stunned even those accustomed to corruption, and also "de-stroyed the credibility of longstanding claims by political leaders that large amounts of money are needed to conduct political activities."[12] For a two-year election cycle, the average member of Japan's Diet raises and spends more than four times (about $2 million) as much as an average United States House member reports spending, even though the former has roughly half as many constituents and does not use television adver-tising.[13]

Because the government of Kiichi Miyazawa was unable to pass a re-form bill to restore public faith in government, on June 18, 1993, the Japa-nese Parliament passed a vote of no confidence in Miyazawa's Govern-ment. Consequently, Prime Minister Miyazawa dissolved the government and called for elections that were held in July 1993.[14] Within months, the new Premier, Morihior Hosokawa, was reported to be making progress toward election reform.[15]

Brazil. Although corruption has been a fixture of Latin American gov-ernance since colonial times,[16] Brazil's corruption scandal is a traumatic, ironic, and yet positive political experience. It is traumatic because it led to the resignation of its first democratically elected president in three decades. Also, as a candidate, Fernando Collor de Mello, ran and won on a platform of clean government, but ironically, was forced to resign after the lower house of Congress had impeached him and the Senate had begun trial proceedings on corruption charges. Nonetheless, Brazil's experience could be positive because it may portend a new beginning for Latin America's "new democracies:"[17] "never before had the same political and legal system that brought a president to power turned around and judged him for such offenses and forced him to resign."[18]

Congressional investigators claimed that computer files maintained by Paulo Cesar Farias, the President's friend and former campaign treasurer, revealed that President Collor ran an influence-peddling ring in which businesses winning state contracts had to pay kickbacks of up to 40 percent on multi-million-dollar deals.[19] Collor was charged with receiving $8 million in bribes solicited by his family and friends in return for political favors; the influence-peddling ring netted more than $55 million.[20] It was disclosed that $2.5 million in proceeds from the scheme had been spent on building the President an elaborate garden with waterfalls, a swimming pool, and a lagoon.[21] Investigators also have established that Farias managed to net $32 million out of the pockets of taxpayers and businesses, some 10 to 30 percent of the total cash flow.[22] Long after Collor's resignation, Farias testified before Brazil's Supreme Court that the $8 million he had deposited in various bank accounts for the personal expenses of Collor's family were part of $28 million left over from $100 million collected to finance campaigns of Collor's allies.[23]

Mexico. Although the Institutional Revolutionary Party (*PRI*) has been governing Mexico for the last 65 years, winning a 1992 governor's contest in Michoacan cost 120 billion pesos (U.S. $38.4 million). At that rate, the next national presidential election would cost 2.58 trillion pesos (more than $900 million), according to Mexico city's *El Financiero Internacional*.[24]

Although for decades Mexico's opposition parties have accused the government of financing the PRI and rigging elections in its favor,[25] political contributions remained effectively unregulated and reforms were not contemplated seriously. Opposition protest and public outcry grew louder after the disclosure that President Carlos Salinas de Gortari presided over a private dinner on February 23, 1993, at which nearly 30 of the country's most powerful business people were asked to donate $25 million each to the PRI.[26] Critics charged that most of the guests solicited by President Salinas profited from the purchase of state companies or received special consideration from government negotiators of the North American Free Trade Agreement (NAFTA).[27]

Government officials confirmed Salinas' action. However, they explained it as an effort to break the governing party's historic dependence on state resources by establishing a party endowment fund.[28] Seeking to dispel domestic criticism and attempting to gain the ratification of NAFTA by the United States Congress, President Salinas proposed a series of political changes, including limits on campaign spending, requirements that parties disclose the source of their funds, and measures to provide the opposition with more equal access to the news media.[29]

United States. The United States has strict federal election laws. However, contributions of hard and soft money[30] demonstrate that the reality of political finance may not always conform to the intended goals of those laws. A case in point is the $1.3 million in political contributions made by the Lincoln Saving & Loan's president, Charles H. Keating, Jr., and his family and associates.[31] Under government pressure to close Lincoln, Keating made numerous political contributions to five U.S. or to soft money recipients they designated.

The senators, dubbed the "Keating Five," received direct contributions of $324,000: Alan Cranston (D) received $47,000; Dennis DeConcini (D), $55,000; John Glenn (D), $34,000; John McCain (R), $112,000; and Donald Riegle (D) received $76,000.[32] In addition, soft money contributions were made to committees working on voter registration and turnout; some of these tax-exempt committees were related to the five senators.

The five senators were accused of having engaged in an extraordinary effort to help Keating fend off regulators. Although the senators claimed that they were performing constituency service and denied doing favors for Keating because of his political donations, there can be little doubt that Keating made those contributions in order to gain political favors. In a news conference, Keating articulated his position as follows: "One question, among many, has had to do with whether my financial support in any way influenced several political figures to take up my cause. I want to say in the most forceful way I can: I certainly hope so."[33]

South Korea. In South Korea, the founder of the Hyundai industrial group and formal presidential candidate, Chung Ju Yung, was charged with election fraud, embezzlement, and campaign funding violations. Chung was accused of ordering Hyundai executives to embezzle about $60 million from the company and illegally funnel the money to the party to underwrite his 1992 presidential bid.[34] He denied the accusation, claiming that the fund was created with the proceeds of stock he had sold.[35]

In 1992, Chung, his company and his family were forced to pay almost $181 million in back taxes and fines. His son was arrested, as were two of his closest aides. However, Chung tried to implicate other politicians in the scandal, claiming that he could prove that the last three South Korean presidents were secretly taking money from Hyundai industrial group. His proof was that he had personally paid some of it.[36] He was sentenced to three years in prison.[37]

West Germany. The 1987 conviction of two former West German Economics Ministers, and the former deputy chairman of the Flick holding company, on income tax evasion had ended a wide-ranging political pay-off scandal which came under investigation in 1981.[38] The investigation provided a glimpse into a vast network of illegal corporate payments to the three major parties, often through tax-free "donations" to dummy charities. Although the defendants were acquitted of the principal charges of bribery and influence-peddling, the scandal eroded popular trust in West Germany's three established parties and contributed to the rise of the Green Party.[39]

In 1985, the three major German political parties supported the enactment of a law that made corporate donations to political parties tax deductible; the small Green Party opposed the legislation at the time.[40] In 1986, in an eight-to-six vote, the Federal Constitutional Court of West Germany declared such a law unconstitutional. At the time, contributions by individuals were tax deductible up to the equivalent of $545, while corporate donations were limited to two-tenths of 1 percent of a company's total sales and salaries.[41]

Spain. Although on a much smaller scale than any of the countries discussed, Spain has witnessed the eruption of a scandal that might engulf some high ranking politicians. The scandal, which surfaced in 1991, involves charges of illegal funding to the ruling Socialist party in the late 1980s. The revelations led to the resignation of the former Socialist finance chief, who stated that he alone was responsible for party funds and that he was confident he had not committed any illegal act.[42]

The Tokyo Roundtable

Most of the corruption scandals discussed here have occurred, have increased in scope, or have been disclosed, only after the Tokyo Roundtable conference on "Theories and Practices of Political Finance and Election Administration" took place in 1989. The discussion was held under the auspices of the International Political Science Association's Research Committee on Political Finance and Political Corruption and the Institute for Political Studies in Japan (IPSJ).

Information about the size and intensity of most of these scandals was not available to the participants;[43] thus, they were not so alarmed. Despite the absence of such information, the participants held a detailed and comparative discussion of legal and institutional regulations concerning political finance, electoral systems, and electoral administration. All present agreed on the need for fair and democratic election procedures to maximize the participation of the voters. In that spirit, they adopted the "Tokyo Declaration on Elections and Election Administration in Democratic Countries," although not all of the participants agreed with each of the following recommendations.

Electoral Systems:
1. In general, the principle of "one person, one vote, one value" should be paramount as a basis of fair representation, though the details of electoral systems may be varied.
2. Fair representation also means setting the boundaries of electoral districts in an impartial way. In order to achieve this, organizations free from partisan pressures are recommended.
3. In general, the voting age should be lowered in accordance with the advancement of education. Normally, the vote should be given from the age of 18.

Electoral Administration:
1. Every government should realize that effective electoral administration is basic to democracy. They should, therefore, assign sufficient staff to administer elections efficiently.
2. Government should take an active responsibility to ensure that the rolls of electors entitled to vote are accurate and up-to-date.
3. It is undesirable to make a long period of residence at one address a condition of being placed on the electoral roll.
4. In general, citizens living abroad should have the right and should be able to vote at least in national elections in their home countries.
5. Foreigners residing permanently in a country should have the right to vote in local elections.
6. In general, the publication of public opinion polls should not be restricted, but polling organizations should be obliged to release relevant technical information, such as the size and methods of sampling used and the specific wording of questions asked.

Legal and Institutional Regulations of Political Funding:
1. There were various opinions about whether financial aid should be given out of public funds for election campaigning and/or for party

organization. However, most scholars favored the provision of free advertising time for parties and candidates on television and radio.

2. The names of large scale political donors to parties and candidates should normally be open to public inspection.

3. Small scale political contributions by individual citizens should be encouraged. Political contributing should be considered a positive act of political participation.

4. Financial reports of the parties, candidates, and public office holders should be made on a regular and periodic basis, and should be submitted to public inspection and audit.

5. There should be separation of political activities of the candidates and public office holders which are financed by political funds and their private lives which should be financed by their private funds.[44]

The "Tokyo Declaration" represents a framework within which the participant scholars provided individual assessments and analyses of political finance problems for particular countries and expressed collective agreement on some recommendations to remedy the problem. The Declaration can serve as a point of departure for further research by those interested in understanding the nature and the role of money in politics. Its proposed recommendations serve as a reference point for those interested in achieving a more level playing field in the democratic process in general and the electoral process in particular.

It is interesting to note that some recent campaign reform proposals, especially those advocating full disclosure and free access to the media, advanced and endorsed by political parties and public officials of the different countries having scandals recounted above, resemble those recommendations articulated by the scholars of the Tokyo Declaration.

Notes

1. Gian Franco Ciaurro, "Public Financing of Parties in Italy," in Herbert E. Alexander, ed. *Comparative Political Finance in the 1980s,* (Cambridge: Cambridge University Press, 1989), pp. 153-171.

2. John Moody, "Sick of It All," *Time*, March 8, 1993, p. 48.

3. William D. Montalbano, "Corruption Scandal Fells More High-Profile Italians," *Los Angeles Times*, February 26, 1993.

4. Alan Cowell, "An Italian Defense Official Arrested in Bribery Scandal," *The New York Times*, April 11, 1993.

5. George Armstrong, "Scandal-Plagued Italy May Be Worth Saving—But Not Its Politicians or Parties," *Los Angeles Times*, March 21, 1993.

6. Alan Cowell, "Broad Bribery Investigation Is Ensnaring the Elite of Italy," *The New York Times*, March 3, 1993.

7. Alan Cowell, "Italy's High Drama," *The New York Times*, November 5, 1993.

8. See Shiratori chapter in this book," Political Finance and Scandal in Japan," pp. 187-205.

9. Sam Jameson, "Japan Kingpin Gets Second Indictment," *Los Angeles Times*, March 28, 1993.

10. David Sanger, "$50 Million Discovered in Raids On Arrested Japanese Politician," *The New York Times*, March 10, 1993.

11. Teresa Watanabe, "$84 Million in Hidden Loot: Scandal Mounting in Tokyo," *Los Angeles Times*, March 10, 1993.

12. Sanger, "$50 Million Discovered in Raids on Arrested Japanese Politician."

13. T.R. Reid, "In Japan, Too, Money Is the Mother's Milk of Politics," *The Washington Post National Weekly Edition*, September 14-20, 1992.

14. David Sanger, "Japan's Government Falls; Party in Peril," *The New York Times International*, June 19, 1993.

15. James Sterngold, "Japan's Premier Wins a Key Test on Vote System," *The New York Times*, November 17, 1993.

16. Jorge G. Castaneda, "Is Latin Corruption Finally to Be Punished?," *Los Angeles Times*, September 16, 1992.

17. In the same article professor Castaneda asked if Venezuela's Carlos Andres Perez will survive a congressional investigation, "a congressional search-and-destroy mission like the one Collor fell victim to in Brazil?" The compelled resignation of President Perez in May 1993 not only answered professor Castaneda's question in the negative, but also may be considered as further evidence to the "new" way Latin America's democracies have chosen to deal with corruption.

18. Castaneda, "Is Latin Corruption Finally to Be Punished?"

19. Alexander Cockburn, "The Bankers' Brazilian Myth Turns to Ashes," *Los Angeles Times*, October 5, 1992.

20. Nathaniel C. Nash, "Brazilian Leader Quits as His Trial Starts in Senate," *The New York Times*, December 30, 1992.

21. James Brooke, "Looting Brazil," *The New York Times Magazine*, November 8, 1992, p. 31.

22. Ibid.

23. "Aide to Deposed Brazil Chief Admits Depositing Funds," *Los Angeles Times*, June 22, 1993.

24. *PACs & Lobbies*, August 19, 1992, p. 14.

25. Marjorie Miller, "Mexico's Ruling Party Sets Limit on Donations," *Los Angeles Times*, March 10, 1993.

26. Tim Golden, "Mexican Leader Asks Executives To Give Party $25 Million Each," *The New York Times*, March 9, 1993.

27. Ibid.

28. Ibid.

29. Ibid.

30. Soft money is raised and spent outside the restraints of federal law and is determined by state laws, many of which are less stringent than federal law.

31. Herbert E. Alexander and Monica Bauer, *Financing the 1988 Election* (Boulder: Westview Press, 1991), p. 79.

32. Ibid.

33. Ibid, quoted from Jack W. Germond and Jules Witcover, "Looking for a Smoking Gun on Campaign Funds," *National Journal*, Vol. 21, No. 48, December 2, 1989, p. 2956.

34. "Korean Industrialist Indicted in Fraud and Embezzlement," *The New York Times*, February 7, 1993.

35. Donald Kirk, "A Contest of Wills That May Sink an Economy," *Los Angeles Times*, February 7, 1993.

36. David Sanger, "A Korean Rich a la Croesus and Running a la Perot," *The New York Times*, October 29, 1992.

37. "Hyundai Founder Sentenced for Violating Election Laws," *The New York Times*, November 2, 1993.

38. James Markham, "Political Graft Trial Ends in Bonn With Three Notables Punished Lightly," *The New York Times*, February 17, 1987. For further reference to the Flick investigations, see in this volume, Christine Landfried's "Political Finance in West Germany, p. 8.

39. Ibid.

40. John Tagliabue, "Court in Bonn Bars Tax Break on Gifts to Political Parties," *The New York Times*, July 16, 1986.

41. Ibid.

42. "Spanish Socialist Out; Party Scandal Eased," *The New York Times*, April 11, 1993. For a catalogue of scandals in Spain, see Del Castillo chapter in this book, "Problems in Spanish Party Financing," pp. 97-104.

43. Seventeen scholars from twelve countries (Australia, Austria, France, India, Japan, Korea, Netherlands, Philippines, Singapore, Sweden, United Kingdom and United States) met in Tokyo from September 8-11, 1989.

44. *PF/PC Newsletter*, International Political Science Association Research Committee on Political Finance and Political Corruption, Vol. IX, No. 1, Winter 1990, pp. 2-3.

1

British Party Funding, 1983-1988

Michael Pinto-Duschinsky

Following its heavy defeat in the 1983 general election, the British Labor party, under the leadership of Neil Kinnock, mounted a strong challenge to the Conservative Central Office regarding organization and fund-raising. The major unions, despite loss of members, continued to increase their financial support to the Labor party. Conversely, the Conservatives faced financial problems until 1986, when the Conservative Central Office sharply improved its fund-raising performance and increased its seriously eroded lead over Labor's Head Office. In addition, the Alliance parties failed to build on their political success in the 1983 general election. The Alliance's financial failure before and during the 1987 general election was symptomatic of the internal political difficulties that were to lead to the divorce between the Liberal and the Social Democratic parties and to the decline of the new center parties that replaced them.

Conservative Party Finances

The years between 1978 and 1986 were a rocky period for Conservative party fund raising. The Central Office was admittedly successful in the 1983-1984 election year when it raised £9.4 million, which was more than sufficient to cover the national organization's routine costs and campaign spending. However, apart from that year, the Central Office was in almost constant deficit. From 1978-1986, Conservative Central spending was 12 percent greater than income,[1] while Labor's national income continued to catch up. The poor state of the Conservative finances contrasted with the party's strong electoral performance. Beginning in 1986, Conservative Central income improved considerably and the upward trend in donations continued after Thatcher's third election victory in June 1987.

In 1987, Conservative Central Office campaign spending, as described below, was the third highest in the party's history. It is, nevertheless, significant that estimated routine spending in 1983-1987 was, in real terms, nearly 10 percent lower than in the 1979-1983 cycle. The contraction in routine spending in 1983-1987 probably resulted from the party treasurer's policy at that time of concentrating resources on general election spending rather than on the maintenance of the headquarters between elections (See Table 1).[2] In the parliamentary cycle 1983-1987, spending in the 1987 campaign accounted for some 28 percent of total central spending (routine and campaign), compared with 15 percent in the previous cycle.

Statistics of Conservative spending in the 1987 general election supplied by the Conservative Central Office reveal that the party headquarters (including the area offices) spent a total of £9,028,000, in real terms nearly doubling the £3.8 million spent in the 1983 campaign.[3] The main

TABLE 1 Conservative Central Income and Expenditure 1982-1989 (£m)

| | | Income | | | | | Expenditure | |
	Donations	Constituency Quotas	Interest	Affiliation Fees	Total	Routine	General Election	Total
1982/3	3.7	1.0	.0	.0	4.8	4.6	0.1	4.7
1983/4*	8.2	1.1	0.1	.0	9.4	4.9	3.7	8.6
1984/5	3.0	1.0	.0	0.3	4.3	5.6	.0	5.6
1985/6	4.0	1.0	.0	0.05	5.0	5.5	.0	5.5
1986/7	7.6	1.2	.0	0.04	8.9	7.2	0.3	7.5
1987/8*	13.6	1.2	0.1	0.05	15.0	6.9	8.7	15.6
1988/9	6.7	1.2	.0	0.18	8.1	7.8	.0	7.8

*Denotes general election year. The statistics have been drawn up on the same basis as those in the author's *British Political Finance*, Table 28.[4] Interest received is net of tax and net of interest paid. Donations are net of fund-raising costs. Constituency income includes quota credits.[5] Inconsistencies in totals are due to rounding. Allocations of expenditure to routine and general election categories are the author's estimates.

Source: Conservative Central Office annual income and expenditure accounts and supplementary information.

items of spending were press advertising (£4,523,000) and leaflets and posters (£1,834,000). Other major spending categories were staff and administration costs, £818,000; party publications, £714,000; leader's tour and meetings, £417,000; production costs of party political broadcasts, £466,000; opinion research, £219,000; and grants to constituencies, £137,000. The figures may not be wholly comparable to those for 1983 since some expenditures during the run-up to the campaign, categorized in 1983 as routine, seem to have been included in 1987 as campaign items.

Central Conservative spending in the 1987 general election was the highest in real terms since 1964, amounting to £9.9 million at June 1987 values. Whereas, in 1964, a high proportion of expenditures was incurred during the two-year run-up to the campaign, most election spending in 1987 was concentrated into the month between the announcement of the election date and the poll. Indeed, the burst of spending by the Conservative Central Office on press advertising during the week before the vote probably constituted the heaviest short-term central campaign spending in British political history.

The Conservative Central Office, like the other central party organizations, does not issue a list of the corporate or individual donations it receives. Therefore, it is not possible to assess the proportion of the income listed as "donations," which came from companies, large gifts by individuals, and relatively small payments from individuals in response to direct mail appeals. Two general propositions can be made. First, direct mail fund-raising was still relatively undeveloped at the time of the general election of 1987. It was only at a late stage in the parliamentary cycle that the Central Office became active in this new method. The profits of direct mail seem to have accounted for no more than 5 percent of the party's central income in the election year 1987-1988, which was less than the proceeds of the Social Democratic Parties' efforts.

Second, corporate donations appear to have accounted for a considerably smaller proportion, and individual contributions for a greater proportion, of central income than before. In its fund-raising methods, the Central Office would seem to have been trying to exploit both the old-fashioned method of a personal approach to wealthy individuals and, to a much lesser extent, modern methods of direct mail.

Constituency payments of the central party organization made up a smaller proportion of Central Office income than in recent parliamentary cycles (barely 12 percent of total income in 1983-1987, compared with 17 percent in 1979-1983, and 20 percent in 1974-1979). During the 1980s, constituency quota payments were smaller in real terms than in the 1970s. This may reflect a decrease in the membership and activity of local Conservative parties during the 1980s.

In the 1983-1987 parliamentary cycle, routine Central Office income was marginally higher in real terms (11 percent) than in 1979-1983.[6] If overall routine and campaign income is included, the rise in real terms was 23 percent. Over the longer term, income in 1983-1987 was slightly higher (about 10 percent) than in parliamentary cycles between 1951 and 1964.

Labor Party Finances

Like the Conservatives, Labor increased its central income during 1983-1987. Routine income averaged £5.4 million (at June 1987 prices), 15 percent higher in real terms than in 1979-1983. Overall income (routine and campaign) was more than a fifth higher than in 1979-1983 and nearly 50 percent higher than in 1974-1979.

The improvement in Labor's Head Office finances resulted mainly from the increase in routine affiliation payments by trade unions. The affiliation payments rose from £2.9 million in 1984 to £4.2 million in 1987. Prior to this, these payments totaled £2.0 million in 1980, and £272,000 in 1969. Taking into account the rate of inflation, the value of these payments in 1987 was nearly two and a half times greater than in 1969.

The 1980s saw a significant improvement in affiliation payments to the Head Office by constituency Labor parties. Constituency payments to the Head Office reached £897,000 in 1987, compared with £570,000 in 1983, £378,000 in 1980, and a mere £143,000 in 1978.

In addition, Labor's direct mail fund-raising activities, established in 1984, constituted another useful s ource of income by 1987, though less was raised by this method than by the Conservatives or by the SDP. In 1987, direct mail fund-raising produced an income (net of costs) of £573,000 of which £252,000 was for the general election fund. (See Table 2).

Besides increasing its routine income and expenditure, Labor's Head Office spending in the 1987 general election was at a level only equaled in real terms, in 1964. According to the 1988 annual report of the National Executive Committee, Labor's Head Office campaign expenditures totaled £4,210,000. In addition, according to information supplied by the Home Office, Trade Unions for Labor (TUFL)[7] contributed £170,000 toward the costs of the leader's tour. If the separate funds of regional Labor parties are included, the total rises to about £4.7 million. The central Labor budget was two-thirds greater in real terms than in the 1983 elections.

The main items of Head Office campaign spending (according to revised information supplied by the Labor's Head Office) were: advertising, £2,114,000 (including national press advertisements, £1,356,000; regional press advertisements, £363,000; cinema advertisements, £86,000 and posters, £309,000); campaign rallies and leader's tour, £67,000 (net of the

TABLE 2 Labor Central Income and Expenditure 1982-1988 (£m)

	Income					Expenditure		
	Trade Union Affiliation Fees	Constituency Affiliation Fees	State Aid	Other	Total	Routine	General Election	Total
1982	2.8	0.6	0.3	0.3	3.9	4.0	--	4.0
1983*	3.0	0.6	0.3	2.4	6.2	4.1	2.1	6.1
1984	2.9	0.7	0.3	0.2	4.2	4.2	--	4.2
1985	3.5	0.7	0.4	0.2	4.9	4.8	--	4.8
1986	4.0	0.8	0.4	0.8	6.1	6.2	--	6.2
1987*	4.2	0.9	0.5	4.5	10.0	7.0	4.4	11.3
1988	4.1	1.0	1.0	0.5	6.7	6.7	--	6.7

* Denotes general election year. Totals include special funds as well as the general fund. Separately collected regional funds are not included. The total has been drawn up on the same basis as in the author's *British Political Finance*, Tables 16 and 38. State aid ("Short Money") is included. "Other" income in general election years consists largely of trade union contributions to the National Executive Committee's general election fund.

Source: Labor Party annual reports and supplementary information.

press conferences), £139,000; grants to constituency campaigns, £423,000; cost of literature (net of proceeds from sales), £263,000; opinion research, £168,000; and administration, organization, staff, and other costs, £890,000. The trade unions contributed 93 percent of the Labor's Head Office's general election income, while direct mail fund-raising produced a net profit of £252,000 (6 percent of the total raised). Although, in 1987, the Labor's Head Office general election income (£4.2 million) was much higher than in 1983, it fell short of campaign expenditures by £159,000. Similarly, routine Head Office spending rose faster than income from trade union and constituency affiliation fees. The deficit in the general (routine) fund totaled £497,000 in 1986 and the Head Office's overall deficit between 1984 and 1987 totaled £1.3 million.

Over the entire 1983-1987 parliamentary cycle, Conservative central spending (routine and campaign) was about 30 percent greater than Labor's. The Conservative margin over Labor was only 15 percent in terms of routine spending, but Conservatives spent twice as much as Labor in the election campaign.[8] Labor devoted 18 percent of its overall spending during 1983-1987 to the 1987 campaign, whereas the Conservatives spent 28 percent of their budget on the 1987 election.

TABLE 3 Liberal Party Organization Routine Income and Expenditures, 1982-1988(£)

	Income	Expenditure
1982	258,000	268,000
1983	383,000	385,000
1984	456,000	386,000
1985	486,000	449,000
1986	488,000	597,000
1987-88*	1,017,000	825,000

* Denotes general election years. General election spending is excluded. Separately collected regional funds are not included. By-election guarantee fund are not included. Statistics for 1987 are estimates. State aid is not included in this table but in the Liberal Central Association's accounts. Years 1987-88 including the period of January 1, 1987, to March 8, 1988, when the party was merged into the new SLD.

Source: Liberal Party Organization Annual Reports and supplementary information.

Liberal and Social Democratic Party Finances

The resounding political success of the Liberal-Social Democratic Alliance in the election of June 1983 was not matched by a similar fund-raising success in 1983-1987. The Alliance election budget in the 1983 campaign was, in real terms, six times greater than the total spent centrally by the Liberals in the 1979 election. In the period following the 1983 election, Liberal central funds advanced while those of the Social Democrats declined (though they were still larger than those of the Liberals). While the parties of the Alliance remained in a healthier financial position than the Liberals had been in the period before the formation of the Alliance in 1981, they were not able to take advantage of their notable electoral performance in 1983. The poor fund-raising by the Liberals and Social Democrats in the June 1987 election reflected the internal rivalries that eventually resulted, after the campaign, in the disintegration of the Alliance. (See Table 3).

Seemingly, the decentralized structure of the Liberal organization affected the party's financial structure. The Liberal Party Organization accounts shown in Table 3 do not correspond to those of the Conservative and Labor headquarters. They exclude campaign spending as well as spending by the Liberal Central Association (shown in Table 4), regional party organizations, and bodies such as the Association of Liberal Councillors. The main sources of Liberal Party Organization income in 1986 were listed as constituency affiliations, £210,000; donations and grants, £146,000; and assembly appeal receipts, £82,000.[9]

TABLE 4 Liberal Central Association Income and Expenditures, 1982-1986(£)

	Income			Expenditure
	State Aid	Other	Total	Total
1982	52,000	10,000	62,000	63,000
1983	57,000	8,000	65,000	69,000
1984	n/a	n/a	n/a	n/a
1985	89,000	3,000	92,000	89,000
1986	89,000	10,000	99,000	113,000

In 1987-1988, the Liberals in the House of Commons and, after the merger, the Social and Liberal Democrats received the following money: State Aid, 328,000, and Other Income, 24,000. Expenditures totaled 310,000.

Source: Reprinted from the author's "British Party Funding 1983-87" in *Parliamentary Affairs: A Journal of Comparative Politics*, Vol. 42, No. 2, April 1989, p. 203, citing Liberal Party Organization Annual Reports and supplementary information.

The Social Democratic Party's organizational centralization contrasted with the decentralization of the Liberals. When the SDP was formed in 1981, it was a London-based organization and central fund-raising was predominant. In its first year, the SDP raised the healthy total of £905,000, of which £760,000 came from individual membership subscriptions payable by credit card over the telephone. After this initial enthusiasm, SDP membership fell. In 1984-1985 and 1986-1987, income from subscriptions averaged £445,000. The £469,000 raised in membership subscriptions in 1986-1987 was less than half, in real terms, than the amount collected in 1981-1982, and large individual contributions came to play a more important role in SDP funding. In particular, David Sainsbury, a major shareholder in the family chain of supermarkets, was active as a participant in the party and reportedly was its largest contributor.

In the 1983-1987 cycle, the SDP's routine central expenditure was 64 percent greater than that of the Liberal Party Organization. However, in 1981 and 1982 it was 285 percent greater. Taking account of inflation, the combined central income of the Liberals and the SDP in 1984-1986 was less than two-thirds of the value of the parties' central incomes in 1981 and 1982. This fall was due to the decline in the level of SDP funds.

The task of assessing central Alliance spending in the 1987 campaign is complicated by the existence of several different funds. On the Liberal side there was an LPO fund and a separate leader's fund. There was an SDP fund run by the former Liberal MP John Pardoe and an Alliance Fund run by Lord Diamond. Also, additional monies were reportedly earmarked by individual contributors for special purposes, such as last-minute advertising and production costs of broadcasts, which may not have been

TABLE 5 Social Democratic Party Head Office Income and Expenditures, 1982/83-1987/88
(£)

| | Income | | | Expenditure | | |
	Members' Subscriptions	Other	Total	Routine	General Election	Total
1982/83	584,000	928,000	1,512,000	962,000	397,000	1,359,000
1983/84*	424,000	1,178,000	1,602,000	670,000	1,124,000	1,794,000
1984/85	381,000	398,000	779,000	669,000	--	669,000
1985/86	486,000	402,000	888,000	750,000	150,000	990,000
1986/87	469,000	522,000	991000	928,000	66,000	995,000
1987/88*	469,000	306,000	775,000	924,000	--	924,000

*Denotes election year. By-election year insurance fund is included. The party's share of state aid to opposition parties is excluded. The SDP's share of this aid was 25,000 in 1983, 45,000 in 1984, and 63,000 in 1985 and 1986. Statistics for 1987-88 exclude general election spending. 1987-1988 includes April 1, 1987 - December 31, 1988.

Source: Reprinted from the author's "British Party Funding 1983-87" in *Parliamentary Affairs: A Journal of Comparative Politics*, Vol. 42, No. 2, April 1989, p. 205, citing SDP Annual Reports.

included in any of the official accounts. This division of financial respon-sibilities for the election was a symptom of internal rivalries within and between the Liberals and the SDP. Consequently full accounts relating to all the funds were not prepared or published, a reflection of the problems caused by the breakup of the Alliance following the election.

The SDP spent £217,000 on preparations for the campaign. The party also spent an additional £1,074,000 during the election, totaling £1,291,000. The largest SDP campaign expenditure was £617,000 given in grants to parliamentary candidates. Other major categories were: opinion polling, £102,000; leader's tours, £72,000; and newspaper advertising, £33,000. The SDP's central campaign fund was raised through three direct mail ap-peals to party supporters. These raised about £122,000 net of fund-rais-ing costs of £700,000. Most of the remaining £300,000 came from larger individual donations, such as those from David Sainsbury.

The Liberal Party Organization's campaign budget amounted to ap-proximately £0.2 million. A separate Liberal account spent another £80,000, mostly on the expenses of the leader's tour and the "Battle Bus." Of this sum, £50,000 was raised in fees from journalists accompanying the tour and most of the remainder came from the Joseph Rowntree Social Service Trust Ltd.[10]

The Alliance fund spent about £250,000. It was responsible for orga-nizing the "Ask the Alliance" rallies, press conferences, and the produc-tion costs of party election broadcasts. Also included was an advertisement in the *Independent*. The main contributions to the Alliance fund were payments amounting to £105,000, from the Joseph Rowntree Social Service Trust Ltd. and Sainsbury Associates.

In combination, the different Alliance funds spent a total of about £1.75 million on the 1987 campaign, compared with £1.9 million spent in 1983. While the two established parties spent exceptionally heavily in 1987, Alliance expenditure was a quarter less, in real terms, in 1987 than in 1983.

1987 General Election

Election costs consist of three elements: (1) central spending, (2) local spending, and (3) the value of subsidies-in-kind, such as free postage for candidates, free use of halls for election meetings, and free broadcasting time. In the 1987 election, Conservative, Labor, and Alliance each received five slots of ten minutes on all television channels as well as facilities for free radio broadcasts. Escalating costs of television advertising greatly increased the value of this free broadcasting time. The value of each party's election and political broadcasts during the run-up to the campaign was an estimated £12.5 million.[11] As shown in Table 6, the subsidies-in-kind limited the financial advantage enjoyed by the Conservatives.

The value of the newspaper advertisements purchased by the Conservative Central Office at a cost of £4.5 million was, according to the above calculation, outweighed by the value of the free party election broadcasts which were equally available to all three main parties. As far as local campaign spending is concerned, 1987 went against the postwar trend in that average expenditure by candidates of all the main parties increased in real terms.

Parliamentary candidates were restricted in 1987 to a total campaign expenditure of £3,370 plus 3.8 pence per elector in county constituencies and £3,370 plus 2.9 pence per elector in boroughs, a limit of £5,000-£6,000 in most constituencies. Conservative candidates spent an average of 78 percent of the legal limit (compared with 72 percent in 1983), Labor candidates also spent 78 percent (63 percent in 1983), and Alliance candidates spent 61 percent.[12] In 1983, SDP candidates spent 62 percent of the permitted maximum and Liberal candidates 50 percent).

Trade Union Versus Company Donations

After 1983, two developments threatened to curtail trade union payments to the Labor Party: the Trade Union Act, 1984, and the continued

TABLE 6 Estimated Total Conservative, Labor and Alliance Expenditure in the General Election of 1987

	Conservative	Labor	Alliance
Central campaign expenditures (excluding grants to constituency campaigns from central party organizations)	8.9m	4.0m	1.0-1.2m
Local expenditure (including grants from central party organizations)	2.8m	2.5m	2.2m
Total (excluding subsidies-in-kind)	1.7m	6.5m	3.2-3.4m
Estimated value of subsidies-in-kind	13.2m	13.2m	13.2m
Total campaign costs (including subsidies-in-kind)	24.9m	19.7m	6.4-16.6m
Votes received	13.8m	10.0m	7.3m
Expenditure per vote (including subsidies-in-kind)	85p	65p	45-47p
Total cost per vote (including subsidies-in-kind)	180p	197p	225-227p

Sources: Information supplied by party headquarters and for local expenditure from Butler & Kavanagh, *The British General Election of 1987.*

fall in union membership. Neither of these threats materialized and, as has been mentioned, the level of union payments continued to increase during 1983-1987.

Part Three of the Trade Union Act, 1984, required all unions with political levy funds to ballot their members every ten years to secure approval for the continued existence of such funds. If a majority of those in the ballot voted against the maintenance of a political levy fund, a union would not be permitted to make payments for political purposes. The Act required every union which had not held a ballot within the previous ten years to do so by March 1986 if it wished to continue to make political payments. In order to protect their political levy funds, the 37 unions affiliated with the Trades Union Congress set up a Trade Union Coordinating Committee to organize the campaign to retain the political fund. The campaign among unionists made little mention of the fact that the bulk of money raised by the political levy was used mainly to support the Labor Party. Instead, it stressed that the defeat of the political levy fund would prevent the union from representing members' interests in Parliament.

The Trade Union Coordinating Committee spent nearly £200,000 and achieved a resounding success. Despite the fact that the Labor Party undoubtedly enjoyed a minority support in a number of unions, every single ballot resulted in a vote to maintain the political levy. The effect of the ballot was to underline the legitimacy of union political levies and to raise questions about the desirability of additional regulations concerning political payments by companies.[13]

Trade union membership fell sharply during the 1980s. The total membership of unions with political levy funds fell from 9.94 million at the end of 1979 to 8.06 million in 1983, and 7.29 million in 1986. Moreover, the numbers contributing to the political levy funds fell even faster (probably because unions have retained a higher proportion of retired or unemployed members on their rolls); whereas 8.1 million members contributed in 1979, the number in 1986 was only 5.60 million, a drop of 31 percent.

However, this did not lead to a decrease in the sums collected. Most unions compensated for falling membership by raising subscriptions and by taking advantage of their accumulated reserves. Political levy fund income grew from 58 pence per member in 1979 to £1.38 in 1983, and £1.86 in 1986. This represented an increase in real terms of 17 percent per member in 1983-1986 and 81 percent between 1979 and 1986. Total political levy income in 1986 (£10.3 million) was 13 percent greater in real terms than the income of £4.67 million in 1979. In 1987, trade union political levy spending totaled over £15 million, of which at least £10 million was used to support the Labor Party at national, regional, and local levels.

Companies are legally obliged to declare in their annual directors' reports all political donations in excess of £200. A review by the Labor Party's Policy Development Directorate of the annual company reports revealed contributions in 1987-1988 totaling £3.85 million to the Conservative Party and to related funding organizations, such as British United Industrialists.[14] This compares with a total of £2.1 million revealed by a similar exercise in the non-election year, 1986-1987, and £3.3 million in the general election year, 1983-1984.

There are two striking features about corporate political contributions. First, the largest political payments by companies in 1987 (as in other recent general election years) were less than the political fund expenditures of the main unions; the four largest unions spent £9.3 million from their political funds. Additionally, the political expenditures in 1987 of the largest union (Transport and General Workers) exceeded the combined political payments of all the companies included in the Labor Party's survey, based on the 1987 annual reports of more than 1,300 of Britain's biggest public companies. TGWU political fund spending (excluding administrative costs) totaled £4,169,886. According to the Labor Party's research, donations by companies to political parties, related funding bodies such as British United Industrialists (BUI), and other political organizations, such as the Economic League, Aims, and the Centre for Policy Studies, amounted to £4,060,758.

Second, the political payments to the Conservatives declared in the company reports covered by the study constituted a surprisingly small percentage of the total received in donations by the Conservative Central Office in the election year 1987. Since the Labor Party review did not cover all company reports, it obviously underestimated Conservative reliance on corporate funds. Nevertheless, a comparison between the Labor Party's survey for 1978-1979 and similar surveys for the election years 1979-1980 and 1983-1984 demonstrates the downward trend in political payments by public companies. This trend is all the more surprising in view of the considerable rise, in real terms, in the total collected by the Central Office. Net donations to the Central Office in 1987-1988 (from all sources), amounted to £13.6 million, compared with £9.8 million (at June 1987 values) in 1983-1984 and £8.3 million in 1979-1980.

Donations thus increased by more than 60 percent in real terms, between the election years 1979-1980 and 1987-1988. Yet, total company political contributions to the Conservative Party (including payments to BUI and industrialists' councils) recorded by the successive Labor Party surveys fell. The £3.85 million contributed in 1987-1988 by the companies included in the survey compared with £4.0 million (at June 1987 values) in 1983-1984 and £4.7 million in 1979-1980.

A rough indication of the declining importance of corporate donations is given by expressing political payments by companies recorded in these admittedly incomplete surveys as a percentage of total donations to the Conservative Central Office.[15] In 1979-1980 recorded company payments to the Conservative Party, BUI, and industrialists' councils constituted 57 percent of donations to the Central Office. This fell to 41 percent in 1983-1984 and to 28 percent in 1987-1988. The number of companies recorded as making donations to the Conservative Party also fell from 370 in 1979-1980 to 249 in 1987-1988. The total of recorded company political payments to BUI fell even more steeply, from 46 in 1979-1980 to 27 in 1983-1984 and to 16 in 1987-1988.

In short, the Conservative treasurers considerably increased the haul of central party income to pay for the expensive election campaign in 1987. But the extra money did not come from large companies. The Conservative Party may have turned more to private companies, smaller public companies or professional partnerships for support. Their payments were not included in the Labor Party surveys. Another possible explanation may be that larger sums are being raised from foreign corporations whose payments did not need to be disclosed under the provisions of British company law. The most likely reason for its declining reliance on company money is that the Conservative Central Office was notably successful at the time of the 1987 election in collecting contributions from individuals. The lower rates of personal taxation and the increasing opportunities for wealth creation in the 1980s may have encouraged this development.

Apart from donations to the Conservatives, at least twenty-five companies donated in 1987 to the Alliance fund, the Liberals, or the SDP, from which two major conclusions emerge. First, total political donations by trade unions in 1983-1987 (as in 1979-1983) considerably exceeded those of companies. Second, though such donations still provided the core of central Conservative and Labor funding, they accounted for a smaller proportion of income than in the recent past. Trade union payments provided 74 percent of total central Labor income in 1983-1987. If the "Short Money," such as the state grant to opposition parties to aid their parliamentary activities, is excluded, the proportion provided by the unions rises to 79 percent. Assuming that 50 to 60 percent of "donations" to Conservative Central Office came from companies and other institutional sources, these then provided 43 to 52 percent of its total income in 1983-1988.

Developments in 1987-1989

Within days of the June 1987 election, a quarrel erupted that led to the end of the Alliance between the Liberals and the Social Democrats. In March 1988 two new center parties were created: the Social and Liberal Democrats (later renamed the Liberal Democrats) formed out of a merger between the Liberals and a majority of the Social Democrats, and a rump Social Democratic party, consisting of those who refused to join the new SLD.

These party changes have had some unfortunate consequences for the student of political finance. For months after the 1987 general election, the staffs of the respective Liberal and Social Democratic party headquarters were in a state of confusion and uncertainty. This made it difficult to obtain accurate statistics for the various Alliance accounts for the 1987 general election.

As far as the two new parties were concerned, the rump SDP, under the leadership of David Owen, was soon in serious financial straits. The party published no accounts at all in 1989, since it was felt that to reveal the accounts would confirm that the party was no longer a serious political force.

Conversely, the Social and Liberal Democrats started with an ambitious fund-raising plan. The new leader, Paddy Ashdown, hoped that a well-funded party would make a strong electoral impact and would be able to absorb the remnants of David Owen's Social Democrats. The SLD planned in 1988 to employ a central staff of sixty and to raise a central income higher than the combined revenues of the former Liberal and Social Democratic parties. But by spring 1989 it was proving impossible to meet this target, especially as the party decided to spend heavily on by-election campaigns. In May 1989, a senior party committee was already considering how to reduce a burgeoning deficit. The financial situation worsened following the party's poor showing in the June 1989 elections for the European Parliament, when the SLD lost heavily to the Greens.

In the first ten months of its existence, to December 1988, the Social and Liberal Democrats' central income, net of fund-raising costs, totaled £0.8 million; spending was £1 million. In September 1989, a document presented to the party conference proposed a budget for 1990 based on an income of £8 million and an expenditure of only £0.5 million. The staff at the Cowley Street headquarters was to be reduced to fifteen persons. The SLD, like the Social Democratic Party, was considerably dependent on its share of the "Short Money" for its parliamentary expenses, which amounted to an extra £0.2 million a year. The new party's main financial problem was that, without reserves or backing from industry or unions, it was reliant on membership subscriptions. The failure to attract more than 80,000 members, therefore, had an immediate effect on the national party organization.

Apart from these changes relating to the center parties, questions about reforms of the laws relating to political finance were again raised in the late 1980s. The Thatcher government's introduction of the Trade Union Act, 1984, led to demands for parallel legislation for political donations by companies. Whether union and company donations are comparable is open to debate. However, in January 1989 the House of Lords voted 106 - 93 for an amendment that boards of directors should not, without separate shareholder approval, spend shareholders' funds on non-commercial purposes. The Lords, who are not as subject to party whips as are members of the House of Commons, agreed that a "sense of fairness" required this change. The Conservative government used its majority in the House of Commons to overturn the amendment.

Also, officials of the Conservative and Labor headquarters became increasingly concerned in the late 1980s about the levels of expenditure at by-elections. These occasional polls have considerable importance as tests of public opinion. The national party organizations therefore, give heavy assistance to their candidates with staff from the headquarters or from surrounding constituencies appointed as full-time helpers for the duration of the campaign (and sometimes for months before the date of the poll is announced); computer facilities and national speakers flow into the constituency. Were all the costs to be counted, they would far exceed the legal limits for a parliamentary candidate's election expenses.

The party organizations avoid incurring expenses in a number of ways, such as professional agents employed by the headquarters taking an unpaid leave of absence in order to work in the by-election, or visiting speakers from London making a stopover in an adjacent constituency, thus avoiding the need to include the expense of a long-distance fare. It is unclear, however, whether such devices are legal. Though the main parties have not challenged each other, a minor-party candidate could theoretically initiate an election petition. In order to avoid this risk, the expense limits for by-elections were raised in the Representation of the People Act, 1989, to four times the level for parliamentary campaigns during general elections. Moreover, the Home Secretary undertook to review the broader field of election expense law, though this did not lead to any further changes in the laws concerning candidates' expense limits.

Notes

1. From 1977-1978, the Conservative Central Office accounts no longer included information about the party's reserves.

2. For statistics of expenditure in the April 1992 election, see the author's "Labour's £10 million campaign spending closes the gap with the Tories," *The Times*, November 30, 1992.

3. In addition to campaign funds collected for the Conservative Central Office, one of the party treasurers, Lord McAlpine, raised separate funds to pay for independent private opinion polling for the Prime Minister. See D. Butler and D. Kavanagh, *The British General Election of 1987* (London: Macmillan, 1988), p. 35. This extra fund was probably a five-figure sum.

4. Calculations have been made on the same basis as those for the 1979 election as described in the author's *British Political Finance, 1830-1980*, (Washington, D.C.: American Enterprise Institute, 1981), pp. 264-67.

5. The sums actually transferred from constituency parties to the Central Office amounted to about 85 percent of the totals given in Table 1, which include "quota credits." The quota credit scheme was discontinued from the time of the 1987 general election and "quota credits" were included in the statistics for constituency payments made in 1987- 1988 only for those sent before the election. Apart from this discontinued scheme, constituencies were also credited for the interest on loans made to the party headquarters.

6. Routine expenditure was lower, however, as mentioned earlier. In 1979-1983, spending considerably exceeded income.

7. For further information on Trade Unions for Labor, see the author's "Financing the British General Election of 1987," in I. Crewe and M. Harrop, eds., *Political Communications: The General Election Campaign of 1987* (Cambridge: Cambridge University Press, 1989).

8. The task of comparing party spending is complicated by the fact that the Conservative accounts run from April to March while Labor's correspond with the calendar year. Calcula-

tions for routine spending in the 1983-1987 cycle have been based for the Conservatives on three-quarters of Conservative routine spending for 1983-1984 and one quarter for 1987-1988 (and the three intervening years) and for Labor on one-half for 1983 and 1987 (and the intervening years).

9. Information about some sources of Liberal donations was revealed by the Labor Research Department (a separate organization not connected with the Labor Party) in *Labour Research*, May 1985. BSM Holdings, the parent company of the British School of Motoring, gave £188,000 to the Liberal Party in 1983, £5,000 in 1981-1982, and £25,000 in 1982. Its chairman, Anthony Jacobs, was the Liberal treasurer.

10. These statistics are based on information from Liberal and Social Democratic Party officials.

11. See the author's *British Political Finance*.

12. See Butler and Kavanaugh, *The British General Election of 1987*.

13. There is a detailed account of the Trade Union Act, 1984 and of the subsequent political levy ballots in Keith Ewing, *The Funding of Political Parties in Britain* (Cambridge: Cambridge University Press, 1987). Shortly after the Act, seventeen new union political funds were established, mostly in white-collar, public sector unions. They included the Inland Revenue Staff Federation, National and Local Government Officer's Association (NALGO), National Union of Civil and Public Servants, and the National Association of Teachers in Further and Higher Education. Though these funds were not used to make contributions to the Labor party, some of them, particularly that of NALGO, were to be sued in the advertising with a clear anti-Conservative message.

14. About 80 percent of donations to BUI are passed on to the Conservative Central Office, constituency associations, and other party organizations. Although BUI has functioned mainly as a conduit for the Conservative Party fund-raising there have been rivalries between BUI and Conservative Board of Finance, as shown in documents leaked to *Labour Research*, July 1988. If 20 percent of donations are excluded from the reckoning, then the total of donations reaching the Conservative Party either directly, or through BUI and the industrialists' council, was £3.8 million. A larger survey of donations by 6,000 companies in 1987-1988 revealed total donations to the Conservatives and allied funding organizations of £4,743,303 (Labour Research, December 1988).

15. This measure is only rough for a number of reasons: (1) the Labor Party surveys do not cover all company reports; (2) different companies have various dates for beginning and ending their financial year (April 1-March 31); (3) some company donations go to constituency associations, not to the Central Office. Despite these provisions, the declining importance of corporate payments emerges clearly. Donations to the Central Office in 1987-1988 totaled approximately £ 4.5 million. Less than £4 million came from the companies covered by the survey of 1,300 company reports. The sources of donations totaling more than £10 million remain to be explained. Speculation about these "missing millions" grew both before and after the 1992 general election and was the subject of articles in a magazine, *Business Age* (May 1993) and the anti-Conservative national daily, *The Guardian*, regarding alleged funding from foreign sources. In the summer of 1993, a parliamentary committee, The House Affairs Committee, conducted an investigation into the funding of political parties and the author was one of the witnesses. At the time of writing, the Committee's report has not yet been issued. The large newspaper coverage and speculation of 1993 has so far produced much heat but little light since all three main parties have refused to list individual contributions in the periods before the election sof 1987 or 1992.

2

Developments in Australian Election Finance

Ernest A. Chaples

After several years of attempting to resolve major problems in Australian election financing, the national government enacted legislation to do so in December 1991. The Political Broadcasts and Political Disclosures Act of 1991 had the potential to radically alter the nature of campaigning at both the national and state levels.

The 1991 Act resulted from four years of parliamentary study and negotiation. It limited the use of electronic media in national and state elections, regulated the nature of this use during the period leading up to an election, and attempted to apply principles of private funding disclosure to most political parties, groups, and individual candidates participating in Australian elections.

In 1980, the Wran Labor Government adopted the first public funding scheme in Australia's biggest state, New South Wales.[1] When Labor was elected to the national government in 1983, it quickly enacted a similar scheme for partial public funding of national elections.[2] The 1991 legislation attempted to correct several problems that rendered the disclosure of donors' contributions virtually meaningless. Among these problems was a provision intended to allow the Australian Electoral Commission to perform spot audits on party returns. When the commission attempted to exercise authority under Section 316 with respect to the Liberal Party and National Party returns, the parties refused to cooperate. The Attorney-General's department advised the commission that registered parties could not be required to comply with the 1984 Act.[3]

Another loophole allowed unreported donations to be made to a party's administrative accounts. Publicity-shy donors could simply be redirected to the non-campaign accounts of a party or candidate. This resulted in damaging publicity for the Labor Party, which had actively supported it. During the 1987 federal election, a controversial Japanese woodchipping export company, Harris-Daishowa, contributed $10,000 to the Australian Labor Party (ALP) which was then channeled into the state party's New South Wales (NSW) administrative account. This donation was revealed during the 1988 NSW election campaign and ALP State General-Secretary Stephen Loosley was convicted of violating the national law. However, the only fallout was the dismissal of a clerk in the Labor Party bureaucracy responsible for receipts; Loosley's appeal against his conviction was successful.[4]

The apparent distinction between election-oriented and non-election-oriented activities for political parties is artificial.[5] It is impossible to separate the administrative and electoral activity of the major Australian parties. The 1984 Labor government legislation created this distinction solely to allow for secret donors to contribute to Labor Party activities. These donations were also exempted from the New South Wales law by amendments to disclosure provisions passed by the Labor state government before the 1988 election.

The election-related activities of interest groups were not covered by the national law. Those which became involved in elections could do so without public responsibility to report their activity. The 1984 Act (Section 305) required that gifts of $1,000 or more to interest groups be reported to the commission and that electoral spending (Section 309) of $100 or more be publicly reported. But, again, when the commission attempted to investigate the electioneering of the right-wing and anti-union H. R. Nicholls Society after the 1987 elections, it was not able to proceed because of alleged drafting deficiencies in the Act.[6]

Legislation to close these loopholes was originally proposed by the Labor government and was supported by the Australian Democrats.[7] The Liberal Party and National Party members of the Joint Committee strongly opposed it, maintaining that spot audits "trespassed on the rights of privacy and association...[and] would introduce a further increment of bureaucratic power that would be intolerable to democracy."[8]

In addition, the opposition MP's argued that "there is no case for forcing any voluntary organization to disclose all of its income and expenditure. This sort of detailed information about a political party could not be of interest or value to anybody, except perhaps the party's political opponents."[9]

Extending commission audits to non-party interest groups, the MP's contended, would be a "thoroughly deplorable intrusion on free speech."[10]

Regarding disclosure at the state-level, the minority members maintained that

> [I]t is doubtful these matters fall within the proper jurisdiction of the Joint Committee. It is even more doubtful that the centralizing effect of these recommendations...would be in the best interests of our political processes.[11]

Tony Eggleton, then Liberal Party national director, agreed with the coalition party parliamentarians in their opposition. Corporate contributors, said Eggleton, "are not interested in public disclosure" of their political contributions.[12] Liberal Senator Jim Short argued that the committee was trying to use the Australian Electoral Commission to "impose Labor's totalitarian socialist, big-brother agenda on the electorate."[13]

A major change in Liberal Party's attitude toward disclosure of party funding occurred after John Hewson became the Liberal Party parliamentary leader following the 1990 national election. Despite a continuing reluctance by most non-parliamentary functionaries in his party to disclose contributors, Hewson pledged Liberal Party support for full and fair disclosure of campaign funds. This contributed to the change in disclosure provisions in the Political Broadcast and Political Disclosures Bill of 1991.

According to this new legislation, full disclosure of all income, expenditure, and debts for all nationally registered political parties is required as are any gifts from interest groups to such parties. The Electoral Committee has been given the power to conduct spot audits of registered parties and interest groups, and this legislation is intended to apply to both state and national elections.

It remains to be seen whether the secrecy surrounding major sources of private funding of political parties and candidates has been affected by this most recent legislation. The results of these efforts may be more apparent after the first annual disclosure reports, due on July 1, 1994, are published.

Funding National Elections

Reported spending on the 1990 election by registered parties and candidates totaled $32.8 million (approximately $24.6 U.S. million in January 1992), an increase of 48 percent from publicly declared spending for the 1987 election.[14] The total bill for public funding subsidies rose from $7,806,778 in 1984, to $10,298,657 in 1987, to $12,878,920 in 1990. The amount of expenditure covered by public funding, however, fell from 58 percent of all declared expenditures in 1984, to 46 percent in 1987, to 39 percent in 1990. Labor and the major opposition parties, the Liberals and Nationals, accounted for 92.5 percent of the declared spending and received 86 percent of the public funding subsidy for the 1990 election.[15]

Elections and the Electronic Media

Advertising through the electronic media, especially commercial television, constituted the major declared expenditure in 1990. The Labor Party reported that 57 percent of its total election budget had been spent on television and radio advertising, the National Party, 52 percent; the Liberal Party, 42 percent; and the Australian Democrats, 30 percent. Overall, 48 percent of the more than $32 million reported expended on the 1990 election was spent on this type of advertising.[16]

This large increase in expenditure for television advertising was focus of attention in the hearings of the Lee Joint Committee in 1989. Chairman Michael Lee suggested that commercial advertising rates for television had increased in the last decade at a rate far in excess of the Consumer Price Index and that television advertising was the main factor leading to runaway election costs in Australia.[17] The Lee Committee recommended free television and radio time during the period of electioneering after an election date had been declared, with the amount of advertising comparable to that contracted for during the 1987 national elections.[18]

Liberal and National Party members on the Joint Committee were entirely opposed to these recommendations. They maintained that "the political parties should be grateful for any 'free time' that the commercial stations made available" and, if further free time was required by law, the parties would be "abusing their privileged position in the Legislative process."[19] The committee majority's claim that broadcaster access to the airwaves carries some obligation to the political parties was completely rejected by the Coalition party members, who maintained that a system of free time allocation would be "virtually unworkable."[20]

The television broadcasters' lobby group, FACTS, was predictably opposed to any free time provisions. FACTS maintained free time was unnecessary since "the public are informed through news services, commentaries, and interviews in current affairs programs."[21] FACTS argued that free time provisions would adversely affect costs and profits, resulting in major party advertising budgets being redirected to the print media at election time, thereby continuing the high cost of campaigning.

The advertising lobby group, AFA, also strongly opposed free time "on both practical and philosophical grounds." Free political broadcasting would be required at the expense of standard commercial advertising. Individual proprietors would be deprived of the right to decide what advertising to accept or reject, "a concept foreign to the Australian way of life."[22]

Typical of the opposition to the free time recommendation was the lead editorial in the *Sydney Morning Herald* on August 9, 1989. Titled "Another Grab by Politicians," the writer maintained that

> it is dishonest to pretend that $15 million worth of television time has no cost simply because it is appropriated rather than bought.... The dishonest suggestion that compulsory advertisements will cost noone anything helps avoid inconvenient questions about just how far public assistance to political parties should go.[23]

However, Milton Cockburn, the *Herald's* chief national political reporter, disagreed. He wrote that the free time and disclosure provisions would be "a further step toward reducing the potential for corruption.... For that reason [they] deserve to be supported."[24]

The federal opposition parties and the television and advertising communities remained opposed to any limitation on the existing practice of unencumbered political television advertising as the debate proceeded. But the Labor Government's viewed the Lee Report's free time provisions as not going far enough. Labor proposed a complete electronic media ban on all political advertising at all times and by all individuals and groups. The 1991 election legislation passed the House of Representatives on May 20, 1991, with this ban included.

While Liberal and National Party reactions were predictable and manageable, the legislative situation in the Senate, where the Labor Government held only thirty-two of the seventy-six Senate seats, was different. To pass such legislation, the government had to win the support of the Australian Democrats, who have continually held the balance of power in Australia's Senate since 1983.[25] The Australian Democrats initially opposed the total ban on advertising in the electronic media and insisted on major renegotiation with the Government before it was passed by the Senate in December 1991.

The outstanding features of the Political Broadcasts and Disclosures Act as it affected both state and national elections in Australia were:

1. All paid political advertising by parties, candidates, governments or interest groups was prohibited on commercial television and radio during the period immediately before an election campaign.[26]
2. Free television and radio broadcasts were required of commercial licensed operators for the same election periods as above. Actual broadcasts were limited to the period after nominations had closed.

3. Strict limitations were placed on these "free" broadcasts. Only a single speaker who was a candidate at that election, could be included in the free broadcast. Images, vocal sounds, or other material that used impersonations or dramatic effect were not allowed. The transmitted image could only be the head and shoulders of the speaker.
4. The free television broadcasts would last two minutes each; the radio broadcasts would last one minute.
5. Allocation of 90 percent of these political broadcasts would go to existing parties from the prior parliament, in proportion to the formal first preference votes they received at the prior election.
6. The remaining 10 percent of the free time would be reserved for other groups that were new at the election in question or otherwise unrepresented in the prior parliament.
7. Free broadcasts on television were limited to three per day for national elections and two per day for state elections.
8. One-time party policy speeches of up to thirty minutes could be broadcast by parties eligible to be included in the free time pool; this broadcast time was not to be counted as part of the free time itself.
9. Administration of these free time provisions was placed under the direction of the Australian Broadcasting Tribunal.
10. Income tax deductions of up to $1200 per taxpayer were allowed for contributions to registered political parties.[27]

These provisions and prohibitions were challenged by New South Wales and the commercial television industry before the full bench of the Australian High Court, which had to decide three questions:

1. Whether the national government has the constitutional power to limit advertising for state and local elections;
2. Whether the Australian Constitution provides an implied guarantee of political process which is violated by a ban on advertising in elections; and
3. Whether it is legal for the national government to reduce the incomes of licensed commercial television stations in the way legislated by this Act, and whether the national government has the power to require free advertisements of these broadcasters.[28]

On August 29, 1992, the High Court of Australia ruled these provisions of the 1991 Act unconstitutional. The decision was unanimous and was handed down during the Queensland and Victorian state election campaigns, throwing both of those campaigns into disarray. The ban and the free time provisions had already been applied at the Tasmanian state election and the Australian Capital territory Assembly election earlier in 1992 and also at several state by-elections. The disclosure provisions in the 1991 legislation were not affected by the decision and will apply to registered parties for the fiscal year 1993-1994. No substitute legislation is anticipated before the next national election in early 1994.

Political Monies in the Australian States

Unaccountable political money has been a particular concern at the state and local levels where land development and the awarding of contracts for basic state services are largely concentrated.

Unaccountable political gifts were a major factor in a complex story that began to unfold in the state of Queensland in 1989. The investigations of Special Commissioner Tony Fitzgerald dealt almost daily blows to the state's long-time National Party government of that state. The Police Commissioner was convicted of taking bribes and several ministers were implicated in the misuse of state funds and the questionable receipt of private monies.[29] The Premier, Jon Bjelke-Petersen, was forced into retirement by the revelations of the Fitzgerald Commission.

The commission uncovered questionable donations to Kaldeal Party, Ltd., a front company set up to fund the private electoral ambitions of Bjelke-Petersen, managed by his closest political associate, Sir Edward Lyons. Kaldeal received $824,000 before the 1986 Queensland elections and went into operation again in 1987 when Bjelke-Petersen considered a run for control of the conservative coalition parties in the national parliament. This was thwarted in part by an unexpected mid-winter federal election in which Labor was returned to control of the national government. Among the Kaldeal receipts were found anonymous brown bagged cash donations of $50,000, $60,000, and $160,000, made directly to the premier. Further evidence of cash gifts of $250,000 by a French owned company, Citra Constructions, to the National Party also attracted attention from the Fitzgerald investigators. Citra later received state contracts in excess of $50 million from the National Party Queensland Government.[30] Bjelke-Petersen stood trial on corruption charges, which ended in a hung jury.

In his report, Commissioner Fitzgerald recommended changes in Queensland's electoral system, including disclosure of the pecuniary interests of parliamentarians.[31] Greater accountability for political contributions has been implemented under the new Queensland Labor Party government elected in late 1989.

Questionable party donations in New South Wales have also been featured in the early public testimony before the Independent Commission Against Corruption (ICAC). ICAC was established by the Greiner Government, modeled upon the Hong Kong Crime Commission, as part of the coalition parties' program to examine public wrongdoing after they replaced Labor in 1988.

Again, it has been the National Party which has suffered most of the bad publicity. An investigation of public land development on the state's north coast (involving Deputy Premier Wal Murray, the state's Natural Resources Minister, Ian Causley, and local MP Don Beck—all National party parliamentarians) has revealed that sizable donations were made to the National Party from applicant developers. These donations could go unreported according to the disclosure legislation in effect at the time.

These investigations focused primarily on Ocean Blue Resorts Party, Ltd., its main operative, Dr. Roger Munro, and on his gifts to both the Labor Party (before they lost government in 1988) and the Nationals (after the 1988 election). Deputy Premier Murray maintained that these donations were unknown to the politicians and that ignorance of the donor's identities was an acceptable protection from corruption. Minister Causley, meanwhile, admitted that if the Ocean Blue donations were known their application would have been withdrawn. National Party General-Secretary for NSW, Jenny Gardiner, revealed that about one-half of total donations to her party were processed in a manner to avoid disclosing the donor's identity under federal or NSW law. She also confirmed that $12,000 of the Ocean Blue monies was passed to the Party directly through Murray's office. Gardiner was charged and convicted for her role in handling campaign funds in this case. Even so, she was elected to the State's Upper House in 1991.

The ICAC assistant commissioner for this investigation, Adrian Roden, Q.C., concluded that the NSW Public Funding Act has failed to achieve disclosure and that the Act "should be amended with a view to removing the loopholes and strengthening its enforcement provisions."[32] Roden observed that campaign disclosure laws in NSW were "something of a joke,"[33] and proposed specific changes. His proposals were being studied by a joint parliamentary committee as of February 1992.

The Western Australian Government has not escaped scrutiny; it was the subject of a detailed royal commission investigation into political corruption during 1991-1992. That commission heard public evidence and colorful stories involving huge contributions to the Labor party in exchange for political favors and contracts emerged. Findings by this royal commission were handed down late in 1992.[34]

Conclusions

The series of highly visible state government commissions that have documented political corruption in Queensland, New South Wales, and Western Australia, and the continued pressure of increasing campaign expenses in Australia, forced radical action by the national parliament of Australia in late 1991. Most of the state governments are still working with the issue, but national legislation dictates major changes in state-level campaigning and in how monies are to be handled by state parties as well.

It will take some time to see how well this new legislation will work. The Liberal/National Party Opposition in the national parliament strongly opposed the severe restrictions placed on advertising through the electronic media in national and state elections. Since they are strongly favored to win government in early 1993, and have the backing of the High Court, the future of these provisions is hardly secure.

Nevertheless, there does seem to be broad, non-partisan support for greater openness and accountability in private donations to election campaigns. The new Act gives reason to hope that this goal might be achieved during the next few years. But with the high cost of elections and the hesitation regarding spending limits, Australian election funding remains a serious question for the future.

Notes

1. See the author's, "Public Funding of Elections in Australia," Herbert E. Alexander, ed., *Comparative Political Finance in the 1980s* (Cambridge: Cambridge University Press, 1989); "The Evolution of Public Funding of Elections in Australia," Unpublished paper presented at the XIVth World Congress of the International Political Science Association, Washington, D.C., August 1988) and "New Issues in Australian Election Finance," Unpublished paper presented to the Research Committee on Political Finance and Political Corruption, IPSA, Tokyo, September 9, 1989.

2. Differences are discussed in the author's chapter in Alexander, *Comparative Political Finance*, pp. 83-84.

3. Joint Standing Committee on Electoral Matters, *Who Pays the Piper Calls the Tune: Minimizing the Risks of Funding Political Campaigns*, Report No. 4., (Canberra: Australian Government Publishing Service, June 1989), pp. 71-72.

4. The judge in the original trial held that Loosley had made an "honest mistake" but that as Chief Administrative Officer, he had failed to install appropriate procedures to avoid such errors. Loosley's original conviction did not prevent him from being selected for the Australian Senate in 1990 or from becoming national Labor Party president in 1991.

5. See the author's, "Campaign Donations: The Real Issues," *Current Affairs Bulletin*, Vol. 64 (March 1988); see also the author's testimony before the Joint Committee on New South Wales Electoral Funding, November 1991.

6. *Who Pays the Piper*, pp. 77-78.

7. The Australian Democrats are a party of the center, capable of tipping the balance in the Australian Senate (elected by proportional representation in state-based constituencies). Their support has been critical for the passage of Labor Government legislation in the Senate since Labor was elected to the national government in 1983.

8. *Who Pays the Piper*, p. 126.

9. Ibid., p. 130.

10. Ibid.

11. Ibid. pp. 132-133.

12. Prudence Anderson, "Showdown on Poll Funding," *The Bulletin*, July 4, 1989, pp. 118-119.

13. Television interview, "7:30 Report," ABC, August 8, 1989.

14. All dollar amounts are reported in Australian dollars; the Australian dollar floats broadly across a wide currency exchange band but was trading at about $U.S. 0.75 as of January 1992. All official figures taken from the appropriate reports of the Australian Electoral Commission produced after the 1984, 1987, and 1990 elections.

15. The Labor and major opposition parties received 92 percent of the public funding subsidy in 1987. The six percent reductions in 1990 were due to the substantial increase from 8.1 percent in 1987 to 17.4 percent in 1990 of first preference votes from minor party and independent candidates in House of Representative contests in 1990.

16. Figures from *Election, 1990: Election Funding and Financial Disclosure Report*, pp. 38-39.

17. *Who Pays the Piper*, p. 26.

18. Free time for state and national elections was already being provided by the public radio stations and the television channel funded by the government, the Australian Broadcasting Commission. For a full discussion of the Lee Committee proposals, see *Who Pays the Piper*, Chapter 10.

19. Ibid., p. 123.

20. Ibid., p. 124.

21. Ibid., p. 123.

22. Ibid., p. 61.

23. Editorial, "Another Grab by Politicians," *Sydney Morning Herald*, August 9, 1988, p. 14.

24. Milton Cockburn, "Political Advertising and the Lure of Public Money," *Sydney Morning Herald*, August 11, 1989, p. 17.

25. The states each elect twelve senators and the two territories elect two senators each. The senators elected from the states are normally chosen for set, three-year terms in groups of thirty-six (six from each state) on a proportional representation basis, using an optional lists system and exhaustive preferential voting. An occasional double dissolution of the entire House and Senate occurs (most recently in 1987) and all seventy-six Senators are chosen in such an election with one-half of the seventy-two state-elected members serving for three years and one-half chosen for six years. The four territory senators face re-election after a three-year term.

26. The "election period" is normally defined as the period between when an election is announced and the close of voting on election day, a minimum of thirty-five days. Some exceptions were included in the Act for special types of elections. The ban applied to referenda campaigns and by-elections as well as regular elections for state and national parliaments. Public information materials sponsored by the relevant Electoral Administration, and certain other minor exceptions, were allowed in the Act.

27. Provisions are summarized here from the Political Broadcasts and Political Disclosure Act of 1991 as adopted by the Australian Parliament in December 1991 and proclaimed in January 1992. Provisions of the Act were to be subject to administrative regulation and implementation by the Australian Broadcasting Tribunal and the Australian Electoral Commission. Most of these regulations and documents were still forthcoming as this chapter was being written.

28. These implications are discussed intelligently by David Solomon in the *Weekend Australian,* February 1-2, 1992, pp. 23-24.

29. G. E. Fitzgerald, chairman, Report of a Commission of Inquiry Into Possible Illegal Activities and Associates Police Misconduct (Brisbane: Queensland Government Printer, 1989), pp. 89-91.

30. Ibid., p. 90.

31. Ibid., pp. 133-135.

32. See Chapter 25, "Political Donations, The Parties and the Law," in Independent Commission Against Corruption, *Report on Investigation into North Coast Land Development,* (Sydney, 1990), pp. 530-531.

33. Ibid., pp. 492-537.

34. Much of the material on political corruption in Western Australia in the 1980s has been canvassed in a series of feature articles, "Oath of Office," in the *Sydney Morning Herald,* February 8, 1992, pp. 33, 39; and February 10, 1992, p. 6.

3

American Presidential Elections, 1976-1992

Herbert E. Alexander

The decade of the 1970s ushered in a new era of campaign financing in the United States; the laws regulating federal election campaign financing underwent a dramatic transformation. The Federal Election Campaign Act of 1971 (FECA),[1] the first comprehensive revision of federal campaign legislation since the Corrupt Practices Act of 1925, established detailed spending limits and disclosure procedures. In 1974,[2] in the wake of Watergate, the Act was strengthened by amendments which set new contribution and spending limits and created the bipartisan Federal Election Commission (FEC) to administer election laws. In 1976,[3] the FECA was fine-tuned by amendments which conformed the election law to the findings of the Supreme Court decision in *Buckley v. Valeo*. Additional amendments passed in 1979[4] were designed, in part, to rejuvenate the activities of party organizations in the electoral process.

Regarding presidential campaigns, the Revenue Act of 1971[5] provided the basis for public funding through a federal income tax checkoff plan. Amended in 1974, the law provided for public matching funds for qualified candidates in the prenomination period and for public treasury grants to fund the major parties' national nominating conventions and the major party general election candidates. The law also established criteria whereby minor parties, and new parties and their candidates, can qualify for public funds to pay nominating convention and general election campaign costs; minor party candidates can qualify for pre-nomination funding in the same manner as major party candidates.

Public funds were intended to help provide, or to supply in entirety, the money serious candidates need to present themselves and their ideas to the electorate. Public funds also were meant to diminish, or to eliminate, the need for money from wealthy donors and interest groups, thereby minimizing opportunities for undue influence on officeholders by contributors. In the pre-nomination period, public funding was intended to make the nomination process more competitive and to encourage candidates to broaden their bases of support by seeking out large numbers of relatively small, matchable contributions.

The federal income tax check-off is the cornerstone of the public financing program for the presidential nomination and election campaigns. It supplied tax dollars—$1 on a single return and $2 on a joint return, checked-off voluntarily on individual income tax returns—to the Federal Election Campaign Fund. Through the 1992 elections, taxpayers earmarked sufficient funds to cover the costs of all presidential public funding programs. However, projections raised doubts about a sufficiency of public funds for 1996 and the Congress raised the checkoff amounts to $3 and $6 in the Omnibus Budget Reconcilation Act of 1993.[6]

Although the tax checkoff has survived since its introduction on federal income tax forms in 1973, based on 1972 income, it has suffered declining participation rates during the past decade. Indeed, the percentage of individual tax returns checked off has been decreasing steadily since it peaked at 28.7 percent in 1980, reaching a low of 17.7 percent in 1991.

Since the 1976 election, excepting the 1992 election, there has been a steady increase in the total amount of public dollars certified for candidates and conventions. Certifications by the FEC totaled $70.9 million in 1976, $100.6 million in 1980, $133.1 million in 1984, $177.8 million in 1988, and $175.3 million in 1992. The amount certified by the FEC for the 1992 election year signifies a slight decrease from that certified in 1988. There were eleven presidential candidates eligible to receive pre-nomination matching funds in 1992, compared with fifteen in 1988. While approximately $67.1 million were certified in matching funds in the 1988 pre-convention period, only $42.7 million were certified in the same period in 1992.

In the early 1970s, contribution and expenditure limits were enacted, although the Supreme Court subsequently ruled that spending limits are permissible only in publicly-financed campaigns.[7] These laws were intended to control large donations with their potential for corruption, to minimize financial disparities among candidates, and to reduce opportunities for abuse. In addition, laws requiring full and timely disclosure of campaign receipts and expenditures were enacted to help the electorate make informed choices among candidates. Finally, the FEC was established to administer the laws and monitor compliance.

Five presidential elections have now been conducted under the FECA, its amendments, and its companion laws, a sufficient experience from which to draw some conclusions about the impact of the laws and to determine whether they have had their intended effects.[8] The general conclusions are that the laws have accomplished some of their aims, but they also have had unintended, and not always salutary, consequences. The degree to which the laws have failed to achieve their intended effects may testify as much to the inventiveness of political actors in circumventing the laws and to the intractability of election campaign finance, as to the deficiencies of the laws themselves.

The Pre-Nomination Campaigns

Under the FECA, candidates who accepted public matching funds in 1992 were permitted to spend no more than $27.6 million plus 20 percent ($5.5 million) for fund raising. In addition, the 1974 FECA Amendments limit candidate spending in each state to the greater of $200,000 or sixteen cents per eligible voter, plus a cost-of-living increase. Moreover, contributions made by the candidates for legal and accounting services to comply with the campaign law are exempted from the law's spending limits, but candidates are required to report such payments.

Although candidates who do not accept public funding are not bound by the overall or individual state expenditure limits, all candidates are bound by the contribution limits stipulated in the FECA. No candidate is permitted to accept more than $1,000 from an individual contributor or $5,000 from a multicandidate committee.[9] Candidates who accept public funding are allowed to contribute no more than $50,000 in personal or family funds to their own campaigns.

As in elections since 1976, to qualify for public matching funds available under the FECA, the 1992 candidates were required to raise $5,000 in contributions of $250 or less from individuals in each of twenty states. The federal government matched each contribution made by an individual, up to $250 to eligible candidates, although the federal subsidy to any one candidate could not exceed $13.8 million, half the $27.6 million pre-nomination campaign spending limit. These threshold requirements serve as a screening device whereby candidates who do not demonstrate widespread support are ineligible for public financial support.

The pre-nomination campaign contribution and expenditure limits and matching fund requirements take effect once a candidate declares his or her intention to run and registers a principal campaign committee with the FEC. Actual payouts of public funds are made only in the election year, but candidates may submit claims for matching funds and be qualified by the FEC in the prior year.

The Overall Spending Limit

The public financing program in effect for presidential candidates imposes limits on the amounts their campaigns can spend. In the general election period, the expenditure limits apply only to the candidate's campaign organization and to the national party. Additional types of related spending, which stem from legitimate sources (not from loopholes in the law, as some critics and reformers contend), were and are available to publicly funded presidential candidates. Independent expenditures in parallel campaigns, for example, are constitutionally protected rights according to Supreme Court decisions. Soft money—money raised and spent outside the restraints of federal contribution and spending limits—is also an available source for those candidates.

The inflexibility of the campaign law to respond to highly competitive campaigns in both parties, and to the rising costs of conducting those campaigns, is a major problem manifested in the pre-nomination phase of the presidential selection process. Since 1976, some candidates who have had a realistic chance to remain in the race through the convention have complained that the overall spending limit is set too low. Although the limit is adjusted to account for inflation, the costs of many of the items and services that campaigns must purchase, such as television advertisements, increase at a rate far exceeding that of inflation.

In the 1992 general election, the issue of expenditure limits became more salient when billionaire candidate Ross Perot vowed to spend as much money as it took to win the election. Some feared that publicly funded candidates could not compete with Perot, precisely because of their spending limits. In retrospect, however, this was not the case as Perot spent less than either major party ticket. Indeed, if the 1988 and 1992 elections are any indication, no independent candidate is likely to put either major party candidate at a disadvantage, regardless of the amount spent. This is because major party candidates have substantial allied and related spending on their behalf in parallel campaigning by various sources.

First, each party has fifty state committees, approximately 3,100 county committees, plus uncounted municipal committees to register voters, distribute absentee ballots, and get out the vote on election day. In addition, many committees can be successful in raising soft money which, in turn, enhances the effectiveness of these activities. Moreover, labor unions can undertake parallel campaigning among their members and families. Thus, the expenditure limits give the illusion of limiting spending without actually doing so.

State Limits

Like the overall spending limit, the ceiling established by the FECA for spending in individual states in the pre-nomination period also is the subject of criticism by candidates and campaign officials. Indeed, there is a wide disparity between the overall spending limit imposed on publicly funded candidates and the far greater sum of the individual state limits. If individual candidates could raise sufficient funds to spend up to the limit in all fifty states—a total of almost $86.7 million in 1992—they would exceed the national spending limit almost three times over. The two sets of limits are inconsistent, thus they force candidates to pick and choose which states will receive the greatest spending.

Aware of the need to do well in the early pre-nomination contests, which are customarily assigned more importance by the news media than the number of delegates at stake would otherwise warrant, candidates want to spend as much money as they can to assure their success. The low spending ceilings in early contests in less populous states, such as Iowa or New Hampshire, force campaigns to centralize control of spending and to impose strict budgetary restraints, thereby discouraging grass-roots efforts and volunteer involvement in their campaigns. Candidates complained that the expenditure limits prevented them from spending the amounts of money most experts said was necessary in order to campaign effectively. To justify dodging the limits and/or to point out the need for raising them, many candidates complained that the rules and formulas adopted by the FEC for allocating expenditures to individual states were not only arbitrary but also illogical.

In 1991, the Federal Election Commission promulgated regulations to loosen the restrictions on how much presidential campaigns can spend in each state.[10] By exempting certain advertising, travel, and consulting costs, considered part of a campaign's spending in a state, the newly adopted rules, which took effect in November 1991, were designed to end the practice of subterfuge to which some candidates resorted to circumvent the state limits in important early primaries or caucuses. The practices included, among other things, the arrangement of overnight accommodations for the candidates' staffs in a state bordering on a primary contest state (the costs could be counted against the bordering state's spending limits), and the purchase of television time in cities outside a primary state when the cities' media markets included portions of the primary state (again, costs could be applied in part to another state's limit). Preliminary statistics indicate that the regulation has had some positive effect in the 1992 election; there were fewer major subterfuges and circumventions of the spending limits.

Under the 1991 regulations, fees for placing television, radio, or print advertisements do not apply to the state expenditure limits. Candidates' staff salaries in the state and their travel expense no longer apply to the state limits. Moreover, neither fees paid in a state for consultants advising on national campaign strategy, nor a candidate's travel expenses, apply to the state limits.

Contribution Limits

The skyrocketing costs of many of the items candidates need to purchase, and services they must acquire, compounded with the constant increase in the Consumer Price Index (CPI), have exacerbated the problem of contribution limits. Under the 1974 FECA Amendments, an individual may contribute no more than $1,000 per candidate for presidential nomination to a maximum of $25,000 annually to all federal election campaigns. However, even though all expenditure limits are indexed to account for the rate of inflation, the individual contribution limit remained the same. Measured by the CPI, a $1,000 contribution in 1992 was worth a little more than one-third of its purchasing power in 1975 when the limit went into effect. In all presidential elections held between 1974 and 1992, the limits achieved their intended effect of eliminating large direct contributions from wealthy donors to presidential candidates. But by prohibiting candidates from gathering seed money for their campaigns through large donations, the contribution limit gave an advantage to well-known candidates who had already achieved significant name recognition and forced lesser-known candidates to begin fund-raising for their campaigns as much as eighteen months before the nominating convention. The limit also altered fund-raising patterns in significant ways. The role once filled by large contributors now is filled by well-connected volunteer fund raisers who can persuade a large number of persons to contribute up to the maximum $1,000 amount.

Multicandidate committees, popularly known as political action committees (PACs), are another source of contributions up to $5,000 per candidate per election. They play a minimal role in the financing of presidential campaigns, however, in part because PAC contributions are not matchable under federal law.

Circumventing the Limits

The expenditure and contribution limits have forced candidates to seek other avenues through which they can raise and spend money. Methods to circumvent the limits are not necessarily illegal. While some methods, such as delegate committees, are established in congruence with rules promulgated by the FEC, others, such as independent expenditure, have their basis in Supreme Court rulings. Still others, those of presidential political action committees and soft money, have become additional tools.

Delegate Committees. According to rules promulgated by the FEC, if several persons, acting as a group, support the selection of one or more delegates by receiving contributions or making expenditures in excess of $1,000 per year, the group becomes a political committee.[11] These committees may accept no more than $5,000 from any individual or other political committee and must report all contributions and expenditures. Any expenditures they make for political advertising advocating the selection of a delegate and referring to a candidate for presidential nomination is considered either an allocable in-kind contribution to the presidential candidate or an allocable independent expenditure on that candidate's behalf.

Ostensibly, these committees are established mainly to further the selection of national nominating convention delegates supporting the candidate who ordered their formation, hence the name "delegate committees." Although he did not invent the idea of delegate committees, Walter Mondale in 1984 was the first to effectively employ them as an additional means of avoiding the federal campaign contribution and spending limits. Delegate committees have not been used significantly since.

Independent Expenditures. In its 1976 *Buckley* decision, the Supreme Court ruled that individuals and groups could spend unlimited amounts on communications advocating the election or defeat of clearly identified candidates provided that the expenditures are made without consultation or collaboration with the candidates or their campaigns.[12] Conforming to the Court's ruling, Congress's 1976 FECA amendments imposed no limits on independent expenditures on behalf of, or in opposition to, federal candidates. Individual donations to independent committees, however, remain restricted to a maximum of $5,000 to each multicandidate committee, and $1,000 to each single-candidate committee. Moreover, contributions to committees making independent expenditures are counted against the individual contributor's annual overall donations limit of $25,000 to all federal campaigns.

In July 1980, concerned with the political impact and validity of independent expenditures, reaching $2.7 million during the nomination period, both Common Cause and the FEC filed suit against a number of groups that had announced plans to spend money independently on behalf of Ronald Reagan in the general election. The plaintiff's primary argument stipulated that the proposed independent spending would violate a provision of the Presidential Election Campaign Fund Act that prohibited organized political committees from spending more than $1,000 on behalf of a candidate who accepts public funding. The specific provision, Section 9012(f)(1) of the Internal Revenue Service Code, never was directly considered by the Supreme Court in *Buckley* and was left untouched when Congress rewrote the election law to conform with the Court's ruling. A three-judge federal court in the District of Columbia rejected the suit, striking down that section of the code as an unconstitutional restriction on First Amendment rights of individuals.

Although it was too late to affect independent spending in the 1980 general election, the plaintiffs appealed the decision to the Supreme Court. In January 1982, the Court reached a 4-to-4 deadlock decision, the practical implication of which was to uphold the 1980 lower court decision. Because the vote was equally divided, however, the Court's decision had no value as precedent and applied only in the District of Columbia circuit.

In 1983, the FEC and the Democratic National Committee (DNC) took the issue of independent expenditure back to the courts. Once more, a district court refused to permit the FEC to implement section 9012(f)(1). The FEC appealed the case to the Supreme Court which declined to expedite the appeal and did not hear oral arguments in the case until late November 1984, after the general election. In March 1985, the Court, in 7-to-2 vote, struck down Section 9012(f)(1) of the IRS Code as unconstitutional. Writing for the majority, Justice William Rehnquist declared that the provision failed to serve a compelling government interest, such as avoiding corruption or the appearance thereof, and that, accordingly, the provision's restrictions of the First Amendment rights could not be upheld. In dissent, Justice Byron White took issue with the Court's identification of money and speech, arguing, as he had in *Buckley*, that the First Amendment protects the right to speak, not the right to spend.

Presidential PACs. Another way to circumvent pre-nomination campaign contribution and expenditure limits is by forming presidential political action committees (PACs) to support pre-candidacy political activities.[13] The ostensible function of such committees is to raise and spend money on behalf of favored candidates and party committees. Although presidential PACs can undoubtedly be helpful to the candidates who receive support from them, they are mainly instrumental in furthering the ambitions of the prospective presidential candidates who sponsored them. They allow their sponsors to gain the favor and support of federal, state and local candidates, and of state, and local party organizations, through the direct and in-kind contributions that the presidential PACs make.

Presidential PACs also allow the prospective presidential candidates to travel extensively throughout the country attracting media attention and increasing their name recognition among party activists and the electorate in general, without having the money raised and spent counted against the spending limits that would apply once the presidential hopefuls began their candidacies.

Reagan was the first to use such a personal PAC to fund efforts he made after his 1976 pre-nomination defeat, thereby laying the grounds for his 1980 successful bid for the nomination of his party and, eventually, for the presidency. In 1981, Mondale added a new dimension to presidential PAC fund raising. In addition to the Committee for the Future of America, which was registered with the FEC, four state-level PACs were formed to raise and spend money in ways that would be helpful to the prospective presidential candidate. These PACs were able to collect contributions under the laws in the individual states in which the PACs were registered. Often these laws gave a freer rein than the federal law to individual contributors and permitted contributions of amounts, or from sources, that would be prohibited under federal law. The greatest use of presidential PACs occurred prior to the 1988 campaigns, and because of the nature of the 1992 candidates, no significant presidential PACs were operative prior to their campaigns.

Soft Money. Whereas "hard money" is raised, spent, and publicly disclosed under federal supervision, "soft money" refers to funds raised from sources outside the restraints of federal law but spent on activities intended to affect federal election outcomes. Soft money was sanctioned by the 1979 amendments to the Federal Election Campaign Act and is therefore not a loophole, as some have suggested, but a conscious effort on the part of the Congress to empower state and local party committees in federal campaigns.

Soft money is mainly used in the presidential general election campaigns. Accordingly, some have called the use of soft money a healthy development because it has spurred citizen participation and has helped to revitalize state and local party committees. However, in the wake of the disclosure that large amounts of soft money were used in the presidential campaigns, and was given by a leading figure in the savings and loan scandal, others have called for federal regulation, or even the complete prohibition, of such donations. As noted earlier, soft money is now required to be disclosed to the FEC.

Matching Funds

Since the federal matching fund system was first employed in the 1976 presidential pre-nomination campaigns, matching funds have provided potential candidates who lacked name recognition or access to large amounts of private campaign funds the opportunity to compete effectively for presidential nomination. If it were not for the combination of contribution limits and public funding, Jimmy Carter, who lacked access to traditional sources of large Democratic contributions, probably would have lost out early in the 1976 primary season to candidates, such as Senator Henry M. Jackson, who enjoyed such access. Public funds also helped John Anderson to become an influential force in some early 1980 Republican primaries and, more significantly, to start building the name recognition and national organization needed to mount his independent candidacy for the presidency.

Matching funds also helped keep Jesse Jackson's underfunded, but well-publicized, campaigns afloat in 1984 and 1988. Perhaps there was no more evidence of the utility of public matching funds than in Jerry Brown's 1992 pre-nomination campaign. His self-imposed $100 contribution limit was a key element of his campaign and the toll-free "800" telephone number, through which donations were made, proved successful. In all these experiences matching funds opened up the electoral process to some candidates whose campaigns otherwise might not have been able to survive.

In all publicly financed presidential campaigns, candidates who accept matching funds are required to supply the FEC with substantial documentation to demonstrate their compliance with spending limits and contribution limits and the law's disclosure requirements. Lawyers and accountants who can lead candidates through the complexities of election campaign finance law and devise systems to keep track of receipts and expenditures are as prominent in some campaigns as are political operatives. Efforts to comply with the law, of course, impose additional expenses on campaigns. Even though these expenditures are exempt from the overall spending limit, they divert funds and fund-raising energies from the campaigns themselves.

The Nominating Conventions

The FECA provides for federal grants to help finance the national conventions of the major political parties. A minor political party also is eligible to receive a federal subsidy for its convention if its candidate received more than 5 percent of the vote in the previous presidential election. Since 1976, no minor party has qualified for federal funding of its convention. Under the 1974 Amendments, the major parties were each eligible to receive a grant of $2 million plus a cost-of-living increase from the presidential checkoff fund. The 1979 FECA Amendments raised the basic grant to $3 million. In mid-1984, Congress increased the base amount to $4 million. With adjustment for inflation, 1992 convention grants were a little more than $11 million for each major party.

The federal grants, which are used to pay for convention-related expenses, were intended to replace the previous methods of convention financing whereby host cities and local businesses furnished cash and services to party conventions. FEC advisory opinions, however, have permitted certain types of outside contributions to convention arrangements committees, and expenditures on their behalf, in addition to the federal subsidy.

State and local governments where conventions are held are permitted to provide certain services and facilities, such as convention halls, transportation, and security services, the costs of which are not counted against the parties' expenditure limits. In addition, local businesses and national corporations with local outlets may contribute funds to host committees or civic associations seeking to attract or assist the political conventions, so long as they can reasonably expect "a commensurate commercial return during the life of the convention."[14] Moreover, both parties are able to arrange reduced-cost services, such as airfare for delegates and telephone and data processing services, by agreeing to designate the providers as "official suppliers" for their conventions.

The mix of public and private financing (including tax-exempt funding) for the nominating conventions satisfies the parties because it provides sufficient monies and involves local participation. But the development every four years of new means of introducing private money clouds the premise in the 1974 law that public funding would essentially replace private funds. Each year, the FEC has opened more avenues for private—often corporate and labor—funds. Besides questioning the rationale for the use of public funds, the infusion of large amounts of private dollars makes the accompanying expenditure limits meaningless.

The General Election Campaigns

The Revenue Act of 1971 and the FECA Amendments of 1974 banned private contributions to major party candidates who accept public funding in the general election period. However, private contributions given to help candidates defray compliance costs are exempt from the ban, provided they do not exceed $1,000 per donor. Minor party candidates who receive at least 5 percent, but less than 25 percent, of the previous presidential election vote are eligible for pre-election payments of public funds. The laws also provide that minor party candidates are entitled to post-election federal grants if they receive 5 percent or more of the total number of popular votes cast for the office of president in the current election.

In 1992, each major party candidate was entitled to a direct grant of $55.2 million, and each national party spending limit, based on the voting-age population of the nation, was $10.3 million. Thus the combined total of $65.5 million could be spent under the direction of each major party nominee's campaign organization. This public funding could be supplemented by soft money raised privately by each of the major national parties for spending on behalf of its presidential ticket.

Conclusions

The experience with five presidential campaigns indicates that the FECA has achieved mixed results. In the pre-nomination period, the campaign law's public funding provisions have improved access to the contest by supplementing the treasuries of candidates who attain a modest degree of private funding. In addition, the public matching fund provision has increased the importance of contributors of small amounts in financing prenomination campaigns, without significantly reducing the role of organized groups. Making PAC contributions non-matchable does not necessarily impede the expenditure of interest group money seeking to influence the pre-nomination campaign result. Although many organized groups traditionally avoid becoming deeply involved in intraparty contests to determine a party's nominee for president, some PACs do make independent expenditures.

Moreover, the law's contribution limits have reduced the possibilities wealthy contributors may have to exert political influence. Its disclosure provisions have resulted in more campaign finance information than has ever before been available to the public, and its compliance requirements have caused campaigns to place greater emphasis on money management and accountability. These effects suggest that, in some ways, the laws have succeeded in altering the behavior of candidates, committees, and contributors to achieve some of the goals of campaign reform.

However, the low individual contribution limit, and the expenditure limits, have reduced campaign flexibility and rigidified the election campaign process. The contribution limit prevents potential candidates from mounting a campaign late in the pre-nomination season because it makes it extremely difficult to raise sufficient funds in a short time. The expenditure limit makes it difficult for candidates who have spent close to the maximum allowed to alter campaign strategy and tactics to fend off new challenges or to take new developments into account.

Instead the contribution limit works to the advantage of well-known candidates capable of raising money quickly, perhaps forestalling others from entering the contest. It forces lesser-known candidates to begin their fund-raising earlier than ever before, thereby lengthening the campaign season. Also, contributing to the lengthening of the campaign season in 1984 was the decision of the Democratic Party to compress the primary and caucus period. A number of states then moved their election contests to the early portion of the period to increase their importance to the candidates and the media, consequently putting pressure on the candidates to establish their credibility and to fill their campaign treasuries earlier than usual. Thus many candidates participated in expensive straw polls and competed for group endorsements through much of 1983, seeking the momentum they hoped would carry them through the front-loaded primary and caucus season in 1984. However, such pre-election year activity was minimized in 1987 and 1991.

The relatively low expenditure limits have encouraged candidates to favor mass media advertising, which is more cost-effective and less time-consuming than grass-roots campaigning, but may not be as informative. It has caused candidates to centralize control of their campaign efforts in order to assure that they remain within the expenditure limits, but this centralization comes at the expense of local authority and direction. The low expenditure limits also have led candidates to resort to a variety of subterfuges to circumvent the limits.

Despite the increase in campaign finance information available to the public because of the FECA's disclosure provisions, there has been some significant erosion in the ability of these provisions to bring important data to light. For example, in December 1983, the FEC voted 4-to-2 to allow candidates who contract with outside vendors to conduct campaign-related activities on their behalf to meet their disclosure obligations merely by reporting payments made to them.[15] The commission failed to heed a warning from its own legal staff that, under such a ruling, campaigns could defeat the purpose of public disclosure of all campaign expenditures simply by contracting with a professional consulting firm to conduct campaign activities on their behalf and reporting only the sums paid directly to the firm.

The FEC decision to consider contributions to convention city promotion and services, funds exempt from FECA limits and therefore non-reportable, means that contributions to provide certain kinds of support for the political parties' quadrennial conventions may be collected from any source whatsoever, and that the contributors may never be known to the public. Finally, the complexities of the law's compliance requirements have contributed to the professionalization of campaigns, possibly chilling enthusiasm for volunteer citizen participation in politics.

In the general election, public funding combined with a ban on private contributions to the major party nominees—except to defray compliance costs—was intended to equalize spending between major party candidates, to control or limit campaign spending, and to eliminate the possibility of large individual or interest group contributions influencing presidential election results. In 1976, with a few exceptions, those purposes appeared to have been achieved. But in 1980, and in later election years, due in large part to increased familiarity with the law's provisions as well as some changes in the law, political partisans discovered a variety of ways to upset the balance and reintroduce substantial amounts of private money into the campaigns.

The low contribution limits have encouraged the development of a variety of ways to frustrate the intent of the limits, including presidential PACs, delegate committees, and independent expenditures. Expenditure limits have served only to constrain the presidential campaign leadership because they have restricted the amounts the central campaign organizations are able to spend directly, and have placed outside of the campaign's control potentially unlimited independent expenditures disbursed, quite legally, to influence the election result.

As in the pre-nomination period, the disclosure provisions have led to increased information for the public regarding political campaign money. But here, too, there are gaps. Some political money does not have to be reported. In this category, for example, is the substantial labor spending on non-reportable communications and other activities that have helped Democratic candidates in all five publicly funded election campaigns. So, too, are the contributions made to, and expenditures made by, tax-exempt, nominally non-partisan organizations that conducted voter drives. Other spending to influence the presidential election result is difficult to trace, such as the soft money raised under national political party committee auspices since 1980 which is channeled directly to state party organizations to finance state and local volunteer-oriented activities on behalf of the presidential tickets. Only since 1991 has soft money been required to be reported.

Experience strongly suggests that in a political system such as that of the United States, animated by a variety of competing interests each guaranteed freedom of expression, a tightly drawn system of contribution and expenditure limits does not work well.

America's system of public funding that has served five presidential elections has demonstrated many problems that need fixing. None of the problems, however, is so severe as to undermine its survival.

It is clear that the campaign finance reforms of the 1970s do not represent a panacea for all the ills that afflicted the presidential campaign financing system before the reforms were enacted. The present campaign finance system has flaws, some of which are quite serious. Nevertheless, for all its shortcomings, the current system represents a notable improvement over the previous system. The aims of the reformers were enormously ambitious, and quite probably not all of them can be achieved. Those that are will be reached only step-by-step, as new approaches to campaign finance regulation are tested in the crucible of the quadrennial contest for the presidency.

Notes

1. Public Law 92-225, 86 Stat. 3 (1973) (codified as amended in 2 U.S.C. 431 et seq. and in scattered sections of 18 and 47 U.S.C.).

2. Public Law 93-443, 88 Stat. 1263 (codified in scattered sections of U.S.C.).

3. Public Law 94-283, 90 Stat. 475 (codified in scattered sections of U.S.C.).

4. Public Law 96-187.

5. Public Law 92-178, Section 701-703, 801-802, 85 Stat. 497, 560-574 (1972) (codified as amended in scattered sections of 26 U.S.C.).

6. Public Law 103-66, 107 Stat. 567, Sec. 13441.

7. *Buckley v. Valeo*, 424 U.S. 1 (1976).

8. For a thorough analysis of the impact of federal campaign finance laws on the conduct of presidential campaigns, see the author's *Financing the 1976 Election* (Washington, D.C.: Congressional Quarterly Press, 1979), *Financing the 1980 Election* (Lexington, MA: D.C. Heath, 1983), and Herbert E. Alexander and Monica Bauer, *Financing the 1988 Election* (Boulder, Colorado: Westview Press, 1991).

9. To qualify as a multicandidate committee, a committee must have been registered with the appropriate federal officer for at least six months, have received contributions for federal elections from more than fifty persons, and have contributed to five or more federal candidates.

10. *Federal Register*, Vol. 56, No. 145, July 29, 1991, p. 1.

11. *Federal Election Commission Record*, December 1983, pp. 1, 4-6.

12. 424 U.S. at 51.

13. For an extensive discussion and excellent analysis of presidential PACs, see Anthony Corrado, *Creative Campaigning: PACs and the Presidential Selection Process* (Boulder: Westview Press, 1992).

14. Federal Election Commission, AO 1975-1, *Federal Register*, July 15, 1975, pp. 26, 660.

15. Federal Election Commission, AO 1983-25, *FEC Record*, February 1984, pp. 4-5.

4

U.S. State-Level Campaign Finance Reform

Ruth S. Jones

Concerns about money in politics are like the tide; they ebb and flow. The 1970s provided a decade of action on campaign finance in the United States, while the 1980s were largely a decade of consolidation: refining, enhancing, and implementing the policies of the preceding decade. However, the decade of the 1990s began with a new round of scandals at both the federal and state levels that once again propelled issues of campaign finance to the forefront of public discussion.

The practical, political context of U.S. campaign financing has particular features that may be unique, including single-member districts, and partisan elections by a simple plurality vote. But perhaps the most important contextual feature of the U.S. electoral system, with respect to campaign finance, is the role federalism plays in structuring U.S. elections. Given the presence of fifty state-level Democratic and Republican parties that have various levels of association with the two national party committees, and literally thousands of local, county, and congressional district organizations that have minimal contact with state or national campaigns, the national party "system" is more appropriately described as one of atomized party organizations sometimes connected by relationships of convenience.

Federalism is central to understanding campaign finance reform because it dictates where reform must take place. Federal regulations govern the election of one President and Vice President, 100 Senators and 435 Representatives. Yet there are well over 520,000 elected officials in the

United States for which primarily state, not national, law determines the electoral process. Thus, the Federal Election Campaign Act actually applies to only a small fraction of elections held in the United States each year. Almost two decades ago, David Broder, a politically astute journalist, suggested that, in considering campaign finance reform,

> the place to begin might be at the level of the state legislature, where candidates today typically have no alternative but to go to special-interest groups for whatever money they need.[1]

Efforts to speak to financing are frequently successful at the state level where comparable activities have failed in the national arena. This may be due to the fact that states are smaller and often more homogeneous, that the political cultures of specific states are receptive to campaign finance reform, or that the process of identifying equitable and politically feasible solutions is not confounded by as many interests. Whatever the reasons, the fact remains that the states provide fifty different laboratories for reform.

Sources of Private Funds

The Federal Election Commission data are the primary source of information about the funding of campaigns for President and Congress, but no comparable agency coordinates the collection of data on state-level elections, so research on state-level campaign finance depends on access to the recordkeeping agencies in each state. Moreover, there is limited comparability across states regarding basic concerns such as definitions of "political action committee" (PAC) or "political party," requirements for reporting and disclosure, or the frequency, detail, and format of state-mandated reports. Yet, it is this autonomy of the individual states that is the very reason we can look to the states for innovative policy alternatives.[2]

Reporting

Policies that establish the requirements for reporting and disclosure lie at the heart of campaign finance reform. Without public access to accurate and reliable data, there is no way to assess the implications of suggested change or to determine if new policies are working. The states differ in terms of who is required to report, how often and when the reports are due, and the dollar threshold that triggers reporting requirements.

Almost all candidates or candidate committees for statewide and state legislative office must file campaign finance reports. County candidates or candidate committees must file reports in four-fifths of the states; municipal candidates or candidate committees must file in three-fourths of the states. State political party organizations file in all states except Arkansas and New Hampshire. Three-fourths of the states require committees that provide campaign financing through independent expenditures to report their financial transactions, and PACs are required to file in all states.

States also differ in terms of when and what must be reported. For example, Ohio requires only one report before and after each election, whereas Connecticut requires quarterly reporting of both pre- and post-election contributions. Some states specify reporting dates seven or fourteen days before the election, yet others require that exceptionally large contributions be reported within 24 or 48 hours during the last days of the campaign. Moreover, states such as Florida, New Mexico, West Virginia, and North Carolina are among those that require itemized reporting of all contributions and expenditures, whereas Nevada requires itemized reports of contributions only of $500 or more.

Most states now have experienced several election cycles under these reporting and disclosure rules and have had the opportunity to make adjustments to initial policies. Many states have added a requirement that the name and address of the campaign treasurer, the candidates, and their offices, be recorded. Several states have gradually included specific county and local candidates under the reporting requirements. Still others have adjusted the thresholds which trigger the reporting requirements so as to exclude low-cost campaigns from the burdens imposed by reporting procedures. In general, however, the thrust of most changes has been to require more inclusive, comprehensive, and timely reporting for the entire campaign cycle.

In the short run, the emphasis is likely to be on efficiency through computerized data-archiving, electronic transmission, and analysis. More states will probably expand reporting requirements to political parties as well as PACs and independent expenditure committees.

Over the long-term, state agencies seem more likely than federal agencies to recognize the interrelationships between campaign finance, lobbies, public ethics, and conflicts of interest and act to coordinate reporting and recordkeeping. For example, candidates for state offices in three-fifth of the states must file financial disclosures as a condition of running for office. In eleven states, even nominees for important public positions must disclose their financial activities before they can be appointed.

As machine-readable techniques and documentation have simplified obtaining, recording, and auditing reports, agencies have been freed to provide wider access to the data and enhance information dissemination. Almost all states publish some summaries or aggregations of data based on the personal disclosure records. Almost three-fifths prepare a comparable publication for lobbying activities. However, fewer than half of the states currently publish a synthesis or summary of campaign finance data and it is the rare agency (New Jersey, Washington, Minnesota, and California) that ventures to provide position papers, analyses, and policy-relevant summaries or recommendations.

Such publications, of course, are likely to plunge administrative agencies into sensitive political waters. The logic and spirit of public records is to make information available to the voting public, but the elected officials who have created this legislation are likely targets for publicity about campaign financing. Hence, state officials generally have been very cautious about what they have directed (or permitted) the recordkeeping agencies to do with campaign finance data once it is collected. Whether through partisan pressures, budgetary appropriations, or formal legislation, analysis of the data has been severely restricted in many states.

Contribution Limits

Campaign finance reports publicize sources of campaign contributions, and aid in enforcing contribution limits imposed by state statutes and the conditions under which funds can be received. Although potential contributor groups are very similar from state to state, the states differ in the amount and focus of regulation imposed on contributions. The approach states have taken towards corporate, labor, PAC, party, and individual contributions, as well as regulations on loans and cash donations, indicates a myriad of policy orientations available for limiting campaign contributions.

Corporations and Labor Unions. The evolution of campaign finance reform influencing corporate and labor union contributions reflects both the degree of interest-group involvement in state politics and the relative power balance between these two political forces. The history of corporate and bank involvement in U.S. electoral politics has not always been a model of pluralist democracy. Consequently, early legislation in campaign finance attempted to limit the political power of these forceful economic interests. Populist traditions are prominent among states that currently restrict or even prohibit corporate contributions. However, in many states both corporations and labor make financial contributions directly, and indirectly, through PACs.

Twenty-six states limit, and ten prohibit, contributions to candidates or candidate committees directly from union treasury funds. Twenty-one limit, and another twenty-one prohibit, campaign contributions from corporate treasury funds. Four states prohibit direct corporate contributions but place no special restrictions on union giving; six states prohibit corporate contributions and limit labor union contributing; and two states limit corporate contributions but not union gifts.[3] This unequal treatment has been challenged in several states. Recently a Michigan court upheld the state's statute prohibiting contributions from incorporated entities while only limiting non-incorporated union contributions.

In North Carolina and Tennessee there have been efforts recently to permit greater corporate involvement in state-level campaign funding. At the same time, legislation has been proposed in New Jersey and New York to prohibit all direct corporate and union contributions for election campaigns. In general, however, legislative activity to change the status of these contributions has been pre-empted by the rise of state-level PACs representing corporate and union interests.

PACs. There is no definitive accounting of the number of political action committees active in state-level elections, nor the full amount of their collective contributions. In states where direct contributions from labor unions or corporations are permitted or only minimally restricted, PAC development has been less than in states that are more restrictive. This implies that PACs may simply be surrogates for traditional funding sources. However, all fifty states report ever-increasing PAC involvement in campaign financing. The state of New Jersey, for example, reported a 118 percent increase in the number of state-level PACs and an 87 percent increase in the amount PACs contributed to state legislative candidates between 1983 and 1987.

Just as state PAC development lagged behind that of national PACs, states have been slow to regulate their activity. In 1992, only twenty-eight states had enacted statutes that explicitly restrict PAC contributions in some way. During recent legislative sessions, almost half of the remaining states gave some degree of attention to PAC-related legislation, most of which was directed at limits on the amounts PACs can contribute per candidate or per election cycle, and on the total amount candidates can accept from all PACs. In Arizona, state legislative candidates are limited to aggregate total PAC contributions of $5,000 plus cost-of-living increases.

Proposals to eliminate PAC contributions generally are the result of frustration from unsuccessful attempts to limit the perceived flow of special-interest money to state-level campaigns. Legislatures are likely to be cautious about enacting absolute prohibitions as the U.S. Supreme Court has ruled that political contributions are a form of political expression protected by the First Amendment. In order for such legislation to survive, legislators will need to present a convincing case that the dangers of PAC contributions warrant restrictions on the freedom of political expression.

Political Parties.   Only eighteen states have explicit restrictions on direct campaign contributions from political parties. Among the states that do seek to limit political party contributions, Arkansas, Maine, and Montana treat contributions by parties the same as PAC contributions and impose very stringent limits. Similarly, Massachusetts limits parties to $3,000 per calendar year, while West Virginia limits party, PAC, and individual contributions to a maximum of $1,000 per candidate. Most of the other states simply specify contribution limits for specific offices.

The historic norm in the United States has been to view legally recognized political parties as quasi-private organizations and to restrain government involvement (including regulation) in their activities. In the 1980s, however, parties were increasingly caught between those who sought to continue the tradition of autonomous and independent political parties and those who saw the reemergence of party organizations as a threat to existing and future legislation to control campaign contributions and expenditures. This latter concern has been fueled by three simultaneous developments:

1. There has been an increased use of "soft" money. This is money legally collected and spent outside the parameters of federal regulation in congressional and presidential campaigns, by funneling funds to state-party organizations for use in virtually everything, except the direct support of federal candidates.
2. The role of the national committees in providing in-kind, coordinated, or direct contributions to state party organizations has grown stronger. In the past, the states were the major sources of funds and services for the national organizations.
3. There has been a nationalization of state-level politics through (a) the shifting of complex national issues (like abortion and environmental issues) to the state policy-making arenas, and (b) the involvement of national party organizations in state-level issues of reapportionment and redistricting, especially as related to congressional districts.

Party advocates see the increasingly vigorous and disciplined party system as the key to addressing the problems of rising campaign costs and special-interest group influence. Under the party-system alternative, parties would be given funding advantages over individual wealthy contributors and special-interest PACs. This, they argue, will help provide institutional responsibility and accountability through recognized political processes and organizations. What state campaign finance legislation does to, or for, political parties will be determined by a range of factors, including the traditions of the state vis-a-vis political parties, the relative strength and cohesion of state party organizations, and the future role of soft money in federal campaigns.

Discussions of state actions regarding soft money take two distinct approaches. One limits direct party contributions and requires detailed reporting of in-kind and coordinated expenditures and "agency agreements." These agreements are between state and national party organizations and enable the national party to assume the state party's legal "contribution" quota for federal candidates. The other approach is to limit the amount any political party organization may accept from individuals or groups. There is even some discussion of making different restrictions, depending on whether the contributions come from an individual, a party (or group) that is indigenous to the state, or from interests and individuals that operate and reside outside the state's boundaries.

Individuals. One of the concerns shared by many who want to change the campaign financing process is the growing tendency for PAC contributions to overwhelm direct contributions by individuals. In state after state, the proportion of funds received from PACs is increasing while the proportion from individual contributors is decreasing. The reformers' goal is greater direct linkage of individual voters, rather than special interests, to individual candidates and the campaign process.

At the same time, there is a parallel concern that exceptionally large individual contributions create obligations for those who receive them. Although states have tried to balance the tension inherent in trying to raise more funds from more individuals, thirty-two have chosen to place limits on the amount of money an individual can give to particular campaigns. The modal individual contribution limit in these states is $1,000 per campaign, but the limits run from as low as $250 for the lower state chambers in Arizona, Connecticut, and Montana, to as high as $20,000 for the governor/lieutenant-governor slate in Minnesota and an aggregate of $150,000 per calendar year in New York.

States that resist campaign finance regulations tend to be especially reluctant to put limits on individual contributors. Aside from a desire to protect the opportunity for individuals to use campaign contributions as political expression, some legislators have voiced concern about one of the loopholes associated with legislation limiting contributions. Specifically, contribution limits on money given to campaign organizations leave independent campaign expenditure by an individual or organization untouched.

Under current rulings of the U.S. Supreme Court, contributions to fund actual campaigns may be limited to avoid the appearance of impropriety. However, campaign spending that is totally independent (not under the influence of a political candidate or campaign committee) cannot be limited because it is a form of free speech. Consequently, a major means of circumventing contribution limits is through independent expenditures, which were pioneered in federal elections, but are now common in state campaigns. Wealthy individuals and PACs that have given the maximum under existing state contribution limits may make sizable expenditures on their own to assist the election of preferred state-level candidates. Moreover, these independent expenditures often have been the source of negative campaigns that are of growing concern to state election officials.

In states where independent expenditures have already become an issue, lawmakers have instituted two different types of policies. One is a generic requirement, applicable to both individuals and groups, for full disclosure of the sponsorship of any political ad or campaign materials. Such requirements may even include a disclaimer that indicates not only who paid for the ad but that it was not approved by or made in cooperation with any political campaign or candidate. The other approach is to require registration and reporting by all individuals and groups that engage in any fund-raising or spending related to political campaigns. Two-thirds of the states already have such requirements, but they vary considerably in terms of the detail and timeliness of the reports. While both of these approaches provide information on the financial sources for independent expenditures, they do little to discourage the use of independent expenditures as a means of circumventing contribution limits.

Cash, Loans, and Surpluses. Because cash contributions can be particularly difficult to trace, half of the states regulate or prohibit cash contributions in excess of a specified amount, which varies from $20 in Michigan to $2,000 in Hawaii. States are moving towards mandating reports of a full and legible name, address, employer, and occupation for each contributor. Moreover, most states require itemized reporting of all contributions exceeding a relatively nominal amount, making it difficult to conceal cash contributions through sleight-of- hand reporting.

The use of loans to fund campaigns is susceptible to abuse. The most common tactic is for a would-be contributor to make a sizable "loan" which then is forgiven after the campaign. As a result, half of the states have put a dollar ceiling on personal loans for political campaign financing. Most states also require that commercial loans, even when subject to the going-market interest rates and conditions, be reported as such on campaign finance disclosure forms. States that require candidates to file personal financial disclosure reports usually also require outside commercial and personal loans to be reported as well. The net effect is to create a public record of direct and indirect assistance given to political candidates.

States are also beginning to look more closely at how debts are retired. The former governor of Arizona was impeached, in part, because of financial irregularities involving personal campaign loans and the misuse of monies in his "protocol" fund, originally created to dispose of funds improperly collected to retire a campaign debt. Kentucky recently passed legislation that prohibits elected officials from fund-raising activities designed to retire old campaign debts.

Although most campaign finance regulation operates under the assumption that candidates never have enough money, the fact is that an increasing number of state-level candidates, usually successful incumbents, end campaigns with a surplus of funds. In part, this is because incumbents can raise funds with relative ease, and often engage in an almost continual cycle of fund-raising in order to build large campaign war chests, with which to preempt any serious challenge. Unless a challenger emerges, the incumbent has little need to spend the large sums accumulated.

State restrictions on the use of surplus funds run the gamut from prohibiting any personal use of surplus funds to merely declaring the surplus as income, thereby freeing it for any purpose. Most states provide several alternative uses for surplus funds, including giving them to the political parties, charities, or the state's general fund. With the amount of surplus campaign funds increasing, despite higher campaign costs, state regulation of surplus funds is likely to grow.

Expenditure Limits and Public Funding

Media costs are one of the primary expenses in most statewide campaigns. However, controlling media expenditures by limiting spending or subsidizing campaigns are not policies that readily could be applied in the United States, because of the very strong societal norm of free enterprise associated with the press and electronic media. Even the "equal time" provision of the Federal Communications Act (an attempt to ensure equity and balance in the political use of electronic media) provided only for the equal opportunity for the candidates to buy equal time. The centrality of commercial radio and television, combined with the rhetoric of the free enterprise ethic, eliminates serious talk of public subsidies for commercial broadcast time.

The biggest stumbling block to limiting any type of campaign expenditure has been the clear pronouncement of the U.S. Supreme Court against such limitations. In the *Buckley* decision, the landmark case for U.S. campaign finance, the Supreme Court made it clear that campaign contributing and spending must be protected under the First Amendment, as they are both forms of political expression.

However, the Court made two exceptions to this blanket rule. One was that regulations to prevent corruption, or even the appearance of corruption, would be permitted; consequently, limits on contributions were upheld. In sum, the potential danger to the larger democratic electoral system warranted restrictions on individual and group contributions.

The other exception made by the Court was that when public money is involved, there is adequate justification to impose expenditure limits. The court did not want to create a campaign finance "black hole" into which unlimited tax dollars might be funneled. The net effect of the *Buckley* decision, then, was to prohibit restrictions on campaign spending except when campaigns are funded with public dollars.

The *Buckley* ruling, of course, also applies to the states. There is a strong undercurrent of suspicion in state legislatures (as well as in the U.S. Congress) that is hostile to government activism generally, and toward government intervention in campaign politics in particular. Yet, state policymakers have been more willing than their federal counterparts to enact public subsidies that, in turn, make campaign expenditure limits possible. The politics of enacting public financing in each state make interesting telling, but in terms of general advocacy and opposition, the goals and criticisms in the several states have been relatively similar.

Sources of Public Funds

In 1907, Theodore Roosevelt advocated public funding of congressional elections, but a subsidy program has yet to be implemented. The history of state-level enactment of public subsidies is equally long. Colorado enacted a campaign subsidy program in 1909, but it immediately was declared unconstitutional and was never implemented. Nevertheless, by the time the first presidential election using public funding took place in 1976, several states had already conducted elections using public funds. Although the 1970s was the decade in which most public funding programs were enacted, each year public financing of campaigns remains on the legislative agenda in several states. In 1988, for example, three state subsidy programs were enacted; in 1990, sixteen other states gave serious consideration to implementing some form of state-level public campaign financing. At the same time, legislation prohibiting candidate use of public funds was passed in Delaware.

The twenty-four states where campaign subsidy provisions have been enacted can be categorized according to how the subsidy money is raised. States use a tax add-on, a tax checkoff, a general funds appropriation, or some combination of these mechanisms to generate campaign funds.

Tax Add-on. Tax add-on programs call for the minimal commitment of public funds or resources. In fact, the only government involvement is that the state agrees to use state income-tax agencies to collect voluntary contributions for political parties or candidates. Taxpayers make a political contribution by adding a designated sum to the amount of tax they owe. They write one check to the state in payment for taxes and the state transfers the appropriate amount to the political account designated by the taxpayer.

Eight states use add-on programs as the only way to raise money for public funding of campaigns. Although these state programs differ in specific details, they are all singularly unsuccessful as mechanisms for raising campaign funds, as very few taxpayers (generally less than 1 percent) choose to increase their tax payment. The add-on programs are viewed more as symbolic gestures on the part of state legislators than as meaningful policies to alter the existing patterns of campaign financing. In several states, political campaign add-on options are listed on the tax form alongside add-on programs designed to assist the arts, protect the environment, or prevent child abuse. Campaign financing is thus presented as one more worthwhile "cause" rather than as a fundamental component of democratic elections.

Tax Checkoff. More serious legislation has sought to label a small portion (usually one or two dollars per income tax form) of general tax revenue for campaign financing. In this arrangement, taxpayers can choose to earmark part of their tax obligation for a particular campaign or political party fund or can simply direct all of their tax payment to remain in the state's general fund.

Twelve states currently have tax checkoff programs. Even among these programs, however, taxpayer participation varies greatly. Only 5 percent of taxpayers participated in the North Carolina program in 1974 while 54 percent participated in a parallel program in Hawaii in 1984. The amount of money available depends on the amount states permit for a checkoff contribution and how many taxpayers participate. In some states, such as New Jersey, Hawaii, and Iowa, taxpayer participation rates have remained relatively constant, but in others, like Wisconsin and Kentucky, there has been a marked decline in taxpayers' willingness to earmark tax dollars for campaign purposes.

Direct State Appropriations. The use of direct state appropriations for campaign purposes appears the most straightforward way to create state-level campaign subsidy programs, and is an option in all states (states that do not have an income tax cannot establish a tax checkoff). Nevertheless, campaign finance reformers have avoided relying on the appropriation process because its "political" nature makes it an unstable funding arrangement. The state of Florida initially chose to establish a public funding program based solely on state legislative appropriations. When the fervor for campaign finance reform was high, the appropriation received wide support, but once the reform was enacted, it was easy for the legislature, faced with growing budgetary problems, to put other needs ahead of campaign financing. Reformers then unsuccessfully sought to use a variety of assessments and fees to fund the Florida Election Campaign Financing Trust Fund. In 1996, Nebraska will use general state funds to subsidize elections for the first time, and in 1995, Kentucky is scheduled to fund slates of candidates for the gubernatorial election.

Combination of Approaches. Combining two of these approaches has been a successful formula for a few states. New Jersey, for example, has been one of the leading states in terms of the scope of, and participation in, a gubernatorial funding program. Although taxpayer participation rates in New Jersey have been among the highest in the nation, the reform legislation also specifies that, if the campaign fund does not have sufficient money to fund primary and general campaigns, general state treasury funds can be used to supplement the tax checkoff fund. In recent campaigns, Rhode Island and Wisconsin also have had the option of drawing funds from the state treasury to supplement the tax checkoff based public subsidy account.

Iowa and North Carolina have developed dual systems whereby the tax checkoff program is complemented by an add-on option. Taxpayers can use the tax form to add a second contribution to the campaign subsidy account. In practice, however, the pattern is one of modest participation in the checkoff programs and minimal use of add-on options available to the taxpayers. Montana and Oregon provide examples of state checkoff programs that were scaled back to become add-on programs, and then Oregon abandoned the system entirely. In Maryland, the add-on program languished for years before the legislature finally abolished it and put the accumulated funds into the general treasury.

Recipients: Candidates and Parties

Eight states follow the federal model of providing funds only to individual candidates.[4] Three states, Kentucky, Rhode Island, and North Carolina, have created programs that provide funding to both individual candidates and political party organizations. Ten states have chosen political parties as the sole recipients of public funds. This latter program is especially noteworthy, given the historic record in the United States of not supporting strong political parties. It is equally interesting to note that most of these public funding programs were enacted during an era in which political parties were viewed by many as declining in importance. States have shown creativity in designing public funding programs to support their unique objectives.

In states where public funds are allocated to specified individual candidates, the tax form generally includes a generic "campaign fund" designation which taxpayers can mark to indicate that they want a portion of their tax payment to go to support political campaigns. If, however, public funds go to the political parties, taxpayers generally have the opportunity to specify which political party will receive their tax dollars. Some states, including Rhode Island, provide both alternatives: a "general fund" designation plus the opportunity to specify a particular party.

In Michigan, only gubernatorial candidates are eligible to claim tax checkoff funds. In the primary, all candidates who meet the threshold requirements and choose to use public funds can receive "matching" funds for their private contributions. In the general election, however, only Democratic and Republican candidates are entitled to a flat grant from the public fund without any matching requirement. In New Jersey, which also funds only the gubernatorial campaign, a matching-funds system is used for both the primary and the general election.

In Hawaii, Minnesota, Nebraska, and Wisconsin, statewide offices and state legislature candidates are eligible to receive public funds. Built into the Wisconsin program is the stipulation that candidates who accept PAC contributions as well as the public subsidy will have the amount of the public subsidy reduced by the amount of the PAC contributions. Minnesota has one of the more complex public funding systems. Their tax form includes both a party and a general fund option. Funds from the party account are allocated both to candidates and the state party. After the primary, 90 percent of the party account dollars are distributed to the

party's candidates who met certain minimum vote threshold requirements. The remaining 10 percent goes to the state political party organizations. The other general account provides an equal amount to each
qualified general election candidate.

Another variation in state subsidy programs is Kentucky's (and, at one
time, Oregon's) allocation of a portion of the funds collected via the tax
forms to the county political parties according to taxpayer checkoff rates
in each county. An Idaho statute limits the party's use of tax checkoff
dollars to non-campaign activities (party building, voter registration, etc.).
One interesting pattern that emerges probably stems from the impact of
the political parties on campaign finance reform; all programs that allocate public funds to political party organizations prohibit the party organization from making contributions to candidates in primary campaigns.

With two exceptions, all programs that fund candidates also impose
an expenditure limit on the candidates who accept public money. Because
the add-on program in Montana generates very little money, candidates
are not expected to agree to a restrictive expenditure limit. Minnesota, on
the other hand, has added a provision to the public funding program
stipulating that a candidate who uses public funds can be released from
complying with the expenditure ceiling if that candidate's opponent does
not sign and file an expenditure agreement with the state's Ethics Commission. Several other states have given consideration to provisions that
would go even further, suggesting that the non-participating candidate's
share of public funds should automatically be allocated to the opponent
who did agree to spending limits. To date, no such program has been
enacted.

Administration and Enforcement

As is true for all public policies, the success of campaign financing policies is dependent not only on the scope, breadth, and clarity of the legislation, but also on administrative and enforcement mechanisms. A complete understanding of the states' efforts to administer and enforce such
regulations is possible only through consideration of four analytically
distinct, but closely related, topics: campaign finance, public disclosure,
ethics and conflicts of interest, and lobbying activities. The fifty states
vary widely in the status and emphasis given to each of these dimensions. In fact, prior to 1974, only nine states had an independent state
agency assigned to any one of these important areas. However, between
1974 and 1983, thirty new state agencies were created (sometimes more
than one per state) to focus on this nexus of money and politics, and
interest continues to grow. As states revisit the issue of program admin-

istration, three distinct topics are repeatedly discussed: the autonomy of the agency, the inclusiveness of its charge, and the authority of the agency.

Autonomy of the Agency

States have followed one of three models in assigning the responsibility for administrating and enforcing campaign finance laws. Some states, such as Arizona, Vermont, North Dakota, and South Dakota, simply assign all matters involving campaign finance, ethics, reporting and disclosure, and lobbying to a single public official, such as the Office of the Secretary of State. Other states divide the responsibility among several agencies. For example, in Wisconsin, the Office of the Secretary of State handles lobbying, the State Election Board is responsible for campaign finance and elections, and a separate Ethics Commission oversees matters of ethics, conflicts of interest, and disclosure. In both models, the responsibility for campaign finance administration and enforcement is often left in the hands of partisan-elected officials whose primary duties and priorities are not necessarily that of campaign finance. Only eighteen states have created separate, administrative units to deal with campaign finance.

Under this third model, the one that reformers prefer, the agency's priorities are clear and the energies and expertise of the staff are concentrated on campaign finance. States that have such independent campaign finance agencies also are most likely to have established a reputation for expert administration and rigorous enforcement of campaign finance regulations. The size of the agency and the method of selecting the staff or governing board varies across states, but in general, independent agencies or boards are bipartisan, involve staggered terms of office, and are funded by separate legislative appropriations. Only the California Fair Political Practices Commission has constitutionally guaranteed partial budgetary independence.

When new campaign finance laws are enacted and oversight and enforcement are assigned, state legislatures seldom appropriate sufficient funds to provide staff and support services that reformers believe necessary. But this must be put into context. The 1980s was the decade of "new federalism" in which the states were given increased responsibilities for public policies. At the same time, economic woes that faced the federal government were mirrored, often more sharply, in budget problems that confronted state governments. Education, public health, housing, public safety, and economic development were all in need of increased state funding. Yet state revenues were at best holding steady, if not decreasing. It is not difficult to understand, under the circumstances, how the budgets for campaign finance enforcement received low priority in the general process of budgetary negotiations. In any case, the difficulties of administering and enforcing an array of laws related to money and politics involve more than just a well-funded administrative agency.

Inclusiveness

Reformers advocate two goals for agencies overseeing matters of campaign finance. One is to remove the administrative unit from partisan political considerations and influences; establishing a new, independent agency is the preferred method of accomplishing this. The second goal is to develop a comprehensive approach for addressing the full range of issues related to money in politics. Thus, the interrelated nature of problems in campaign finance, public disclosure, ethics and conflicts of interest, and lobbying suggests that effective regulation of money in politics requires an all-encompassing agency. In fact, in twenty-nine states a single agency is responsible for campaign finance and at least two of the other related domains. However, in only ten states is comprehensive coverage of all four domains assigned to a specialized, independent agency. Therefore, in 80 percent of the states, as is the case at the federal level, administration and enforcement of the regulations of money, disclosure, ethics, and lobbying is fragmented. When responsibility is thus divided, it is difficult, and often impossible, to develop an integrated approach to regulating the role of money in campaigns.

Agency Authority

Even the most autonomous and comprehensive agency cannot be effective if it lacks the authority to do its job. At least a third of the state agencies charged with administration and enforcement of campaign finance regulation do not have the power to initiate inquiries into possible irregularities in campaign financing. Almost half of the agencies also lack the authority to subpoena witnesses and records, and thus are limited in their efforts to gather information relevant to their assigned duties. And finally, only slightly more than half of the state agencies have the benefit of in-house legal counsel. This is an important measure of the ability of a politically sensitive agency to carry out its mission. When the agency must rely on the Office of the Attorney General, the county attorney, or some other equally busy state agent, campaign finance becomes just one of many state interests waiting for the attention, advice, and action that only legal experts can provide. In the future, agencies responsible for enforcement of campaign finance laws will be at a decided disadvantage unless they have political independence, comprehensive jurisdiction over all aspects of money and influence in politics, and the authority to initiate, develop, and prosecute campaign finance cases in a timely manner.

Future Trends

It is always dangerous to try to predict future political trends, especially in an area as volatile as the regulation of campaign finance. But, barring extremes, such as the reform-inspiring Watergate scandal, or wide-spread economic crisis, the recent past is probably the most useful predictor of future state behavior.

The trend toward more regulation, and more specific and all-encompassing campaign finance policies, is likely to continue, although it is true that there are those in almost every state who would prefer a laissez-faire approach regulated only by the forces of the "market." Appropriations for campaign finance administrative agencies are often a target of anti-reform forces, with bills to eliminate the enforcement of campaign finance or reduce regulation not being uncommon. However, during the last decade, such direct anti-reform movements have had little success. However, state budget cuts have included reductions in funds for administering and enforcing campaign finance regulation. Consequently, during the 1990s, some state campaign finance officials were forced to reduce the scope or the rigor of their activities. In fact, although it was less publicized than during the immediate post-Watergate surge, the 1980s saw a persistent and strategic extension of campaign finance reform that continues today. While the states remain the most active governmental units in terms of the variety of campaign finance reforms under consideration, the trend also has spread to local governments—from major cities like Los Angeles and New York, to county governments and even small communities such as Seattle, Washington, and Tucson, Arizona.

Within the general domain of campaign finance, there are at least four general topics or issues that can be expected to occupy the reform agenda in the near future. The first is the issue of leadership in shaping the reform agenda. Over the past few years there have been several examples of pro-reform governors successfully overcoming a reluctant, status-quo legislature. In Louisiana, a state notorious for corrupt politics, the governor led a successful effort to pass sweeping campaign finance reform. Governor Cuomo of New York convened a blue-ribbon commission that made exhaustive inquiries into the status of campaign financing in New York state and recommended a far-reaching reform package to a reluctant and wary, but politically vulnerable, legislature. [5]

In many states, citizens have the opportunity to legislate through citizen initiatives. When Governor Clinton was unsuccessful in trying to persuade the legislature of Arkansas to pass a strong ethics bill, he joined forces with citizen groups to put an initiative on the ballot. The voters approved the initiative, thus creating a public disclosure law applicable to public officials and lobbyists. Similarly, when elected officials in California failed to provide leadership on campaign finance issues, citizen and interest groups were successful in putting two competing ballot initiatives before the voters. In short, leadership in campaign finance reform is being supplied by governors, public interest groups, and other grassroot organizations which are losing patience with the recalcitrance many legislators show toward changing campaign finance regulations.

A second topic of reform concerns expanding the coverage, and tightening the enforcement, of contribution limits. At present, only Minnesota and Massachusetts prohibit corporations from using treasury funds to create and maintain PACs. But as corporate PACs continue to contribute increasingly larger sums to state campaigns, more attention will be given to the support PACs receive from contributors as well as from their parent organizations. Several states are giving serious consideration to limiting the amount of money any one candidate can take from PACs and are monitoring the Arizona example of limiting the aggregate amount a candidate can receive from PACs. Wisconsin prohibits PACs from giving to political parties and from acting as conduits for organizational giving.

States also are seeking to define and narrow the funding cycle. Several states have either prohibited contributions from lobbyists or have limited fund-raising activities during the legislative session. Nebraska is representative of state efforts to extend the laws governing lobbying of the legislature to the executive branch as well. Other states are trying to determine how best to regulate "bundling"—that process whereby one individual or group collects many individual contributions and bundles them into a single, large "contribution."

Public subsidy programs provide a third area in which states can be expected to show continued activity because of the growing public concern about ever-increasing campaign costs. In Kentucky, the gubernatorial race in 1967 cost less than $2 million; by 1987, expenditures exceeded $18 million. In 1986, the cost of state legislative campaigns in California was more than $57 million, while the 1990 California and Texas gubernatorial races each cost more than $50 million.

Public campaign financing appears to be the only constitutional vehicle for effectively limiting campaign spending, and many states have looked seriously at partial funding programs. States as diverse as Maine, New York, Washington, and West Virginia have developed strong advocacy groups for public campaign financing, including subsidies for state legislative campaigns. In lieu of direct campaign subsidies, some states are exploring the waiver of filing fees in return for agreeing to expenditure limits. Others seek public pressure to encourage candidates to voluntarily accept campaign expenditure limits. Further underscoring the fact that the states are not backing away from the concept of public financing are efforts in Iowa, Minnesota, and Wisconsin to extend state public campaign financing, and hence expenditure limits, to congressional candidates. However, such state actions are likely to be negated because federal law preempts state law in the election of federal officials. Nevertheless, states stepping in where Congress has failed to act is testimony that public subsidy programs may have more future in the states than pundits have predicted.

The fourth area on which states will most likely focus attention involves the role of political parties in campaign financing. "Soft money" has become an issue largely because states have few regulations on the contribution and expenditure patterns for state-level political party organizations. Two dimensions of party activity are drawing the attention of reformers. One is the use of the state party organizations as dumping grounds for excess funds targeted for federal candidates. Many individuals and interest groups wanting to contribute beyond the limits imposed by FECA do so through contributions to the state political parties. Most often, this money is not only implicitly given to assist a federal candidate but it is given by someone who resides or does business outside the state. One extreme example of an attempt to confront this activity is a legal action in Alaska, which challenged the constitutionality of funds for a candidate raised from outside the candidate's electoral district. Several states have limits on or are considering limiting the amount a state party can give to an individual candidate. Others are simply arguing for full disclosure of all sources of political party funds.

A slightly different aspect of political party funding focuses on the role of party leaders, especially legislative leaders. It is now common practice for the top legislative leaders to become the "bankers" for their party's legislative candidates. These leaders raise very large sums, usually from PACs and special interests, and allocate them to the party faithful. The most common way to counter this practice is to limit the amount any one candidate (or leadership PAC) can "transfer" to another candidate. When transfer fund limits are in place, the power of the legislative middleman is reduced. Advocates of stronger parties denounce such legislation, while campaign finance reformers view limits on transfers as essential to maintaining the integrity of the campaign funding process.

There are many approaches to campaign reform that individual states have taken which may or may not become commonplace among the fifty states. In Indiana, creating a special commission to police political ads and literature has been debated, while in Washington legislation has been proposed to deal with false and malicious political advertising. Legislation has been introduced in Alaska to prevent lobbyists from being directly or indirectly involved in the solicitation of campaign funds. New Jersey law, demonstrating different concerns, requires gubernatorial candidates who accept public funding to participate in two public debates. Clearly, there is no limit to the diversity of state activity in the area of campaign finance. Without much fanfare, the regulation of campaign finance continues to be the focus of interest and activity in the states, with the product of these valuable laboratories providing new lessons in the democratic electoral process.

Notes

1. David S. Broder, "Assessing Campaign Reform: Lessons for the Future," in Herbert E. Alexander, ed., *Campaign Money: Reform and Reality in the States* (New York: The Free Press, 1976), p. 315.
2. The following discussion is based on material presented in *The Book of the States 1988-89*, vols. 27, 28, and 29 (Lexington, KY: The Council of State Governments, 1992); Joyce Bullock, ed., *Campaign Finance, Ethics, and Lobby Law Blue Book 1988-89* (Special Edition); Also see 8th edition, 1990. (Lexington, Kentucky: The Council on Governmental Ethics Laws through the Council of State Governments, 1988); bimonthly issues of *COGEL Guardian* (Lexington, Kentucky: Council on Governmental Ethics Laws, 1988); *Campaign Practices Reports* (Washington: D.C.: Congressional Quarterly, Inc., Vol. 16, No. 16, August 7, 1989), and The Council of State Governments, *State Trends and Forecasts*, Vol. 2, No. 1. (Lexington, Kentucky, April 1993).
3. The states of Massachusetts, Ohio, and Tennessee prohibit corporate contributions but do not restrict most union contributions; Kentucky, Michigan, Minnesota, Montana, Oklahoma, West Virginia, and Wisconsin prohibit corporate contributions and restrict union gifts; Alabama, Mississippi, and New York limit corporate contributions but not union contributions. The majority of states also put restrictions on contributions from banks, insurance companies, and utilities, especially those doing business with the states.
4. Under FECA, public funds provide partial funding for the major parties' nominating conventions but no public money is allocated for any other party activity.
5. New York State Commission on Government Integrity, *The Midas Touch: Campaign Finance Practices of Statewide Officeholders* (New York: New York, June 1989); and *Evening the Odds: The Need to Restrict Unfair Incumbent Advantage* (New York, New York, October 1989).

5

The Cost of Election Campaigns in Brazil

Roberto Aguiar

In every democratic country in the world, election campaigns involve substantial financial costs, although actual expenses are not easy to determine.[1] Even in countries where the campaign costs are relatively low, or subject to strict surveillance by the courts or other agencies, it is possible to observe a discrepancy between "official" and actual spending. In Brazil, this difference is immense, though it is difficult to gather precise data on these costs since many of the financial and commercial transactions concerned are covert and sometimes illegal.

Collection and Reliability of the Data

In order to assure reliable calculations, the researcher must be meticulous and innovative in collecting data and must consider the various specific features of Brazilian elections. Data collection should include information that is verifiable and publishable, and also information that could, in certain cases, even endanger the researcher. Sources may range from account books to conversations lubricated by whiskey. From the viewpoint of the elections proper, the investigator has to bear in mind at least two fundamental features: the direct and clear connection between the method of electing by public vote, and the covert and subtle maintenance of the real power structure regulating the relations between politicians and electors. Expenditures must cover both these fundamental aspects of campaigning, ranging from advertising expenses to the distribution of dentures to electors.

Election Campaigns in Brazil: Costs and Funding

In order to be elected in Brazil, a politician is dependent upon at least two major support groups: the financial backers and the militants. The former guarantee the flow of resources, while the latter are charged with converting the money into votes. However, such a statement is not intended to reduce the process to merely buying and selling votes. The process is more complex than this, although it cannot be denied that the simple purchase of votes does occur.

Parties and candidates are obliged to pay a high price to have their messages disseminated to the public. Election publicity has increasingly been utilizing resources ranging from the distribution of small gifts to the promotion of shows: performers, caps, shirts, buttons, sandals, colored ribbons, pamphlets, posters, billboards, brochures, jingles, newspaper space, pyrotechnics, and presenters. The market rules for this kind of professional expertise are relatively well-known and stable, making it possible to calculate the cost. It should be noted also that most of the contracts are non-written, with frequent under-the-counter payments.

The amount of money spent on funding the militants is far more difficult to estimate accurately. The militants may be volunteers—or simply mercenaries. Volunteer militants within the middle class often cover their own expenses, such as food and transportation. However, those with scanty economic resources are financed by the party or politician during their mobilization. Thus, volunteer militants receive publicity material and also some form of financial help, while mercenaries may receive rivers of money.

The money spent by the politicians and parties, however, does not necessarily reach the pocket of the ordinary elector. It is paid directly to the *cabo eleitoral* (professional vote-getter), someone who has influence over a fair number of people, possibly a community leader or a *coronis* (big shot) whether urban or rural. Although votes are sometimes exchanged for ready money, the ordinary voter can also barter his or her vote for something more palpable and concrete than money. Everything from payment for photographs for old voter's cards to medical prescriptions can be used in an electoral transaction.

A functional change has progressively replaced the *cabo eleitoral* with a system of greater complexity, but his work has not been eliminated. He is still entrusted with the task of "rendering assistance" to the electors, visiting them and seeing to it that their requests are heeded by the politician he serves. The *cabos eleitorais* of old, whose work was almost entirely carried out on an individual basis, now operate predominately as part of an integrated group. A small organization, often based on a family, constitutes a "structure," usually including a town councillor, a mayor, or a community leader. Such personnel cost the politicians and the parties a great deal of money and exercise considerable power over the lives of a significant part of the electorate. Apparently, in the 1986 gubernatorial elections one of the groups that founded one of the main parties in Pernambuco spent about $12 million, most of which was channeled to the aforementioned "structures." However, the ordinary voter saw in this money only the transportation provided on election day, the T-shirts and "colors" (sets of shirts for soccer teams) they received, the beers and barbecues, and the whitewashing of neighborhood schools or the local domino league's building.

There are few politicians with sufficient money of their own to finance the expensive election campaigns in Brazil. The most conservative estimate of expenditures on Pernambuco's 1986 election campaign indicates that no less than $70 million was spent. This figure represents nearly 3 percent of the state's gross domestic product and made the vote in Pernambuco among the most expensive in the world, at about $20 per voter. There are those who see the frenetic economic activity engaged in during Brazilian election campaigns as somewhat of an informal mechanism for the distribution of income, and it is true that small firms and a fair number of unskilled workers do benefit from increased earnings during the election period. However, it also is the case that these financial benefits are most concentrated in the most privileged sectors of the country.

The campaigns are funded mainly by bankers, industrialists, traders, and livestock breeders. Firms providing specialized services to the state have, on the whole, been particularly generous in contributing to political parties and politicians. Among these, the large civil construction firms have played a leading role, earning the reputation of being the major financial backers in the last few elections. It is clear that the money donated is not always officially recorded in the parties' account books, but it does not go exclusively into politicians' pockets. The exchange in question is more subtle and complex.

On the one hand, the way in which power is structured in Brazil has led to its concentration in the hands of a few—generally those of the technobureaucracy in the executive branch of government. On the other hand, it has transformed the legislator into a mere lobbyist, someone who knows the right people and the best way to make things move. In this way, legislators—town councillors, deputies, or senators—are indispensable to ensure that public tenders are held, or won, and above all, that payments by the state are duly made. As resources are always scarce, the state is frequently in arrears with payment of its obligations. Thus, there will always be a legislator willing to obtain the release of the funds in exchange for contributions to his or her party or own election campaign. As a result, the state is indirectly transformed into a source of funds for politicians and parties. For example, the release of funds and settlement of overdue debts by SUNDENE (Federal Agency for the Development of the Northeast) at election time in the Northeast are well-known. Also common is the release of funds by ministers, state governments, or public financing agencies without a clearly specified purpose during the election period. In this way a large sum of money, vaguely labeled as social assistance, may be used to favor the governing party.

The contributions and donations to election campaigns obey certain established rules. Even outside of legal limits, they are not entirely beyond the control of the parties and politicians. In fact, the political parties carefully organize the financial control of election campaigns, which has led to increased prestige and power for their treasurers, who use unofficial books and other unorthodox means to handle campaign funds.

One of the most widely used ploys has been opening a bank account in the names of two persons, directors of a non-existent company. With the bank manager fully aware that the documents and names are false, donations and contributions flow into this account. One such newly-opened account, intended to finance a political party in Pernambuco during the 1986 election campaign, received deposits of more than $4 million in less than a month.

Money from an even more controversial source can help finance politicians and parties in Brazil. Frequently *bicheiros* (operators of the illegal, but widely tolerated, annual numbers lottery) and contraband dealers make sizable donations to election campaigns as a way of laundering their funds. Large traffickers of precious metals and drugs—particularly cocaine—approach political parties and politicians of the most diverse ideologies, as a way of influencing the decision-making process and protecting themselves. Additional contributions are made by international organizations, legal and illegal, of the most varied ideological complexions.

The data suggest a correlation between the amount spent on election campaigns and the value of legislators' earnings. In fact, relatively speaking, Brazilian legislators are among the highest paid in the world. Even if North American legislators receive more actual dollars than their Brazilian counterparts, they enjoy fewer perquisites, pay more in taxes, and have a higher cost of living. The approximately $50,000 that a federal deputy earns per annum in Brazil is a far higher amount in terms of purchasing power than the per annum earned by members of the U. S. Congress.

The explanation for the value of the earnings of Brazilian legislators cannot be found merely in the fact that the upper middle class in Brazil has a level of consumption—and therefore of income—among the highest in the world. It is also necessary to recognize that wages and salaries, regardless of their nature, are directly related to the type of work performed under the mandate granted by the electors. It is the mandate, rather than parliamentary activity proper, that mostly determines the value of the legislator's earnings. In general, mayors, governors, and senators have been the election campaign figures around whom the webs of power and influence are woven, on whom the *cabos eleitorais*, town councillors, and deputies depend. This is especially true of those who occupy posts in the executive branch of government, since the operation of the state machine depends most directly on them. Operating the state apparatus becomes a privileged means of distributing benefits that can be exchanged for votes.

An analysis of the 1986 election results provides a demonstration model of the efficacy and efficiency of the local political bosses as vote pullers. It was they, more than any other combination of political or ideological forces, who were chiefly responsible for the election of almost all the governors in 1986. In the states of Rio Grande do Sul, São Paulo, Minas Gerais, Bahia, and Pernambuco, this support of the mayors and local political bosses was the decisive factor in ensuring electoral success. The power and influence of these local bosses over the behavior of the electorate indicates that political ideologies, as traditionally understood, played a secondary role in the electors' choice of candidate.

Direct elections, following the 1964 coup, were exercises reserved only for filling posts in the state legislatures and local governments of the hinterland. State governors did not start to be elected again by direct suffrage until 1982, and the direct election process of mayors of state capitols resumed only in 1985. Perhaps this was the reason that the local political bosses had their political and electoral functions enhanced by the Brazilian electoral system. It is imperative to add, moreover, that medium-sized towns have shown real progress in recent years throughout the country. Accordingly, the administrative performance of their mayors has received the electorate's strong approval, reinforcing still further the relative weight and influence of such political readers from the hinterland.

For this reason, all available evidence suggests that the local political bosses, particularly the hinterland mayors, were one of the main electoral forces operating in the presidential election of 1989. The figure of the professional politician (frequently linked to that of the legislator) was profoundly discredited and, with no simultaneous elections for the legislature taking place, was less present and showed less interest in this particular campaign. The same cannot be said of the mayors, who would depend on federal grants for at least another year to keep their administrations running. Hence, despite being what has come to be known in Brazil as an *eleição solteira* (single election), the presidential campaign of that year appeared to be strongly tied to the local political leaders. As a result, it is obvious that the more mayors a politician had under his leadership, the greater his chances of influencing the outcome of the election. In view of this, the electoral power of the then governor of São Paulo should come as no surprise: as leader of the national municipal movement he commanded a vast number of mayors from the extreme north to the extreme south of the country.

The Presidential Campaign and Its Cost

A number of important features made the presidential election of 1989 an electoral process without precedent in Brazil. After twenty-nine years the population was electing the president by direct, secret, and universal suffrage. Twenty-two candidates disputed the votes of 82,074,718 electors who for the first time had to exercise their franchise in two rounds of voting. It was thus an electoral event five times as large as that which had elected President Janio Quadros in 1960. Of the 1989 electorate, 63.3 percent (those under the age of forty-six), had never before voted in a presidential election.

In addition, the social and economic changes that took place between 1960 and 1990 had significantly modified Brazilian society. The country was emerging from a dictatorship and launching itself on a competition for votes with an entirely new face. In 1960, Brazil was still an agriculturally-based society, with only about 47 percent of its total population having reached adulthood. Of this adult population, the illiterate 38.8 percent were not entitled to vote.

In 1989, the rate of illiteracy, though still high, had fallen by 54.6 percent and, moreover, the illiterate had won the right to vote. Out of a total of 144,293,110 inhabitants, 107,239,796, (about 60 percent) live in urban areas—the opposite of the prevailing situation three decades earlier. In addition, the per capita income, though still low, had tripled. Industrial production had grown at impressive rates, placing Brazil among the new industrial countries. A young population, 60 percent under twenty-five years of age, in a society renewed by the processes of urbanization and industrialization was launching itself into the new experience of saying no, through the vote, to all that it considered obsolete.

Being an election for a single post, the presidential election should have been a relatively cheaper election than the 1986 state governorship elections. Nevertheless, by virtue of its national character, and probably owing also to its having been held in two rounds, the 1989 presidential election cost much more than those in 1986. However, the unprecedented battle in the electronic media (particularly on television) increased the expenses to even more astronomical figures.

Television has considerably altered the way in which politicians and parties relate to the electors. Through video, the politician becomes an idol. Every appearance is carefully planned and produced, while content matters less. In advance of his appearance on the video, the politician pays a team of pollsters and social scientists to investigate what the viewers would like to see and hear. During the production of the program a team of social communicators and experts on television language see to it that the politician says, in the appropriate media language, exactly what the potential electors wish to hear, resulting in high rates of public acceptance.

There is nothing cheap about this election strategy. Even considering the fact that Brazilian legislation allows for free access to television for politicians and parties, the planning, preparation, and production of the programs consume a great deal of money. It is said that as early as May, five months prior to polling day, a certain candidate had paid out $50,000 for each appearance on television. This money includes the hire of a party label, the only legal loophole permitting an appearance on television.

The election legislation in Brazil allows for each party to request the Electoral Court to grant it free time on a national radio and television network at least once a year. In addition, during the election campaign proper, the parties are allowed two hours per day, divided into two slots, for the presentation of their programs. This mechanism, originally devised as a way of democratizing access to the mass media, has been distorted into one of the chief reasons for the rise in campaign costs. In fact, the large and small networks alike found themselves obliged to cede, for free, a significant part of their peak audience times to parties and candidates. But the competition among parties to present the best politically-marketed program has brought about a huge increase in the cost of actual production.

It is not hard to find examples of political journalists who, owing to the demands of parties and candidates, have specialized in what has become known in Brazil as political marketing. For salaries vastly higher than those of journalists, these professionals form small advertising agencies and undertake to sell the candidate's image, and also disseminate the parties' ideas in a more efficient manner, according to the rules of show business.

In the 1980s, Gallup polls had acquired an unprecedented popularity among Brazilian politicians, parties, and electors. What was formerly the exception became the rule, obliging parties and politicians to rely on data from polls to win the allegiance of the electors. In 1989, the candidate Fernando Collor de Mello prepared a sophisticated strategy for following the trends in public opinion surveys. Other candidates did likewise, but apparently none of them organized such a complete and comprehensive scheme as Collor de Mello. After polls taken in February had shown him to be the preferred candidate of a mere 2 percent of the electorate, Collor de Mello managed to alter this picture by employing the elaborate technology of propaganda, as well as the technically correct use of surveys, and was elected president in December of that year.

Estimating the costs of the 1989 presidential election campaign is very difficult. The shortcomings of Brazilian legislation that exercises practically no effective control over such expenses, plus the singularity of this particular election, contributed considerably to the fact that a significantly large amount of money was spent on the campaign. If one includes the money spent from February, the figure may appear immense. Although the first round of the presidential election of 1989 did not take place until November 15, parties and politicians had clearly been on the campaign trail since the beginning of the year. Collor de Mello, for instance, obtained legal permission to speak on a national television network for three successive months, causing his popularity rating to rise from a negligible 2 percent to more than 20 percent by the end of June. Even in the first semester, expensive, well-produced programs were being used by the parties.

The perception that billions of dollars may have been spent to elect the first Brazilian president since the fall of the dictatorship does not seem at all fanciful. Indeed, in the ten months of real campaigning, many small jets were hired, many trips were made all over a country of continental dimensions, numerous television and radio programs were made, and a great many national and foreign groups and trade union organizations were involved. If one bears in mind that as president-elect, Collor de Mello, traveled in a private jet with a group of friends for ten-day vacation in the Seychelles, calculations indicating that the sum total of money spent on the election campaign for the presidency of the Federative Republic of Brazil in 1989 exceeded $2 billion does not seem farfetched.

And some of the sources of the money led to President Collar de Mello's downfall.

Note

1. This essay is based on a previous work by the author, "O Custo Das Campanhas Electorais No Brasil," in *Cadernos de Estudios Socias*, Vol. 5, No. 1, 1989, pp. 5-13.

6

Regulation of Political Finance in France

Pierre Avril

Until 1988, the relationship between politics and money in France was a contradictory one with legislation theoretically insuring equality among candidates in elections, but political practices occurring almost completely outside the law. However, the situation was not felt to be pathological, but rather an unavoidable compromise between the principles that had to be proclaimed and the practical requirements from which one could not escape.

The first concern for this situation appeared following scandals provoked by what was called the "real estate Gaullism." During his press conference on September 23, 1971, President Georges Pompidou revealed the peaceful skepticism that was prevailing then. He reasoned that the parties' resources "are not very clear in general, for various reasons, and not always for immoral ones for that matter. I do not mind if we regulate them. This will not change much." [1]

Thought about reform began much later, with the successive political changes which brought the Socialists to power in 1981, before the Right regained the majority at the National Assembly in 1986. In 1988, Francois Mitterand called for new elections, and on the eve of the presidential campaign, the first reform was adopted. The process was completed at the end of 1989, after the set of national and local elections that followed.

The Circumstances of the Reform

The rapid rise of electoral expenses, which affected all the political parties, was the convincing factor that the status quo could not last and that change was needed. A campaign cannot be executed without polls, mailings, photo opportunities, consultations with experts in political marketing, commercial bill posting, and numerous other elements. Even though the true efficiency of some of these sophisticated methods can at times be questioned, politicians inevitably feel obligated to use these techniques because their competitors do. The resulting financial escalation started to seriously worry candidates and party leaders.

Thus, on the occasion of the Ninth Conference of the Council on Government Ethics Laws in September 1987, there was new consensus in favor of moderating electoral expenses. Two months later, the principle of a law on political financing was accepted by the Government and all the parties except the Communists, who were hostile to any state interference.

The sudden and unpredictable acceleration of the reform process was due to the immediate need to defuse an explosive judicial inquiry. On November 4, 1987, the daily newspaper of the Right, *Le Figaro*, disclosed the conclusions of an administrative report calling into question the Socialist Party's role in the exportation of shells to Iran by the Luchaire company. Despite an embargo, the office of the Defense Minister was accused of having favored the operation, and the Socialist party, then in power, would have benefited financially from it. The President reacted immediately. On November 16, he publicly invited the Government to propose that Parliament vote on a law regulating and controlling the financing of political life in order to avoid the repetition of such matters. A few days later, the case of the Lyon false invoices, in which personalities of different parties were mentioned, confirmed that the Luchaire practice was not an isolated incident.

The whole system was in danger of being indicted. Prime Minister Jacques Chirac answered Mitterand's invitation and obtained the passage of two laws on March 11, 1988: one dealing with the financing of elections for the President of the state and the members of Parliament, and the other concerning electoral campaigns and the parties. But the new measures proved inadequate and were regarded with skepticism since they had been adopted quickly and under suspicious circumstances (just before the opening of the presidential electoral campaign in which Mitterand and Chirac were going to confront each other). The problem was far from being solved.

The question arose again in May 1989, with the case of the South-East false invoices which involved a very important company of public works, the Société Auxiliaire d'Entreprise (SAE). The principal leaders were arrested, and political personalities from the Right and the Left, who had benefited from the company's "generosity," were charged with the crime. During searches in Marseille, the police discovered documents expounding in detail the financing mechanism, developed by the Socialist Party through a consulting firm (Urbatechnic) and a centralized purchasing body (Grappo) which served as intermediaries between the local elected candidates and the companies.

On May 14, 1989, Mitterand claimed that his initiative of 1987 had been "distorted" by the government of Chirac and that a new strict and complete law needed to be considered.[2] This law, which he asked Prime Minister Rocard to prepare, was supposed to settle the situation. Public financing would be stabilized by insuring public revenues to the parties and candidates. Amnesty would be given to those who had resorted to unlawful practices due to the lack of an organized and controlled method of financing. The opposition were indignant at this measure from which the Socialist Party appeared to be the main beneficiary, but the amnesty secretly relieved many elected candidates who were not Socialists. The Right allowed the measure to pass by the abstention of a sufficient number of its Parliament members.

The Sources of Political Financing

Electoral campaigns today are much more costly than those in the past and cannot be run in the same unsophisticated manner. Public declarations of expenses are always under suspicion because the parties traditionally under-report their expenses. The estimate of one marketing agency, published in 1986 by the Canard enchaîné assessed a constituency's campaign to be ten francs per voter. This meant, for the whole of France, more than 360 million francs for each party. Gérard Monate, the head of the consulting firms supporting the Socialist party, indicated that in 1989, ten to twenty francs per voter were necessary, depending on the population of the constituency. The publicist Jacques Seguela, who invented the slogan "la force tranquille" (The Peaceful Force) for Mitterand, estimated the total expenses of the legislative elections of 1986 to be one billion francs. Costs for the two main candidates in the 1981 presidential election, Valéry Giscard d'Estaing and Mitterand, were estimated to be about 200 million each. All reports indicated that expenses were appreciably higher in 1988, but the declared campaign accounts, which are now required to be published, reported smaller sums, citing 99,842,170 francs for Mitterand and 95,948,005 francs for Chirac. This under-evaluation partly resulted from the imprecision of the applicable rules, as the Constitutional Council later found in its observations of the presidential election.[3]

For a long time, the parties maintained that their resources came from their members' dues, with the candidates discreetly soliciting contributions from a few friends. These assertions have never been taken seriously, primarily because of the small number of party members and the limitations of "disinterested patronage." Among the other sources of funding are the national subscriptions and the contributions made by members of Parliament which sometimes reach high amounts. Before 1986, the 285 Socialist Parliament members each paid about 8,000 francs per month to the Socialist Party, totaling about 28 million per year. In 1989, the number of Socialist Parliament members had fallen to 257, but their donations had risen to 10,000 francs each.[4]

The true sources of ordinary political financing are to be found elsewhere. Some sources are public, but not official. Some lie in the services that the municipalities offer to the candidates of their party (mailing leaflets and brochures, hiring officials paid by the community), in the tradition of political machines. However, less innocent sources have developed, such as utilizing research organizations controlled by friends which intervene in two ways. The municipality may pay for research services at rates higher than their true value (the difference being used to finance the expenses of the Party), as happened in 1982 town-planning operations in Paris. The municipality also may force the companies applying for contracts to hire these research organizations, which then levies a "research fee" of 2 to 2.5 percent of the value of the contract, similar to a tax levied on the public markets. The company Urbatechnic, which supports the Socialist party, contends that it supplies a service equal to the commissions it receives. It also reports that three-fourths of its commission is paid back to the national treasury of the Party after its functioning expenses are deducted.[5]

One form of this levy has arisen around the Royer law, which allows a local agency, the Department Commission for Town Planning and Commerce, to authorize the creation of department stores. This sometimes gives rise to a real racket, as in the case of the false invoices of the city of Nancy, which ended with the imprisonment of the RPR deputy and mayor to the town of Toul in November 1989.[6]

Naturally, the parties in power are well placed to use the resources that power provides, though sometimes skirting the rules of public accounting, such as allocating the communication budgets of different ministries during the elections to their respective agencies. As Prime Minister, Jacques Chirac tried to centralize the financing and ordering of this system, but some members of the Government rebelled because they feared the contracts would be given only to the agencies that worked with the RPR. It is clear that exporting companies are sometimes obliged to pay unofficial intermediaries in order to obtain markets. In the Luchaire case, the office of the Defense Minister was accused of having closed its eyes to the unlawful exportation of shells to Iran, so as not to lose the kickback for the Socialist Party.

The other type of campaign funding is private. Employer associations have always assisted the candidates, usually those supporting favored positions, but sometimes as insurance in all camps. The National Council of the French Employers (CNPF) intervened directly under the Fourth Republic. The entry of the government of André Boutemy, who was the dispenser of the CNPF funds, nearly provoked a crisis in 1953 which forced Boutemy to resign.[7] The CNPF has since dedicated itself to an advisory position through its Legislative Studies Service. The Audit Office has discovered that the employee federations sometimes financed the parties by indirect taxes, levied for the benefit of the branch. Here again, it is mainly the parties of the Right that are privileged; those of the Left benefit from the favors of large mutual insurance companies.

Party treasurers have diversified their contacts at the company level where patronage comes in all forms. A common practice consists of subscribing to candidates' publications or to the parties, and signing advertising contracts unrelated to realistic sales expectations. For example, the Socialist Party newspaper received the equivalent of about 100 advertising pages from an advertiser, of which less than forty had actually been published. In exchange, the advertiser asked for excessive favors.

All these subventions are "under the table," and are sometimes made through fronting companies that allow the donor to remain anonymous. In 1982, during legal proceedings provoked by the "black box" of a famous soccer club, it was discovered that the club's president was contributing to the electoral expenses of the town's two deputies. The proceedings also revealed false invoices from which the value added tax (VAT) could be recovered. These deals, which in September 1983 led to corruption charges against four Communist-elected candidates in the Paris region and the former deputy mayor of Marseille, appear to be only the tip of the iceberg. In 1988 and 1989, charges against mayors and Parliament members of all parties were leveled in connection with the cases of the false invoices of Lyon, of the Southeast and the East, and the region of Rouen.

The Present Legislation

The two laws of March 11, 1988, are concerned with the presidential and legislative elections, the disclosure of the estates of elected candidates, and the subventions to the parties. The laws of January 15 and May 10, 1990, have established a general regulation for all universal suffrage elections excepting the election of senators, which takes place by indirect voting, and local elections in districts of less than 9,000 inhabitants. They also have modified the financing of the parties.

Financing and Reaching a Ceiling of Electoral Expenses

The main deficiency of the traditional regulation of electoral expenses is that it was applicable only during the three weeks of the official campaign preceding the election. Also, it was aimed only at expenses for which reimbursement was secured. The new legislation takes into account the total amount of receipts, and the expenses directly incurred by the candidate or on his or her behalf, during the year that precedes the month of the election.

Limitations. During this one-year period, candidates cannot receive funds to finance their campaigns and can only pay campaign expenses through a financial agent whom they designate. Inspired by the British electoral agent, either an association or an individual must open a special bank account to handle campaign operations. The agent's term of office ends three months after the election.

A variable ceiling on electoral expenses is set for all elections, depending on the nature of the election and the population of the district. For the election of municipal council members, the ceiling ranges from eleven francs per inhabitant for districts of less than 15,000, to five francs per inhabitant for those over 250,000. For general council elections (department), the ceiling varies from three to six francs, and from two to five francs for district council elections. The ceiling for Parliament members is 500,000 francs per candidate, except in districts with populations of less than 80,000, where it is reduced to 400,000 francs. Finally, the ceiling for candidates to the presidential election is set at 120 million francs, expanded to 160 million for the two candidates on the second ballot.

In order to reduce the constantly increasing costs of campaigns, the 1990 law forbids commercial bill posting, press advertising, and free telephone or telematic (Minitel) numbers, during the three months preceding the month of the election. Finally, political advertising is permanently forbidden on radio or television.

Private contributions from an individual are limited to 30,000 francs for a single election, and up to 10 percent of the ceiling or 500,000 francs, from a private corporate body. However, the parties are not included in this limitation. The donors receive a receipt for their contribution from the financial agent. A compromise between the Socialists, who favored publicity, and the Centrists, who preferred confidentiality, resulted in receipts issued for gifts of more than 20,000 francs by individuals. Those receipts issued for a corporate donation indicate the beneficiary of the gift, while the receipts for individual gifts of less than 20,000 francs do not. Gifts to candidates are deductible from personal income tax and from the corporation tax under the same conditions as those that benefit general interest philanthropic or educational organizations.

Reporting and Penalties. Within the two months following the election, the candidates must deliver an account of their campaign finances, along with the accounts of their financial agents, counting all revenues by source and all the expenses according to their nature, incurred for the period of one year preceding the polling. This accounting is forwarded to a National Commission for Campaign and Political Financing Accounts which is composed of three members, named by their chiefs from each of the three superior courts: Conseil d'Etat, Cour de cassation (Court of Cassation) and Cour des comptes (Audit office). The Commission then reviews the accounts and approves, rejects, or corrects them within three months. Two additional months are allowed if the election is disputed in the administrative courts (local elections) or in the Constitutional Council (legislative elections). The accounts of the candidates in the presidential election are forwarded directly to the Constitutional Council.

Faulty reporting may result in ineligibility, criminal conviction, or fines. Ineligibility is declared when a candidate has not handed in his account or has had the account legitimately rejected. The ruling is delivered by the administrative court or the Constitutional Council called upon by the National Commission for Campaign and Political Financing Accounts. If the elected candidate has been declared ineligible, the election is ruled invalid. The election judge also can declare a candidate ineligible for exceeding the ceiling of authorized expenses.

Many decisions concerning ineligibility have since been made by the Conseil d'Etat's decision. One involved the matter of a winning candidate who had exceeded the expenditure ceiling by not including in his campaign account the price of a party-financed poll paid on the electors' attitudes in his electoral constituency. On July 31, 1991, the council refused to declare him ineligible and did not cancel the election because it considered the law imprecise on this point. (The council indicated that in the future such expenditures must appear on campaign accounts.) In another decision, on January 29, 1992, the Constitutional Council declared two candidates ineligible who had not submitted their campaign accounts within the prescribed time limits. The National Commission notifies the public prosecutor when offenses are found during auditing, who then determines the criminality of the offense.

Fines are attributed equal to the amount by which the ceiling was overstepped, as fixed by the National Commission. Furthermore, state repayment of the expenses listed in the campaign account is possible only after its approval by the commission.

Repayment. Besides the expenses traditionally repaid by the State to candidates obtaining at least 5 percent of the vote cast (the printing and mailing of the declaration of principles and ballot papers, and printing of prescribed billboards), the new regulation plans an inclusive repayment equal to one-twentieth of the amount of the ceiling, (6 million francs) for all the presidential candidates, a quarter of the ceiling (40 million francs) for those obtaining more than 5 percent of the vote cast, and one-tenth of the ceiling (40,000 or 50,000 francs, depending on the district) for the candidates to the National Assembly obtaining at least 5 percent of the vote cast.

Transparency of the Estates

The second innovation of 1988 concerns the disclosure of the accounts of the principal elected candidates at the beginning and end of their terms of office.

Each candidate for the Presidency of the Republic must submit to the Constitutional Council a statement of his or her net worth (the totality of his or her estate including communal property and the indivisible property in case of inheritance), in a sealed envelope, with an agreement to file a new statement at the terms' expiration. The statement of the elected candidate is added to the election results proclaimed by the Constitutional Council, published by the *Journal Officiel*. In this manner, it was disclosed that Mitterand owns a Parisian home, a sheepfold in the Landes, and a pond in the Morvan, where he was a long time elected candidate.[8]

Within the fifteen days following the beginning of their term, Parliament members and senators also must file, in the Office of their Assembly, a sworn statement of their financial worth, and a new statement at the end of the term. The Office evaluates the variation in their financial situation by comparing the two statements. The president of the Assembly verifies the report (published in the *Journal Officiel*), at least on each re-election. The first report of the President of the Assembly noted that no "abnormal" variation of estate had been established for the fifty-one deputies whose mandate ceased at the beginning of the legislative session in June 1988.[9] Unlike the statement of the President of the Republic, these statements remain confidential and can only be communicated at the request of the person concerned or of the judicial authorities.

The members of Government, the presidents of the Regional Council and the General Council, and the mayors of communities with more than 30,000 inhabitants file their statements with a commission composed of the chiefs of the three supreme jurisdictions (courts of law) and presided over by the vice-president of the State Council. This commission, the

Commission for the Financial Transparency of Political Life, submits a report at least every three years. The first report, dated December 20, 1988,[10] specified that at that date, there were 397 persons obliged to file statements of net worth to the commission. In its third report, the commission was able to proceed to a comparison of estates of the Rocard Government members whose functions had ended in May 1991 but did not find any abnormal variation compared to their declarations of 1988.[11]

Financing of Political Parties

The law of March 11, 1988, instituted a system of public financing of political parties, depending on their parliamentary representation. The law of January 15, 1990, further enlarged the realm of private financing and modified public financing. Public financing is secured by the inclusion of credits in the Finance Act each year; the amount is, as a rule, proposed by the Government. In 1989, it reached 114 million francs, about three francs per registered voter. However, the French Communist Party refused to accept this allotment and the distributed sum was reduced to 105,602,679 francs.

This sum is divided in two parts, with the first part allocated to the parties that have presented candidates in at least seventy-five districts during the last session of the National Assembly. The funds are distributed proportionate to the number of votes received by their candidates on the first ballot. (In the second ballot, generally only the two leading candidates remain in competition.)

The law specified that parties receive at least 5 percent of the ballots cast in each district for a party to be eligible for funding. But the Constitutional Council decreed that "because of the threshold chosen, [this criterion was] of a sort to hinder the expression of new currents of thoughts and opinions." The council argued that it ignored the requirement of pluralism which constitutes the foundation of democracy and therefore was contrary to the Constitution.[12]

The second part of the sum is allocated to each of the parties based on the number of members of Parliament who are registered with that party or have an expressed linkage to it. The declaration of one's party association takes place in April of each year.

This second mode of allotment has been applied exclusively since the tenth session of the National Assembly, which took place in March 1993, because the first method could only be applicable when candidates remain in the party to which they were linked *before* the election. The system of French parties actually includes regrouping structures, like the Union for the French Democracy (UDF), which unites the Republican Party, the Center of the Social Democrats, the Radical Party, the Social Democrat Party, and the clubs Perspectives and Realities, together with the direct members. These all can refuse the allotment of credits corresponding to their elected members under the UDF seal. This happened in 1989 when sixteen parties participated in the allotment, including a "Union of Non-Registered Senators" (three members who went on to share 381,696 francs). The Socialist Parliament members have proposed that members of the National Assembly be the only ones taken into account for allocation purposes because the senators are not elected by direct suffrage, but retaining the status quo has been one of the conditions of the compromise sought by the Government.

The laws of 1988 and 1990 that require parties to file their accounts with the National Commission of Campaign Accounts and Political Financing, which publishes them in the *Journal Officiel*, first took effect in 1990.[13] The commission noted that six parties which had received credits for registered members of Parliament did not fulfill this obligation and therefore would lose the benefit of public subsidies. There has been an abnormal increase in the number of "parties" in which the members of Parliament have declared themselves registered. There were forty by the end of 1991, more than half of which had only one elected candidate. It is obvious that the law is being misused by some deputies and senators to obtain the credits regularly assigned to finance true political parties.

The private financing regulations detailed in the 1990 law extends to the parties a financial agent similar to the one for electoral campaigns. This agent is the only entity entitled to receive the gifts, which cannot exceed 50,000 francs per year from an individual or 500,000 francs from a private corporate body. They are deductible from corporation or personal income taxes under the same conditions as contributions to the candidates. The financial agent can be designated by a party or by a specialized branch (youth, women, research, etc.), to draw up a statement of the gifts from corporate bodies. The receiving party must file its account with the National Commission of the Campaign and Political Financing Accounts or risk losing the benefit of the public subvention.

The first statement of the new regulations will be found in the report of the Commission of Investigation on the Financing of Parties and Electoral Campaigns under the Fifth Republic. It was developed in May 1991 to end the controversies provoked by the different problems mentioned above. These continue to lead to legal actions on issues not covered by the amnesty law of 1990.[14]

The new system was first applied to the departmental and regional elections of March 22, 1992, and then to the legislative elections of March 21 and 28, 1993. It seems to function properly. From now on, candidates and parties will be aware of the risks involved in rule-breaking: they are automatically declared ineligible for one year if they have not submitted their accounts within the allotted time, and their election may be cancelled if they have won. This control may appear too cumbersome to be effective, but the National Commission of Campaign and Political Financing Accounts has appointed delegates to the various departments to rapidly monitor the accounts and submit those found unacceptable to the election judge (an administrative judge for local elections and the Constitutional Council for parliamentary elections). The March 1993 campaign was noticeably more temperate than the preceding ones. In addition, continuing criminal proceedings (two former treasurers of the Socialist Party were charged as accomplices to corruption in September 1993; several right-wing members of Parliament have been tried or convicted since the beginning of the year) are keeping politicians in line. The era of impunity is decidedly at an end.

Notes

1. *Le Monde,* September 25, 1991.
2. *Le Monde,* May 16, 1989.
3. Textes et documents relatifs a l'election presidentielle des 24 avril et 8 mai 1988, La Documentaion francaise, Notes et etudes documentaires, No. 4865.
4. *Bulletin quotidien,* June 2, 1989.
5. Edwy Plenel, "Urbatechnic á livre ouvert," *Le Monde,* April 17, 18, 19, 1993.
6. *Le Monde,* December 17-18, 1989.
7. Henry J. Ehrmann, *Organised Business in France,* (Princeton, N.J.: Princeton University Press, 1957), p. 196.
8. *Journal Officiel,* May 12, 1988, p. 7,004.
9. Ibid, October 8, 1991, p. 13,178.
10. Ibid, January 11, 1990, p. 422.
11. Ibid, November 23, 1991, p. 15,300.
12. Ibid, January 11, 1990, p. 573.
13. Ibid, January 23, 1992, p. 1,120.

7

Problems in Spanish Party Financing

Pilar del Castillo

Although the history of political party financing in Spain is as short as the new democracy, discrepancies between theory and practice have already developed. The media seem to uncover some new scandal nearly every day in a plot of alleged illegal party finance and political corruption.

While the scope of the corruption may verge on the ridiculous, such behavior deeply affects citizens' trust in political parties which can diminish faith in democracy itself. Spanish political parties already carry a deficit of credibility, partly due to the anti-party and apolitical culture that resulted from the Franco regime. Over the last two years, daily revelations of misconduct in Spanish newspapers have only added to this distrust.[1]

Regulations on electoral financing of political parties began in 1977, including public financing of campaign expenses, freedom to accept private donations (except foreign money), and a very loose disclosure system. This model was applied to the regular financing of political parties in 1978, to municipal elections in 1979, and to regional elections in 1983. The first reform did not occur until 1985, since the electoral financing norms for general elections were provisional and were initially approved only for the elections of a Constitution-drafting Parliament. Since disclosure was vaguely regulated without serious enforcement, very little is known about private sources of party financing between 1977 and 1985.[2]

Drawing from different sources, the general traits of Spanish party financing between 1977-1985 can be determined, from which two distinct periods emerge: 1977-1979 and 1979-1984. The first period coincides with Spain's transition to democracy. Party financing essentially relied on public funds, private donations from business associations and banks (through a policy of loan cancellations), and contributions from foreign organizations (such as national parties, international organizations of parties, and party foundations). German party foundations, for instance, gave considerable material and organizational support to Spanish parties.[3]

After 1979, there was a reduction of international economic aid. German party foundations continued to support their Spanish counterparts, but both the scope and quantity were reduced.[4] Public and private domestic funding continued as in the previous period, although information about the latter is still limited. Membership dues and direct deductions from Members' of Congress salaries, a practice common to most parties, continued to be marginal given the limited scope of party affiliation.[5] In 1981, a socialist-elected city council member from Madrid, who later abandoned that party, publicly charged a trash-collecting company with paying a commission to the parties in exchange for the job. This was the first sign that a new party financing system had begun.

In 1984, the German political-financial scandal known as "The Flick Case" broke, which had ramifications in Spanish politics. Allegedly, the Secretary General of the Spanish socialists (the current President) had received money from the German consortium to finance the 1977 elections. Under Spanish law, parties cannot receive contributions from abroad during electoral campaigns (although they may at other times).

An inquiry commission created by the Spanish Parliament did not uncover any important findings and the secretary general of the Spanish Worker Socialist Party was freed from all responsibility in the case. In the same report, each party in Parliament, except for the Communists, pointed out the importance of the aid they received from German foundations while establishing the democracy.[6] Nevertheless, political party financing became the subject of more focussed attention, resulting in a reform of the rules of electoral party financing.

In 1985, a new norm was approved which brought some substantive changes. The reform limited private sources of funding (1 million pesetas—approximately U.S. $10,000—per individual or group) and electoral expenses (3.3 billion pesetas in the 1989 elections), and exerted greater control over party expenses and income.[7]

In 1987, a more detailed law regulating ordinary party financing was passed.[8] The new rules gave public revenues overwhelming weight in the financing of parties. As in electoral contributions, the 1987 law limited the maximum annual amount which a person or group could donate to a party to 10 million pesetas. A new limitation on private contributions also was introduced: the total amount of private contributions could not exceed 5 percent of the quantity assigned in the state budget for subsidizing political parties. The consequences of this new restriction became clear in its first year of application when the total state subsidy amounted to 7.5 billion pesetas; no party could receive more than 375 million pesetas from private donations in 1987. Since the Socialist party's share of the subsidy was 3.195 billion pesetas, private contributions legally could have amounted only to a maximum of approximately 10 percent of its total income. While this percentage was greater for the first party in the opposition, the Partido Popular, its lower share in the same subsidy made private donations marginal relative to public funds. This legislation delegated a role of authority to the state in the financing of parties, a change without precedent.

The 1985 electoral financing reform and the 1987 financing regulation enjoyed the support of the main parliamentary parties, although some, such as the Partido Popular and the Catalan Nationalists, initially opposed limiting private contributions. The strong sanctions against private financing resulted from parliamentary debate. Along with introducing inequalities among parties, private funds have the potential to be exchanged for favorable treatment, making them ethically unacceptable.[9] To diminish such pressure on political groups, only small amounts of private money should reach political parties; their main support should be based on "neutral" state money (even though neutrality in Spanish politics is questionable, since the criteria used for allocations of electoral and regular public funds clearly reward majority parties).[10]

An underlying attitude about the trinomial society/party/state relationship favors a close tie between parties and the state but leaves links between parties and society undeveloped. Many arguments contend that, in a liberal democratic system, such a relationship should be maintained, if not encouraged.[11] Arguments to this effect can be found in a 1966 German Supreme Court decision on party financing, and in the 1982-1983 report by the Presidential Committee which created the basis for the 1983 political party financing reform.

In February 1991, the rules of party electoral financing were subject to a new reform effort intended to reduce the ceiling on electoral expenses. However, the ceiling increased rather than decreased. While parties are required to use less of their money than in previous electoral campaigns, the state must subsidize their growing electoral mailing expenses. The apparent reduction in party expenses actually represents an increase in public funding.

Since 1986, the Tribunal de Cuentas (a committee in charge of electoral and ordinary party accounting) has published reports about electoral expenses and income (1986, 1987) and ordinary expenses and income (1987).[12] These reports show the same schema of party financing as previously outlined. According to the model based on official data, parties determine their financing almost exclusively on state subsidies. Private donations are practically nonexistent and the majority parties' resources, membership dues, and party congressmen, make up only between 2 and 5 percent of their incomes. Bank loans are used extensively by all parties to finance electoral campaigns. Only part of these loans are repaid by subsidies received after the elections, resulting in ever-increasing party debt.[13] According to official reports, parties have never exceeded the limit set on electoral expenses, nor have any accounting irregularities been found to indicate an electoral criminal offense.

The reality of Spanish party financing presents a very different picture, according to data gathered by the mass media over the last year and a half. Several judicial investigations are now underway dealing with cases of alleged political corruption and illegal party financing. The Socialist party has been most affected by these scandals, but the Partido Popular has been involved as well. Suspicions of unlawful financing have equally extended to other parties, such as the Catalan and Basque nationalists.

On April 17, 1991, several newspapers reported that the Minister of Public Works requested large building companies to refrain from paying commissions to any political party in exchange for contracts for public work. In circles close to the building trade, such payments fluctuating between 2 and 4 percent of the work's total value, have been acknowledged as a common method to obtain work contracts.[14] However, these exchanges are not limited to the building trade. According to press sources, there are many decisions at local, regional, and state administrative levels which seem dependent upon receiving corresponding commissions.[15]

Party financing, insofar as it is based on a "compulsory political tax" such as a commission, is often handled by middlemen, not directly by the parties. Individuals and groups of party members have become sales agents of influence, selling favors to business interests in a variety of spheres of economic activity. Parties receive a percentage of these commissions while the rest is pocketed by the middlemen. Another form of unlawful fund raising consists of charging money for non-existent technical reports. This money raised has provided an avenue of direct funding to the parties which companies seek to influence.[16]

Data is still inconclusive regarding the scope of several alleged corruption and financing scandals which have razed the Spanish political scene for many months. Despite several investigations, it is likely that only a few of these cases will actually be proven, partly due to a lack of adequate legal instruments to control party accounting. The Tribunal de Cuentas does not have the authority to go beyond the information offered by the parties, making it difficult to verify the activities of those companies which act or could act as intermediaries. At any rate, there is abundant evidence that private money plays more than the marginal role prescribed by the financing law.

Summarized below are the most important exposé during 1990-1991, in chronological order:[17]

The Guerra Affair
- First reports: January 1990
- Party affected: PSOE
- Status: Under judicial investigation
- Protagonist: Juan Guerra, brother of the ex-Vice President, Alfonso Guerra. Guerra was assistant to the vice president and occupied an office with the government delegation in the city of Sevella.
- Facts: Alleged utilization of Juan Guerra's political position to obtain favorable decisions from the administration for private companies, from which he would have received a commission partly designated for PSOE financing. This case has innumerable ramifications.
- Political consequences (indirectly, since there has been no official acknowledgment): Resignation of Vice President Alfonso Guerra in March 1991.

The Naseiro Affair
- First reports: April 1990
- Party affected: Partido Popular
- Status: Under judicial process
- Protagonists: elected city council member, the person in charge of party financing, and the person formerly in charge.
- Facts: Alleged charging of commissions to certain companies which would then be awarded public services by the city hall of Valencia, part of which would go to finance the party.
- Political consequences: Request for the creation of a Parliamentary inquiry committee by the Partido Popular, which was rejected by the PSOE, the majority party. Also, the resignation of the general vice-secretary of the party, the person in charge of party financing, and the resignation from Parliament of the person formerly in charge (who also left the party).

The Prenafeta Affair
- First reports: March 1990
- Party affected: Convergencia Democratica de Cataluña (Catalan nationalists)
- Status: Case completed
- Protagonist: Prenafeta, General Secretary of the Presidency of the Regional Government of Catalua
- Facts: Charged commissions for obtaining licenses for casinos.
- Political consequences: Resignation of Prenafeta from office.

The S.A.S. (Andalusian Health Services) Affair
- First reports: May 1991 (growing out of the judicial investigation of the Juan Guerra affair)
- Party affected: PSOE
- Status: Under judicial investigation
- Protagonists: Managerial staff of S.A.S. during 1987 and 1988
- Facts: Alleged irregularities in S.A.S.'s economic management of generating commissions, destined partially for financing the PSOE, resulting from work contracts for services and health equipment to clinics and companies.
- Political consequences: None

The Ceres Affair
- First reports: June 1991
- Party affected: PSOE
- Status: No open investigation at present
- Facts: Ceres Travel Company was awarded the contract for organized trips for pensioners (1988-1989 and 1989-1990) by the Ministry of Social Services, allegedly in exchange for commission for the Socialist Party.
- Political consequences: None

The Filesa Affair
- First reports: June 1991
- Party affected: PSOE
- Status: Under investigation by the Tribunal de Cuentas
- Protagonists: The finance director of PSOE, the Socialist parliamentary group, and other people related to PSOE
- Facts: Filesa, together with Time Export and Malesa, allegedly is tied to the PSOE financing. This group of companies allegedly invoiced several other companies for unwritten reports for large amounts of money to finance a part of the PSOE electoral expenses in the general elections of 1989.
- Political consequences: Resignation of the main person involved and also the temporary removal of the person in charge of national finance. This party has opposed the creation of a parliamentary investigation about the case.

Conclusion

As noted, "public subsidies are expected to contribute to less corruption, more control of lobbying, more equal opportunities in party competition and some control of the cost explosion."[18] These considerations summarize the positive effects public funds could have, but the Spanish experience demonstrates that those consequences depend upon other factors which, together with public subsidies, define a particular system of party financing.

The rules of party finance in Spain prescribe a dominant role for public funding and no comparative legislation punishes the use of private funds as do the Spanish rules of party financing. By imposing a strongly statized system and condemning private financing, continuing private financing operates outside the control of the established mechanisms of the law. This system fosters irregularities and corruption which would be less likely to develop in a framework of complete freedom and disclosure.

Spanish rules on party finances need major reform, and the role of private funds must be reconsidered. If private donations constitute a way to reinforce the party/society relationship in a liberal democratic system, they are more necessary in the Spanish system where affiliation to political parties is loose and dues are not a substantive percentage of their income. Correspondingly, the role of public funds also has to be reconsidered. State revenues can help party financing but cannot be the solution to party finance needs. Other factors, such as setting limits on electoral expenses, developing the instruments needed for effective disclosure, and increasing the state funds that parties annually receive for regular expenses, all need to be revised by the legislature.

A different legal framework for party financing is expected to help in the solution of some of these problems, but much will depend on the parties. Party responsibility is an indispensable element in halting the practices that have been common features of party financing. Under any indicator the Spanish democracy can be considered a consolidated democracy, but its low quality is underlined by the level of political corruption found therein.

Notes

1. While reviewing this article for publication, the Prime Minister has called for advanced national election. Among the factors explaining the Prime Minister's decision was judicial investigation of illegal party finance. The Filesa case, later explained in this article, has played a decisive role in this action.

2. For a detailed description of the Spanish party financing of political parties in that period, see the author's, "Financing of the Spanish Political Parties," in Herbert E. Alexander, ed., *Comparative Political Finance in the 1980s.* (Cambridge: Cambridge University Press, 1989), pp. 172-199.

3. As was recognized for most parliamentary groups in 1985, see "Boletin Oficial de las Cortes," *Congreso de los Disputados.* Madrid, March 14, 1985, pp. 104 and 105.

4. Data on the expenditures of German party foundations in Spain between 1983 and 1988 are reported in Michael Pinto-Duschinsky, "Foreign Political Aid: The German Political Foundations and Their U.S. Counterparts," *International Affaires*, Vol. 67, No. 1, 1991, pp. 38 and 55.

5. Del Castillo in Alexander, pp. 186-188 (see footnote 2 above).

6. The report elaborated by the previously mentioned Inquiry Commission is discussed in detail in the author's, "Lay electoral y financiación de las campañas electorales." Madrid, 1985 (unpublished).   The study was developed with the support of the Centro de Estudios Constitucionales.

7. "Ley origánica del Regimen Electoral General," 5/1985, June 19, on the Regimen Electoral General, *Boletin Oficial del Estado*, June 20.

8. "Ley Organica de Financiación de los Partidos Politicos," 3/1987, July 2, on Financing of Political Parties, *Boletin Oficial del Estado*, July 3.

9. See the author's "Lay electoral y financianción," p. 45.

10. The effects of discrimination against minor parties are shown in the author's, "Financing of Spanish Political Parties," p. 177, Table 2, and "Financiación de las elecciones generales de 1986," *Revista de Derecho Politico*, Vol. 25, 1988, Table 1, pp. 124-125.

11. The report is discussed in Hans-Peter Schneider, "The New German System of Party Financing: The Presidential Committee Report of 1983 and its Realization," in Herbert E. Alexander, ed., *Comparative Political Finance in the 1980s*, pp. 220-233.

12. The Tribunal de Cuentas has not fulfilled its legal duty in annually publishing a report on party ordinary expenses and income.   Currently, the only the one corresponding to 1987 has been published.

13. For example, in 1991, the organization secretary of the government party, the Socialist party, declared that his group had a debt of 5.995 billion pesetas. See *El Pais*, June 23, 1991, p. 19.

14. These statements were published by several newspapers. See, for example, *El Pais*, April 23, 1991, p. 1 and "ABC," April 1991, p. 17.

15. Ibid.

16. These practices have mobilized the Stockholder Association into demanding legal guarantees for shareholder rights since, in most cases, the shareholders did not know about the political donations given by their companies. See *El Mundo*, June 7, 1991, p. 11.

17. At this writing, a new scandal has arisen relating to some of the policies followed by the former staff of the public railroads. The former General Director of the Public Railroad office, now Minister of Public Health, was accused of speculation by artificially increasing the price of some land and selling it to private companies.

18. Karl-Heinz Nassmacher, "Structure and Impact of Public Subsidies to Political Parties in Europe: The Examples of Austria, Italy, Sweden and West Germany," in Herbert E. Alexander, ed., *Comparative Political Finance in the 1980s*, p. 238.

8

Regulation of Party Finance in Sweden

Gullan M. Gidlund

Two types of strategies by which a democracy can address the problematic relationship between political parties and money are judicial and consensus. In countries that have experienced negative aspects of party financing, demands are strong for public control, legal regulations, and accounting requirements. In the United States, the Federal Republic of Germany, and Japan, there are continuing efforts to establish a system of legal standards—the judicial strategy—while Sweden has mainly adopted the consensus strategy to regulate party financing. This strategy entails voluntary agreements among the parties with a minimum of legislation, a strategy based on ethics instead of legalities.

The strategy which operates in a particular country depends upon that country's specific structure of party finance. The consensus strategy seems connected to proportional-representation systems with party-oriented elections, while the judicial strategy better fits candidate-oriented electoral systems. The demand for effective strategies is reinforced by intermittent comprehensive "political exposé" and scandals related to party finance, and by accompanying credibility crises. In such circumstances, the consensus strategy provides a weak response to a crisis.

In political systems with an institutional division of power, judicial trials in the constitutional courts are of decisive significance. In parliamentary systems, such as Sweden, collaboration among parties is an integral part of political life. In these systems, no court can overturn the decisions of the Parliament; the principle of popular sovereignty is upheld, from which the consensus strategy follows naturally. In addition, the deep-rooted and principally successful tradition in the mixed economy of Sweden motivates political parties to negotiate and make agreements concerning collective goods.

The Swedish Party System: A Panorama

The representative democracy of Sweden is usually characterized as "a democracy through political parties," which, in a comparative perspective, holds a strong position in society. Sweden has a multi-party electoral system based upon party, not candidate, support. The parties have complete control over the nomination of candidates, and have the economic resources for campaigning. Over the decades, the established parties have built up strong organizational structures at the national, regional, and local levels.

Sweden is a typically unitary state, which has retained relatively strong local governments. The five-party structure in Parliament (Riksdag) has been extremely stable. However, with 5.5 percent of the vote, the Green party passed the 4 percent threshold and obtained twenty seats in the Riksdag in the 1988 national election. The Green party lost its representation in the 1991 national election, but two other minor parties entered, the Christian Democratic party (5.2 percent) and the new right-wing New Democratic party (6.8 percent).

Another feature of the Swedish political system is the unique position of power held by the Social Democratic party. This party has formed the government for over half of its 100-year existence, though it has sometimes required the parliamentary support of the small Communist party (VPK). The traditional non-socialist opposition, consisting of the Liberal party (Folkpartiet), the Center party (Centerpartiet), and the Conservative party (Moderata samlingspartiet), has experienced great difficulties in forming a unified and strong alternative, although it did hold office between 1976-1982, and again (the Christian Democratic Party) beginning in 1991.

The common image of Swedish parties, although not always realistic, denotes high member participation and organized activity during campaigns and nonelection times. The Social Democratic party, a mass party with strong links to old "popular movements" *(folkrorelser),* has provided a prototype for the entire party system.

The combination of automatic voter registration, liberal advance-voting, and the parties' high capacity for mobilization explains the still high turnout rate in Sweden. In the 1976 national election the record turnout of 91.8 percent was reached. Since then, voting participation has declined; in 1991, the last election to the Riksdag, the turnout was 83.3 percent.[1]

A Tradition of a Minimum of Legislation

In Sweden, legislation regarding election finance is minimal. Legal restrictions exist in only three areas: public funding, bribery, and broadcasting time. Bribery laws are the most stringent. Politicians and office-holders are not allowed to receive even small gifts from companies, organizations, or individuals; a Christmas gift cannot exceed 250 SKR (U.S. $40).[2] Public funding laws relate to the subsidies that are provided at the national,[3] County Council, and municipal levels.[4] Finally, the relationship between the state and the Swedish Radio and Television Company regarding free broadcasting time is prescribed in the Radio Law *(Radiolagen)*. In practice, Swedish Radio and Television may exclude minor parties not represented in the Riksdag from participating in debates and other programs during the election campaigns. Though impartiality is prescribed, this decision belongs to Swedish Radio and Television.[5]

Swedish parties are not bound by any law regarding contributions from individuals or group funds from unions and corporations, campaign costs or other forms of party expenditures, or accounts of income and expenditures. Instead of legislation, the political parties have created a network of voluntary agreements among parties, which also govern decisions within parties—the consensus strategy. Sometimes agreements are a response to the threat of legislation or a result of strong moral pressure, not the least of which is exerted by the mass media.

This strategy has had concrete results, such as an agreement made among the established parties during World War II to reduce the amount of printed propaganda in election campaigns. Another agreement has made public the incomes and expenditures of the established parties at the national level since 1980. One internal party decision to stop accepting direct contributions from companies was made by the Liberal party at the national level in 1971, then at all levels in 1976; the Conservative party followed suit in 1977. The Social Democratic party made a decision at their 1987 party Congress to abolish the collective affiliation of union members to the party starting 1990.

Which Strategy?

In Sweden, the most debated legislative reform has been whether the parties would make public their sources of income in order to inform voters which interests they represent. During the 1930s and 1940s, two scandals occurred that were central to this discussion.

The incident of 1932 was revealed when authorities investigated the failure of the extensive Kreuger corporation following the suicide of the director, Ivar Kreuger. That summer, the Government was hit by a serious political crisis when, in the middle of the election campaign for the Riksdag, it was revealed that the Liberal Prime Minister, C. G. Ekman, had received substantial donations from Kreuger to the minor Liberal Party. Ekman had openly accounted for a certain amount of this money to the party, but apparently retained the remainder. Despite evidence to the contrary, Ekman denied that he had kept the money for himself. He was eventually forced to resign as Prime Minister and leader of the Liberal Party.[6]

Despite this situation, the new Social Democratic government, formed after the 1932 election, made no effort to place the question of party financing on the political decision-making agenda. In 1934, an MP from the Social Democratic party in the Riksdag proposed that political organizations render their accounts,[7] but the Committee of Law and most members of the Riksdag were against the idea of legislation and questioned its positive impact on party finance. As one MP declared "...it would be the most easy thing in the world for these associations to keep the information back from the public, if there was something unpleasant."[8]

Another heated debate about party finance arose during the national election campaign in 1948. The Liberal Party was suspected by its political opponents of having large amounts of secret finances. A Social Democratic newspaper referred to the situation as "a smell of prostitution in political life."[9] However, an investigation by impartial lawyers showed that the accusations were unfounded and that Mr. Molander, the Social Democrat who had "exposed" the affair, lacked proof of the claims. As a result, coupled with demands from the Riksdag, the Experts of Party Financing Committee was set up by the government in 1950 and commissioned to investigate whether organizations dealing with political propaganda should be obliged to account publicly for their incomes and expenditures.[10]

In their report to the government, the committee emphasized that political parties are voluntary organizations and are not under the same obligations as companies and economic associations to render accounts. Because of this, the committee opposed any legislation introducing such obligations for political parties, with the following arguments:

1.   The disclosure of contributors' names would be contrary to the spirit and meaning of the constitution concerning the protection of the secrecy of the ballot.
2.   The parties would risk losing certain contributions, and some donors may be exposed to persecution, if names were made public.
3.   Practical problems related to the control of the observance of the law could arise. The committee maintained that:

> as rich opportunities to evade the legal provisions exist, it seems evident that they would be unable to reach the level of effectiveness

which should be established in order that the respect for such laws and for the legislation on the whole should be preserved.[11]

4. The freedom and independence of the parties should persist in relation to authoritarian bodies. This was seen as a necessary condition in order for the parties to retain the potential to fulfill their important functions in society: "Administrative control over the parties is unfamiliar to democratic principles. Under some circumstances legislation which allows such a thing can place constraints upon our political life." [12]

the committee's final argument was possibly the foremost in the context of party financing: because political parties held a special position in a democratic society, the "last say" should not come from the administration or the authorities, but from the people represented by the parties in the Riksdag. The committee also looked upon contributions to political parties as a form of political participation comparable to voting.

Further, the committee commented on campaign costs. They could think of no effective means of preventing the parties from using propaganda resources "if [the parties] believed in success."[13] During World War II, the Swedish parties had voluntarily agreed to reduce the use of posters and other forms of printed matter in the election campaign, but the committee was doubtful whether such agreements would lead to any significant reduction of campaign costs.

After conducting inquiries among the parties, the 1951 Committee indicated it felt confident that the parties would voluntarily carry out public accounting of their finances. These conclusions formed the official policy for the regulation of party finance in subsequent years, and the consensus strategy was enacted by the political decision-makers. In 1980, parties represented in the Riksdag made a voluntary agreement to account publicly for the income and expenditure at their national levels each year. But no party law or legal regulation concerning party finance (with the exception of the public subsidies laws) has been introduced.

Ethics

An argument for public funding in Sweden during the 1960s was that a national subsidy would make it possible to reduce the parties' dependency upon powerful contributors, primarily companies, which was considered ethically and democratically unsatisfactory. The argument against a national subsidy was that the parties would lose their integrity as free political parties.

The Liberal and Conservative parties occasionally have been the targets of the media and political opponents for receiving money from companies. One occurrence took place during the national subsidy debate in the Riksdag in 1965, when the leader of the Center party, Dr. Gunnar Hedlund, brought forth the fact that 90 percent of the Conservative party's income consisted of company contributions. As a consequence, Hedlund noted that the Conservative party would be somewhat obligated to consider the contributors' point of view to a certain extent. This charge was denied by the Conservatives in the Riksdag.

The critical point for company subsidies occurred when the nonsocialist parties took office after the national election victory of 1976. The media immediately confronted the parties with the question of whether it was appropriate for a party represented in the government to accept these contributions. The response appeared to be "No," as the Liberal Party had already decided to stop accepting money directly from companies at its national level in 1971 and extended the policy in 1976 to include their local level. The Conservative party "voluntarily" stopped receiving direct contributions from companies in 1977.

These decisions by the Liberal and Conservative parties presupposed public funding. The fact that traditional contributors also had displayed a reduced willingness to give money to the parties, probably made it an easier decision.

Currently, no Swedish political party receives money directly from companies—at least not openly. The fear of losing voters makes it difficult for any party to change its policy. However, company money is not entirely excluded from Swedish politics. The bourgeois parties receive their most significant form of indirect support through large, professional public relation campaigns about issues such as taxation, nuclear energy, and collective wage-earners funds, which are paid for and organized by companies and special foundations. This strategy was established in the 1970s and focused on molding public opinion and setting the national agenda. The big companies and organizations have simultaneously built up a network of contacts and direct-access links to decision-makers in the different levels of the government.

Another manifestation of the consensus strategy occurred in 1987, when the Social Democratic party abolished the collective affiliation of union members to the party, a requirement since 1898. The nonsocialist parties occasionally had attempted to prohibit this system by legislation, but never succeeded, because the opposition generally had a majority in the Riksdag. The Communist party (VPK) also had opposed a law against collective affiliation on several occasions, but in 1986 seemed prepared to vote with the bourgeois bloc. The leadership of the Social Democratic party could either wait for a law to pass in the Riksdag, which would force them to change the old system, or they could make a voluntary decision to end the collective affiliation of union members. The national board of the Social Democratic party announced their decision at a press conference immediately before the voting procedure in the Riksdag. The Party Congress of 1987 decided to end the system during 1990. Organizational affiliation would replace collective membership affiliation and each local union organization would make the decision to "join the party" and to pay the special organization fee.

With this decision, the Social Democratic party preserved a measure of traditional autonomy, a principle often emphasized by the party leadership. During the 1984 Party Congress, it was argued that: "It is our collective mission to fight for our autonomy. Nobody outside, and by all means not the bourgeois parties, shall make decisions concerning our internal affairs."[14]

The Consensus Strategy and Public Funding

The proposal for a national subsidy, introduced in the Riksdag in 1965, caused the deepest conflict to date regarding party financing. The proposal by the Social Democratic government was supported by the Center party and the Communist party, while the Conservative party and one section of the Liberal party in the Riksdag strongly opposed it. The debate took on a distinct ideological profile, but particular strategies were manifested in alternative proposals for a national subsidy and in demands for different principles of allocation which would benefit the respective actors.[15]

In 1969, public funding was expanded and decentralized. The Riksdag awarded municipalities and county councils the legal right to subsidize the parties at their local and regional levels.[16] This decision, made by consensus without ideological considerations, was accepted by all parties.

The three main public subsidies were based on fundamental principles, which were not written into the two subsidy laws. Both the "Law about Subsidies to a Political Party" (the national party subsidy) and the "Law About Municipal and County Council Subsidies to Political Parties" are technically-oriented laws which stipulate the rules of allocation between the parties. Yet, the following fundamental principles are incorporated into government bills and official reports which concern party subsidies:[17]

1. Subsidies should only be provided to the parties which have a significant level of electoral support, as demonstrated in general elections;
2. Subsidies should be calculated and distributed according to fixed rules which do not permit any discretionary examination;
3. The size of the subsidy should be proportional to the strength of the party;

4. No official control shall be exercised over how the subsidies are used;
5. The introduction and size of the municipal and county council subsidies should be decided upon by the municipal and county councils themselves, on the basis of the legally prescribed allocation rule; and
6. The greatest possible level of consensus concerning the size and the allocation rules of the subsidies should be sought.

The fourth point emphasizes the general nature of Swedish public funding. Consequently, the subsidies are not intended solely for election campaigns, but can be used freely as each party decides. In fact, the subsidies are so general that there are no legal stipulations that the money should be used only for political work.

The sixth principle resulted from the 1965 debate on national subsidies. At the time, opponents to the proposal feared that the rules might be changed arbitrarily by a parliamentary majority. Advocates for the Liberal party demanded, without success, that the laws be given the same status as constitutional laws.

In 1992, when the municipal and county council subsidies were reformed, adherence to the fundamental principles shifted. The Royal Commission proposed deregulation of the local and regional subsidies. The proposal became law in December 1991. As of 1992, no rule of allocation has been stipulated by the Riksdag; the councils have the right to decide how to designate the financial support to their representative parties. The only restriction is that the subsidy must not be allocated so as to unduly favor or unfairly treat a party.[18] One of the original fundamental principles, that there should be no official control over the use of these subsidies, is still in effect at the local and regional levels. At the national level, adherence to the fundamental principles remains unchanged.

Requests for national subsidy funds must be submitted to a special board consisting of three judges. In accordance with popular sovereignty, the decision of the board may not be appealed. Appeals against decisions regarding the municipal and county council subsidies are possible (as the local government is sometimes subject to the state) and occur intermittently. After the 1992 reform, appeals against different solutions and negotiations at the local and regional level probably will increase before a legal praxis is established.

Conclusion

The consensus strategy of regulating party finance in Sweden is a function of the proportional-representation election system and the principle of popular sovereignty as laid down in the constitution. The strategy relies upon the legitimacy of the party system, a tradition of strong negotiating organizations, and the absence of scandals related to party finance.

The introduction of public funding has made Swedish party financing mostly transparent, but there are significant exceptions: minor parties, especially those without representation in political assemblies, and "big money" (money which comes indirectly from companies and unions in the election campaign and is not recorded in the budgets).

Swedish political parties are heavily dependent upon public funding at all levels of the organizational hierarchy. Even Swedish newspapers with a traditionally strong connection to the political parties have received public subsidies since 1972. In addition to the general subsidies to the parties, a set of small selective subsidies has been introduced.

There is a real risk in Sweden that the established political parties lacking a ceiling on public funding will allow it to spiral out of control, slowly disengaging from the people they are supposed to serve. This risk is reinforced by the lack of an effective judicial control over public funding in Sweden. The real test of the consensus strategy may be yet to come.

Notes

1. See Gullan M. Gidlund and Janerik Gidlund, *Storstadens partier och valdeltagande 1948-1988*. [Tr.: *Political Parties and Electoral Turnout in Metropolitan Areas* (in Sweden) 1948-1988.] (Umea: Political Science Department, University of Umea, 1989).

2. Brottsbalken (BrB) [Tr.: Criminal Code] 17:7; 20:2.

3. *Svensk forfattningssamling* (SFS) [tr.: Swedish Statute Book] 1972:625; 1989:241.

4. SFS 1969: 596; SFS 1991: 1774.

5. It is however, possible to appeal against a program to a special committee (Radionä amnden).

6. See Stig Hadenius et al., *Sverige efter 1900* [Tr.: *Sweden After 1900*] (Stockholm: Aldus/Bonniers, 1967).

7. Motion [tr.: Bill in the Parliament], 1934:455. Protokoll [tr.: Minutes from Parliament], 1934:31.

8. Protokoll, 1934:13, p. 59. Author's translation.

9. Richard Lindstrom, former editor-in-chief of *Morgon-Tidningen* (MT), cited in Ahlmark, Per, *Var fattiga politik* [Tr.: *Our Poor Politics*] (Stockholm: Bonniers, 1964).

10. *Statens offentliga utrendningar* (SOU), 1951:56.

11. Ibid; pp. 59-60, Author's translation.

12. Ibid.

13. *Statens offentliga utrendningar*, p. 47.

14. B. B. Toresson, general secretary of the Social Democratic Party. *Protokoll fran kongressen* [tr.: Minutes of The Party Congress], 1984:184.

15. See the author's *Partistod* [tr. *Public Funding of Political Parties in Sweden*] (Lund: Liber, 1983); and "Public Investments in Swedish Democracy: Gambling With Gains and Losses," in Matti Wiberg, ed., *The Public Purse and Political Parties: Public Financing of Political Parties in Nordic Countries* (Helsinki, The Finnish Political Science Association, 1991).

16. Sweden has 284 municipalities (local government bodies) and 23 County councils. County councils are responsible for the health care facilities. For information on the municipal and county council subsidies, see the author's *Det konnunala partistodet: En studie av kommenernas och landstingens stod till politiska partier* [tr.: *The Public Funding of Political Parties by Swedish Municipal and Council Councils of Domestic Affairs*] Ds C 1985:8.

17. *Statens offentliga utredningar* (SOU), 1972:62, p. 56.

18. *SOU*: 1991:80, SFS 1991: 1771. The regulations are integrated in the Local Government Act.

9

Dutch Political Parties: Money and the Message

Ruud A. Koole

The Dutch Political System

The Netherlands, commonly—but not quite correctly—referred to as Holland,[1] is a parliamentary democracy in a constitutional monarchy. The former republic changed to a monarchy after the French occupation at the beginning of the nineteenth century. This may have been opposite to the "normal" development of an independent state, but the republican value of equal rights for all citizens to participate in politics still developed in the newborn monarchy. In 1848, a new Constitution introduced ministerial responsibility, which established the formal primacy of parliament in the Dutch polity. The right for men to vote was gradually expanded until the beginning of the twentieth century when the general franchise for men was accepted in 1917 and, in 1919, for women. At the same time, the electoral system changed. The majority-vote system with multiple districts was replaced by a strict proportional-representation system with single-member districts. After 1917, the general features of this electoral system remained stable, and according to the proposition made by Rokkan and Lipset, the party system also was frozen for the foreseeable future.[2]

Parties and other societal organizations were grouped under four ideological families or *zuilen* ("pillars"): Catholic, Protestant, Socialist, and Liberal, though not all were fully developed. Only the denominational groupings represented all socioeconomic strata in society. The Socialists counted more adherents among the lower social classes, while the (conservative) Liberals consisted of the nonreligious well-to-do. Within each pillar several parties could exist side by side, such as the Protestant *zuilf* which contained two major parties and several splinter parties from the fragmentation in the Protestant church. The strict proportional-representation electoral system allowed many ideological nuances to find a place within the party system.

No party has ever managed to win a majority. The Netherlands is a country of minorities in which a tradition of segmentation, already present in the seventeenth and eighteenth centuries, has had a great impact on the political culture. Only cooperation among the elites of the various pillars has prevented Holland from falling into political chaos. Coalition governments were often difficult to form but were necessary in order to achieve political majorities. This type of politics, which has been coined "consociationalism", or "the politics of accommodation," lasted until the 1960s.[3]

In the 1960s, the pillarized society began to disintegrate. The ties among organizations within each pillar loosened, as did those between the voters and the parties. Class and religion had become less important in structuring the vote than they had been during the heyday of pillarization. The "floating vote," which has fluctuated between 16 and 24 percent since 1967, and the new voters had become the main targets of the parties' campaigns (especially for leftwing parties, which were determined to alter the political culture). Instead of striving for consociationalism parties, they tried to increase political openness by pursuing a policy of "polarization." This effort proved to be a failure, however, with the formation of the Christian Democratic Appeal (CDA) party, into which two former Protestant parties (ARP and CHU) and one Catholic party (KVP) merged in 1980. Today, the CDA plays a dominant role in Dutch politics, perhaps even more than the Catholic party had done in the period of pillarization. The CDA is the pivot of the present party system and is in a position to form coalition cabinets with the conservative Liberals (VVD), and with the Social Democrats (PvdA). A "Westminster" type of party system, with two alternating blocks, did not evolve and the PvdA dropped the ideal of polarization officially in 1988 to embrace consensus politics again.[4]

Although approximately twenty-five parties participate in each national election for the Lower House of Parliament (the Second Chamber or Tweede Kamer), only about ten win seats. At the right side of the political spectrum, three orthodox Calvinist parties (SGP, GPV, and RPF) constitute a small but stable factor in Dutch politics. At the left, three small parties (the Communist CPN, the pacifist-Socialist PSP, and the radical PPR) have joined into one Green List that was presented for the first time at the September 1984 elections. A center-left position is taken by the Democrats 66 (D66), a group of progressive liberals that formed in

TABLE 1 The Performance of the CDA, PvdA, and the VVD, in the National Elections of the 1980s

Parties	1981 Popular vote	seats	1982 Popular vote	seats	1986 Popular vote	seats	1989 Popular vote	seats
CDA	30.8	48(-1)	29.3	45	34.6	54	35.3	54
PvdA	28.3	44(-9)	30.4	47	33.3	52	31.9	49
VVD	17.3	26(-2)	23.1	36	17.4	27	14.6	22
Others	23.6	32	17.2	22	14.7	17	18.2	25
Totals	100.0	150	100.0	150	100.0	150	100.0	150

Source: R. A. Koole and G. Voerman, "Het lidmaatschap van partijen na 1945", in *Jaarboek 1985 Rocumentatiecentrum Nederlandse Politieke Partijen, Gronigen,* 1986, pp. 115-176. The 1989 figures stem from the *Jaarboek* 1990, p. 20. Reprinted by permission.

1966 with rather unstable electoral support, though its popularity was rapidly growing at the end of the 1980s. The Center-Democrats (CD), a small xenophobic party has occupied one seat since 1989, as it also had done between 1982 and 1986. Even so, three major parties dominate the political scene, as seen in Table 1.

The Extra-Legal Status of Dutch Political Parties

The first nationally-organized political party in the Netherlands was the Anti-Revolutionary Party (ARP) in 1879; the Social Democrats followed suit. Both parties were "mass integration" parties, which organized "the people behind the voters," since the extension of suffrage took place only gradually. It was not until 1904 that the Catholics were to set up a loosely organized national political organization.

The extra-parliamentary party organizations were not, of course, mentioned in the liberal Constitution of 1848. The Constitution of 1917, although introducing the general franchise and proportional representation, did not mention them either.[5] Parties were accepted *de facto* but not recognized *de jure,* and this *extra legem* situation of parties still exists. The term "political parties" is absent from the Constitution of 1983. The constitutional position of parties is still being debated;[6] the fear of too much state influence on the internal life of voluntary organizations, such as parties, has prevented Parliament from adopting constitutional stipulations regarding them.

The situation began to change when political parties were endangered from within when their organizations seemed no longer able to meet the challenges of a changing political environment. This was the case in the 1960s when "depillarization" loosened the ties between the parties and organizations which, in turn, lessened the support the parties had received from these organizations, including financial support. At the same time, the parties lost a considerable number of members and, consequently, some of their membership fees.

As Table 2 demonstrates, the Catholic KVP lost almost three-quarters of its members between 1960 and 1970. A downward trend is apparent in all the major parties. Not surprisingly, when there were calls for state financial support, the initiative was taken by the parliamentary leader of the KVP. After lengthy parliamentary debates, state subvention to the research institutes of political parties was introduced in 1971. After 1975, political parties could claim subsidies for educational purposes, and for their youth movements as well, beginning in 1976.

State Subvention: A "Mess of Pottage?"

The proposal for granting state subsidies to parties' research institutes was defended in 1971 by the Minister of Domestic Affairs who stressed the importance of scientific research and documentation in the formation of the political will in a democratic political system. "Society is getting more and more complex and it changes at an ever accelerating pace. These trends reinforce the need for research as a basis for political thinking and acting."[7] This goal-oriented subsidy had a matching funds provision, in which the maximum amount was related to the number of seats a party occupied in the Second Chamber.

The small GPV, D66 and, to some extent, the VVD, opposed any kind of state subvention. The GPV stated that it was unjust, and not possible, to differentiate between parties while granting them public money. The introduction of state subvention meant that state subsidies eventually could be given to parties with ideas difficult to reconcile with the basic assumptions of parliamentary democracy. This position became relevant when the extreme rightist Center Party entered Parliament in 1982.

The GVP also stressed the danger of petrification of the party system. If parties received money from the state, some of them might continue to exist even after they lost popular support. In this case, public subsidy would become a sort of "political trust for the preservation of historical sites."[8] The argument that subsidies would be given to the research institutes and not directly to the parties was not convincing to the GPV, since the distinction was difficult to make.

TABLE 2 Membership Figures of Parties Represented in the Dutch Second Chamber of Parliament

Party	1950	1960	1970	1980	1989
ARP	102,737	97,980	80,695	54,500	--
CDA	--	--	--	143,000*	125,033
CHU	(40,000)	48,000	28,900	26,000	--
CPN	27,392	(11,200)	(11,000)	15,510	5,700
D66	--	--	6,400	14,638	9,561
GPV**	1,200	6,311	8,702	12,922	13,015
KVP	319,419	385,500	97,300	49,343	--
PPR	--	--	4,000	11,500	6,150
PSP	--	2,700	4,228	8,703	3,612
PvdA	105,609	142,853	98,671	112,929	96,600
RPF	--	--	--	5,545	8,330
SGP	10,500	12,300	15,400	20,300	23,000
VVD	21,271	35,000	38,000	85,881	64,554

Numbers within parentheses are author's estimates. Other round numbers estimates by the national bureau of the party concerned.

* Combined membership of ARP, CHU and KVP plus directly-affiliated members.
** Founded in 1948, but gained its first seat in Parliament only in 1963.

CDA	Christian Democratic Appeal
CHU	Christian Historical Union
CPN	Communist Party of the Netherlands
D66	Democrats 1966 (progressive liberal)
GPV	Reformed Political League (orthodox Calvinist)
KVP	Catholic People's Party
PPR	Radical Political Party (leftwing, ecological)
PSP	Pacific Socialist Party
PvdA	Labor Party
RPF	Reformed Political Federation (orthodox Calvinist)
SGP	Political Reform Party (orthodox Calvinist)
VVD	People's Party for Freedom and Democracy (right-wing liberal)

Source: R.A. Koole and G. Voerman, "Het lidmaatschap van partijen na 1945", in: *Jaarboek 1985 Documentatiecentrum Nederlandse Politieke Partijen*, Groningen, 1986, pp. 115-176. The 1989 figures stem from the *Jaarboek 1990*, p. 20. Reprinted by permission.

The Minister and the other parties agreed that it was impossible to clearly differentiate between parties and their affiliated institutions, but they felt that the institutes should be trusted to make sure that the subsidy was actually used for research purposes. The danger of petrification of the party system was not considered to be very great. The strict proportional-representation electoral system, with its low entry level for new parties, made this argument too far fetched to sway the decision.

The Second Chamber passed the proposal with a large majority, as did the First Chamber (the Senate). The First Chamber questioned why the change was not proposed as a special formal law instead of a minor change to the budget. The Minister answered that some experience had to be gained before a formal law was enacted. The fear of establishing a formal and legal link between the parties and the state also contributed to this reluctance. Only indirect subsidies for specific purposes proved to be acceptable.

General Features of Subsidies for the Research Institutes

The general lines of the adopted proposal read as follows:

1. The research institutes of all parties can claim state subvention up to a certain maximum;
2. Only one institute per party can claim this subsidy, and it is the parliamentary party which decides which institute that will be;
3. The amount of subsidy depends on the number of seats a party occupies in the Second Chamber;
4. The amount of subsidy claimed must be matched by an equal amount of "private resources";
5. Every research institute must formally be a legal entity; and
6. The maximum amount of subsidy is decided by ministerial decree.

The maximum amounts of the subsidies were calculated in such a way that the smaller parties received more money proportionately than the larger parties. This maximum was derived from the sum of a fixed amount for each party represented in the Parliament, and an amount proportional to their number of seats in the Second Chamber. This system changed

TABLE 3 Calculation of the Maximum Subsidy for Research Institutes (in guilders)

	1979	1986
Fixed Basis Amount	89,347	76,998
Each of the First 10 Seats	8,935	7,700
Each of the Second 10 Seats	7.358	6,341
Each of the Third 10 Seats	5,781	4,983
Each of the Fourth 10 Seats	4,205	3,624
For Every Seat more than 40	2,628	2,265

Source: *Handelinger Tweede Kamar* (Proceedings Second Chamber of Parliament), 1986-1987, 19508, nr. 4. Reprinted by permission.

in 1979 and 1986, when the maximum subsidies were calculated accord
ing to the criteria listed in Table 3.

In 1973, the center-left government, led by the Social Democrat Den
Uyl, embraced the idea of state subvention for education institutes, while
the conservative-liberal VVD and the orthodox-Calvinist GVP opposed
it. The government agreed with the arguments, as put forward in a letter
to the Minister of Domestic Affairs, that political education of party members would have a positive impact on the quality of political parties and
hence on the quality of the political system in a parliamentary democracy. The calculation method of the maximum amount of this subvention
was similar to that for research institutes, although smaller parties prof-
ited comparatively less from this subvention because the fixed-basis
amount was considerably lower (in 1986, Dfl. 31,421), and the money
based on the number of seats in Parliament substantially higher. Whereas
research institutes had to have as much "private income" as they received
in public allocations, educational institutes only needed to provide 30
percent in matching funds.

Both educational and research subsidies are paid by the Ministry of
Domestic Affairs. This is not true for the third kind of state subvention
introduced in 1976, the subsidy for the youth organizations of political
parties. This subsidy is paid by the Ministry of Welfare, Health, and
Culture. Its calculation method also is different from the other two in
that, while the number of seats held in the Second Chamber is an important criterion, the number of members in the youth organizations is also
relevant.

Other Forms of State Support to Political Parties

In addition to these state subsidies, all parties represented in the Second Chamber are given free time on television and radio.[9] During the
election campaigns, time is extended to all parties that present lists in all
19 electoral subdistricts. Some money to produce the television and radio programs is furnished as well, but until 1987 this did not equal the
costs. Even so, studies have shown that relatively few people listen to or
watch the programs.

Also, gifts to political parties are tax-deductible. Natural persons can
deduct gifts up to a maximum of 10 percent of their gross annual income;
non-natural persons, such as enterprises (corporations) can do so up to a
maximum of 6 percent of the corporation's profit.[10] Thus, donations to
parties are completely legal. Apart from the membership fees and small
gifts to the electoral funds of the parties, they hardly exist in practice.

Although parliamentary parties do not form part of the party organizations, their financial position has changed considerably in the last two decades. The salaries of the representatives in the Second Chamber have improved considerably since 1968, which may have fostered the ongoing process of the professionalization of Parliament. Today, the income of parliamentary delegates is somewhat more than Dfl. 100,000 per annum. In the 1970s, individual and collective assistance to the parliamentary parties was introduced, which came to a cost of about Dfl. 17,000,000 in 1987. Approximately 300 assistants are also at the disposal of the individual representatives and/or the parliamentary parties.[11]

The Slow and Hidden Process of Codification

Notwithstanding the reluctance to formally recognize political parties, the Dutch legislature began to deal with parties in a more specific manner in the 1980s. The Civil Code and some articles of the Broadcasting Law and the Electoral Law were changed, and plans to adopt a special law on state subventions are now in the advanced phase of preparation.

The rise of racist parties at the end of the 1970s worked as a catalyst in this process. The Netherlandse Volksunie (Dutch People's Union), a party with Nazi sympathies, managed to win some votes at local elections, though it never won a seat in a municipal council or in Parliament. The Volksunie was subsequently put on trial because of its overt racism, directed especially against the immigrant workers from the Mediterranean countries and people from the former colony of Surinam. But although the court of Amsterdam, in its verdict, described the Volksunie as an illegal organization, the party was not dissolved based on technical judicial reasons.[12] The Volksunie has remained active but has never grown to be a party of significance. However, when another extreme rightwing party, the Center Party (CP) managed to win a seat in the Second Chamber in 1982 (which it lost in 1986 and won back in 1989), the public demanded a change.

The existence of the Volksunie and the electoral threat of the CP[13] led to the introduction of stricter legal regulations regarding political parties. The first measure introduced in 1982, was a change in the Broadcasting Law. Until this time, parties only needed to present a list of candidates at the elections in one of the electoral subdistricts. An amendment in the Broadcasting Law required a party to present lists of candidates in the elections in all nineteen subdistricts. This meant that parties had to pay the deposit of Dfl. 1,000 nineteen times, and had to gather twenty-five signatures for each of the districts. (Often, the Center Party was accused of fraud with regard to signatures, although this was difficult to prove.)

A revision of the Electoral Law was proposed by the government in 1987 and adopted by Parliament in 1989. Subsequently, parties must pay an extra--through rather small--deposit before registration at the Electoral Board. The existing deposit was raised to a one-time payment of Dfl. 25,000, instead of nineteen deposits of Dfl. 1,000, regardless of the number of electoral subdistricts in which the party was participating. Both deposits must be paid only by parties that are not yet represented in the Second Chamber. In order to be registered by the Electoral Board, all parties must be fully recognized legal entities and also "associations" subject to regulations in the Civil Code; thus if a party is dissolved by a judge, it is no longer able to participate in the elections.[14]

The verdict of the court of Amsterdam in the Volksunie case in 1978 disappointed many people. Therefore, the Minister of Justice proposed to sharpen two articles in the Civil Code. This proposition in 1982 stated that if a "corporation" (since political parties did not exist formally) is judged to be illegal, it must be dissolved. The Second Chamber hesitated before accepting this idea because freedom of speech and freedom of organization were at stake, but after lengthy deliberations and explanations, the law was adopted in March 1988.[15]

During the discussions, it was suggested that this stipulation be included in a special law regarding political parties, in which state subventions were also to be regulated. But the Minister of Justice did not agree, stressing that the new article in the Civil Code was not intended only for racist or facist parties, but was important also in dissolving fraudulent business corporations. It was agreed that public money should not be given to a "hostile" party, but determination of this has to be made by a judge, not politicians.

A legal procedure to dissolve a political party always takes time, and the problem arose whether or not the State must continue to subsidize an accused party in the interim. In the proposal for the law on state subventions, the Minister of Domestic Affairs argued for the subsidy to be interrupted the day the Public Prosecutor demands the dissolution of a political party and to end on the day of the verdict. If the verdict was to dissolve the party, the subsidy would be stopped altogether; if this was not the case, the interruption of the subsidy would be canceled.

However, interrupting a subsidy before a decision is made on the court was criticized by several parliamentarians from the conservative-liberal VVD and the orthodox-Calvinist SGP and GPV. They argued that only voters should decide about the existence of political parties, and their prohibition must remain an *ultimum remedium* in a parliamentary democracy, under a judge's jurisdiction.[16]

In the meantime, the Center Party continued to receive money from the state for its so-called research and educational institutes until it lost its seats in 1986. The ambiguity of the situation became very clear when, in 1984, the director of the Center Party research institute wrote a racist leaflet called "Holland for the Dutch" (*Nederland voor de Nederlanders*). The judge did not condemn the director and the institute on the grounds that the pamphlet was said to be for internal use only. The expectations of the GPV in 1971 had indeed come true: public subvention of racist propaganda had occurred. However, the fact that the Center Party lost its seats in 1986 showed that the Dutch system of public subsidy did not automatically preserve parties without popular support. The Center Party's re-entry in the Second Chamber in 1989 was achieved without the public subsidy grant.

State Subventions to the Institutes of the Political Parties

In 1984 the Minister of Domestic Affairs published a report on state subvention which proposed to stop the flow of state money to the parties' educational institutes, but to continue subsidies to the research institutes. He defended the distinction between research and educational institutes by claiming that the work of research institutes was more directed than educational institutes to serve "the general interest." This was a remarkable interpretation, since it was educational work that had justified the introduction of this subsidy in 1976. But the coloration of the government coalition had changed (from center-left to center-right) and the reduction of the state deficit was proclaimed to be of the highest priority in the Cabinet's policy.

The Second Chamber refused to follow the Minister and voted, in 1985, for a continuation of both subsidies at the same level. It also advocated the integration of all regulations concerning state subsidies to party foundations into one law. A formal law would allow the institutes to develop financial perspectives for a longer period than the ministerial decrees had offered until then. In 1986, the government made a proposal for such a law, which was accepted by the Second Chamber.

The proposal followed the general structure of the existing regulations but did not include subsidies for the youth organizations. The official reason for this exclusion was that this subsidy formed a part of the general youth policy of the Ministry of Welfare, Health, and Culture, and could not be grouped with a law on subsidies for research and educational institutes without damaging the integrated youth policy. More to the point, this was a demonstration of the difficulty of integrating the policies of two different departments. The Cabinet's general goal to reduce the number of laws and regulations in order to make the administration more open to public scrutiny ("deregulation" and "harmonization") was not reached in this proposal.

The criteria used to calculate the maximum amount of subvention were to be the same for both kinds of institutes, which were generally agreed upon. Except the PvdA and the CDA, whose subsidies increased more than Dfl. 10,000, all parties' subsidization decreased. The D66 was the most affected with a loss of Dfl. 11,457; the CPN, PSP, and SGP lost Dfl. 4,938; the PPR and RPF, Dfl. 2,765; the VVD, Dfl. 1,255; and the CP, KVP, and GPV, Dfl. 592.

According to the proposal, only parties represented in the Second Chamber could claim subsidies for one research institute and one educational institute; their situation at the moment of the election would be the decisive factor. If a parliamentary party split during the parliamentary period, only already "acknowledged" institutes would receive money from the state, and the original number of seats would continue to be the basis for calculating the maximum subsidy. In general, only new elections could induce changes. In an election, the new parliamentary party could "acknowledge" other institutes, while the institutes of parties which lost their seats in the Second Chamber would continue to receive their subsidy for a transitional period of five months. Only in a merger of two or more parliamentary parties would the subsidies for institutes of the original parties cease immediately. The new party would then be able to "acknowledge" one research institute and one educational foundation.

In September 1990, the First Chamber rejected the proposal. The principal reason was that the proposal did not allow political parties represented in the First Chamber, but not the Second Chamber, to claim state subvention.

Meanwhile, the Minister of Domestic Affairs had installed a special commission, presided over by the political scientist Van den Berg, to report on the desirability of direct state subsidies to parties relative to other forms of state support. The report, published in September 1991, argued for a continuation of the existing forms of state subvention for specific purposes (research institutes, educational institutes and youth organizations), albeit in a somewhat different form. It also argued for the inclusion of a public subsidy to parties to maintain contacts with their sister parties abroad.[17] The commission did not support direct subsidies to parties for general purposes, such as campaign spending.

Given the report of the commission, the Minister of Domestic Affairs is likely to present a new proposal, which should reflect, to a large extent, the system of the rejected proposal. It remains to be seen whether it will allow state subvention to parties that are only represented in the First Chamber, since the commission endorsed the Minister in her refusal to do so.

A Move Toward Direct Financing of Political Parties[18]

Until now, the reluctance to grant public money directly to parties has been a dominant feature of the Dutch system of state subvention. But voices have been raised to change this situation, and, as in the 1960s, the shrinking number of members has caused a change in the political climate in this respect.

As Table 2 shows, all parties, except the small orthodox ones, suffered a considerable loss of members in the 1980s. Whereas depillarization accounted for the declining number of party members in the 1960s, the present exodus is nationwide and must be attributed to a phenomenon that has hit all parties except the conservative orthodox Calvinist parties: "individualization." There are no signs of realignment, as was the case in the 1960s and 1970s when the VVD and some new leftwing parties somewhat counterbalanced the loss of other parties. Apparently, people are turning to organizations that defend their interests in a direct manner (trade unions, consumer organizations, or automobile associations) or advocate issues without being identified with a specific ideology (Amnesty International or environmental organizations).

Only a small and rapidly declining percentage of the electorate are members of a political party: 15 percent in 1946, 8 percent in 1967, and 4 percent in 1986. Parties do not need massive numbers of adherents any more in order to reach the voters as television and opinion polls are more efficient in this respect, but they do need members in order to present candidates for political functions. And in the Netherlands, parties especially need members who furnish financial support, since they depend on members' donations for about 80 percent of their budgets.

Dutch political parties do not possess their own profitable enterprises, and receiving money from business circles, although perfectly legal, is just "not done" in the Netherlands. In the face of declining membership, there is only one institution that can come to the rescue: the state. This is what happened at the end of the 1960s and may perhaps take place again.

In 1989, the Christian Democratic Minister of Culture proposed that money from the Fund for the Press should help to pay for party periodicals. However, this proposal was not warmly welcomed. A broader financing system was broached by the chairman of the CDA:

> We are the only country in Western Europe where parties depend completely on contributions by members. In itself, this is a good thing. In other West-European countries political parties are financed by the state and/or by the trade and industry...[But] In my conviction we act too contorted in this respect. I plea for more openness in this discussion in order to realize the societal function of political parties.[19]

And in a speech at the Party Council of the CDA in July 1989, he said:

> Political parties constitute an important element of democracy. They are channels through which the formation of the political will takes place. They are devices to enlarge political consciousness and participation. They counterbalance the big official advisory boards, which give their advice in an apolitical way. The equipment of the political parties in the Netherlands is distressingly small compared with the countries around us. I hope that we will finally have the courage during the new governmental period to analyze how the financing of political parties can be organized in an apolitical manner. Perhaps we deal too sparingly with respect to our democracy...[20]

The CDA may very well be successful in lifting the taboo on this subject. At the beginning of 1990, the major parties formed a committee to report on the desirability of extra state subsidies: the possibility of direct subsidies was to be explicitly part of their deliberations. The special commission, installed by the Minister to advise her regarding state subvention, agreed that the total amount had to remain the same, but was divided regarding whether specific subsidies should be given directly to the parties, or continue to be given to formally independent institutes.

Income and Expenditures of Dutch Political Parties

As long as new sources of income are not introduced, Dutch political parties will continue to depend, to a large extent, on contributions coming from their members, of which membership fees constitute the principle source of income. In addition, all parties transfer a certain percentage of their total income from membership dues to the regional and local party organizations.

About 80 percent of national party income stems from the annually paid fees. Even if one does not include the share that is transferred to the subnational party organizations, this percentage is still very high: 75 percent for all three parties. The national party headquarters' income does not include that of the affiliated organizations. If this income were added to that of the national headquarters, the share of the membership dues would be reduced to about 60 percent.

Party members also support the party financially in other ways. Predominantly, in election years, special fund-raising activities among members are held in order to fill the party's purse. For the most part, the results of these activities are saved as special election funds, which do not figure into the current annual budget. If money from fund raising is not put aside in the election fund, it can be used for the current budget. Also,

those who hold jobs due to their membership in the PvdA, mostly representatives at the local, provincial, and national level, account for about 12
percent of the parties' income; known in left-wing parties as a "party
tax." The smaller PSP, PPR, and CPN also obligate "their" politicians to
pay a share of their income to the party.

Other gifts, those not within the framework of fund-raising actions or
in the form of a "party tax,"[21] are far less important, but all gifts to the
party, as well as the membership dues, are tax-deductible. This is also
true for contributions from business corporations, although the national
headquarters of the CDA, PvdA, and the VVD hardly receive any money
in this manner. The affiliated organizations receive somewhat more, but
in small amounts.

Interest on investments is one other specific source of income, consti-
tuting 4 percent of the PvdA. The PvdA is especially fortunate in this
respect, which is due to the relative wealth of the party; the annual income of the party is the highest of all parties and this is equally true of its
capital reserves.[22]

Dutch political parties spend much more money on their permanent
party organizations than on election campaigns, although the latter have
become more important over the last decades because of the growing
floating vote. The permanent party machinery is the nucleus for each
campaign, but in the end, almost all activities of the party organization
can be considered election-related.

The payment of members of the executive board and the staff constitutes the most important item in the budget of the parties. If the transfers
to subnational party echelons are not included, then salaries account for
30 percent of the total expenditures of the CDA and the VVD, and 46
percent of the PvdA.

The PvdA gives the highest subventions to affiliated organizations, such
as the research and educational foundations, and the youth and women's
organizations. In 1987, the PvdA allocated 20 percent of its funds to these
organizations; the CDA, 15 percent; the VVD, 7 percent.

The research, educational, and youth organizations claim state
subvention, but only on the condition that proves they also receive a certain amount of money from other sources. For these organizations, the
donations by the party are also a means to claim state subventions. The
less money an affiliated organization receives from the party, the more it
needs to raise from other sources in order to be able to claim the maximum state subvention.

Most of the other expenditures are organizational costs, but the publication of party journals accounts for much of this. All three parties distribute a party journal, for which no extra subscription fee is required.

Within the VVD, however, the subscription is earmarked as part of the membership fee.

Conclusion

Dutch party finance still is relatively modest. Major scandals with respect to party finance are absent. The voting turnout at national elections is about 80 to 85 percent. "Golden cords" between parties and the state do not yet exist as such, and entrepreneurial circles grant very little money to parties. But membership figures are rapidly declining; the income of Dutch parties is under pressure. Parties might begin turning to the state or to trade and industry for financial support in order to prevent a decline in citizen political participation. However, money coming from business circles still is suspect because it undermines the democratic principle of "equality of opportunity," since some parties are evidently more popular among employers than others.

The introduction of a direct state subsidy to parties is more acceptable. It will end the present hypocrisy of granting public money to party-affiliated foundations while pretending that party organizations themselves do not profit from it. In practice, no tight lines of separation exist between parties and these institutions. In order to prevent a petrification of the party system, two conditions must be met. The subsidy must maintain to a large extent its goal-oriented character, in order to prevent parties from neglecting their "qualitative" tasks (education, research, etc.) and spend all their money on their "quantitative" tasks (mobilizing the vote, election campaigns). Also, the subsidy must be linked to the number of seats a party occupies in the Second Chamber. Since the electoral threshold is very low in the Netherlands because of the strict proportional-representation system, this criterion is a good one to combine with the principle of "equality of opportunity," mentioned above.

If the government is going to organize party finance on a more structural basis, it probably will make a proposal along these lines. The color of the party message must not be subject to governmental control, but the passage of that message to the voters might be helped with somewhat more public money.

Notes

1. Officially Holland is only a part of the Netherlands. But since this part of the country has been the economic center throughout history, its name has become synonymous with the official name of the country abroad.

2. See S. M. Lipset and S. Rokkan, *Party Systems and Voter Alignments: Cross-National Perspectives* (New York: The Free Press, 1967).

3. See A. Lijphart, *The Politics of Accommodation: Pluralism and Democracy in the Netherlands* (Berkeley: University of California Press, 1968); H. Daalder, "The Netherlands: Opposition in a Segmented Society," in R. A. Dahl, ed., *Political Opposition in Western Democracies* (New Haven: Yale University Press, 1966), pp. 188-236; and H. Daalder, "Consociationalism, Center and Periphery in the Netherlands," in Per Torsvik, ed., *Mobilization, Center-Periphery Structures and Nation-Building: A Volume in Commemoration of Stein Rokkan* (Oslo: Universitets forlaget, 1981), pp. 181-240.

4. For a well-documented overview of the developments during the last decades, see H. Daalder, "The Dutch Party System: From Segmentation to Polarization—and Then?" in H. Daalder, ed., *Party Systems in Denmark, Austria, Switzerland, the Netherlands and Belgium* (London, Francis Pinter, 1987), pp. 193-284; also H. Dadaler and G. A. Irwin, eds., *Politics in the Netherlands: How Much Change?* (London, Frank Casee, 1989).

5. In fact, the very introduction of proportional representation was probably meant to weaken the existing party system. The liberal prime minister, Cort van der Linden, defended the introduction of the new electoral system by stressing the possibility for independent persons to win seats. History has proven him incorrect; "self-starting politicians" are not known in the Netherlands. On the contrary, the new system has promoted the existence of political parties, since it required national organizations to cope with the need for a balanced list of candidates and a common program. Cf.: W.J. van Welderen Rengers, *Schets eener parlementaire geschiedenis van Nederland*, (The Hague, 1948), pt. IV, p. 1532.

6. For a detailed treatment, see D.J. Elzinga, *De politieke partijen het constitutionele recht* (Nijmegen; Ars Aegui, 1982).

7. Proceedings, Second Chamber, 1970-1971, no. 11.105, no. 3, p. 1 (author's translation).

8. Proceedings, Second Chamber, 1971-1972, September 29, 1971, p. 178.

9. See also the author's, "The 'Modesty' of Dutch Party Finance," in Herbert E. Alexander, ed., *Comparative Political Finance in the 1980s* (Cambridge, England: Cambridge University Press, 1989); and "Political Parties Going Dutch: Party Finance in the Netherlands" in *Acta Politica*, January 1990.

10. Wet op de inkomstenbelasting, at. 47.1-3; Wet op de Vennoot schapsbelasting, at. 16.1

11. See D. J. Elzinga, *De financiele positie van de leden der Staten-Generaal* (Groningen, 1985); also D.J. Elzinga and C. Wisse, *De parlementaire fracties* (Groningen, 1988).

12. *Nederlandse Jurisprudentie*, 1978, nr. 281.

13. In the European elections in 1984, for instance, the Center Party won 2.55 percent of the popular vote.

14. *Nederlandse Staatscourant*, January 26, 1987, nr. 17.

15. For a detailed description of this law and the history of the prohibitions of political parties in the Netherlands, see J.A.O. Eskes, *Repressie van politieke bewegingen in Nederland; een juridisch-historische studie over het Nederlandse publiekrechtelijke gedurends het tijdvak 1798-1988* (Zwoll, 1988).

16. In 1991, a special commission, installed by the Minister of Domestic Affairs, pleaded for the ending of facilities (television time) and subventions given by the state, at the very moment the criminal judge) such as condemned a party because of the violation of anti-racist stipulations in the Penal Law. See: *Waarborg van kwaliteit*, report of the Commission on State-subventions to Political Parties (The Hague, 1991).

17. *Waarborg van kwaliteit*, report of the Commission on State-Subvention to Political Parties. The Hague, 1991.

18. Parts of the following sections have also been published in the author's, "Political Parties Going Dutch," *Acta Politica*, January 1990.

19. *CDActueel*, March 4, 1989, p. 23.

20. Speech, partijvoorzitter Van Velzen partijraad July 15, 1989, in het Spant te Bussum, p. 3.

21. In 1983 the Hoge Raad (Supreme Court) concluded that this kind of obligation by the party still is to be considered as a gift, which makes "party tax" tax-deductible as such. Cf., Elzinga (1985), pp. 213-224.

22. Due to the rapid decline of the number of members at the beginning of the 1990s, the reserves of the PvdA shrank at an equal pace.

10

Political Finance in West Germany

Christine Landfried

Political finance in West Germany is characterized by certain structures that contribute to a growing alienation between its citizens and the
political elite: etatization, capitalization, and commercialization. Etatization
commonly describes the influence of public money and the danger posed
when parties become more dependent on the state than on membership
dues.[1] Capitalization refers to the process of increased "big" donations to
political parties in exchange for concessions and privileges.[2] Commercialization expresses the "principle of performance in exchange for
money,"[3] which reduces party member participation and increases the
influence of political consultants.

Political Income: Etatization and Capitalization

A comparison of the laws regulating political finance in 1967, 1984,
and 1988, indicates the influence of public money in West Germany. In
1967, the Federal Constitutional Court decided that campaign costs for
parties receiving 5 percent of the votes in the preceding election should
be reimbursed at 2.50 DM per voter. This figure was raised to 5 DM in
1984. This reimbursement covers approximately one-third of the parties'
total income but the share is significantly greater for each of the party's
headquarters. On average, more than 50 percent of the total income of
each party headquarters comes from reimbursement money. As seen in
Table 1, party headquarters are predominantly financed by public money,
especially in election years.

TABLE 1 Reimbursement of Campaign Costs as a Percentage of Total Income of Party Head-quarters In Four Year Terms, 1968-1991*

	Christian Democratic Union (CDU)	Social Democratic Party (SDP)	Free Democratic Party (FDP)	Die Grunen (DG)
1968-1971	49%	52%	55%	–
1972-1975	37	50	42	–
1976-1979	48	57	44	–
1980-1983	53	62	60	–
1984-1987	66	64	65	65%
1988-1991	63	66	78	69

*The CSU is not included because it is active only in Bavaria.

Source: Reports of Account of the political parties.[4]

A second source of public financing is the equal-protection scheme (*Chancenausgleich*). This plan, initiated in 1984, was intended to equalize the tax privileges given for dues and donations to parties. The law declared that dues and donations to political parties were tax-deductible up to 5 percent of an individual's income or 2 percent of a corporation's turnover. This provision had to be amended due to a decision of the Federal Constitutional Court.[5] The new law of December 1988 made dues and donations tax-deductible up to a maximum of 60,000 DM, favoring wealthy persons and parties which attract large donors. The equal-protection scheme was introduced to compensate for these inequalities by using public money to subsidize disadvantaged parties which gained smaller sums of tax donations from their members and donors. Though this plan is operated by private initiative, by its nature it is a form of public funding.[6] The equal-protection scheme is essentially the same as the "matching funds" program in the United States federal system. The sum paid by the state has more than doubled in the seven years the equal protection scheme has been in existence (see Table 2).

A third source of public funding is the dues from the salaries of Members of Parliament. The Presidential Commission has called this a "hidden form of public funding," as parliamentary salary schedules are calculated to enable Members of Parliament to pay a certain sum.[7] From 1968 to 1983, these kickbacks amounted to 10 percent of the total income of the CDU, 8 percent of the CSU, 9 percent of the SPD, and 7 percent of the FDP. After 1984, these contributions were no longer delineated separately in the Reports of Accounts and can only be estimated. According to a survey carried out among Members of Parliament in 1988,[8] members of

TABLE 2 Public Funding of Political Parties From the Equal-Protection Scheme (Chancenausgleich) in millions of DM

	Christian Democratic Union (CDU)	Christian Social Union (CSU)	Free Democratic Party	Social Democratic Party	Die Grunen	Total
1985	2.8	1.9	1.7	--	3.0	9.4
1986	3.9	3.7	1.1	--	1.7	10.4
1987	--	1.4	4.3	1.9	5.9	13.5
1988	6.4	2.4	2.7	--	--	11.5
1989	6.9	2.9	2.8	9.1	5.1	26.8
1990	8.1	2.4	1.4	9.1	--	21.0
1991	10.1	2.8	4.0	10.1	--	26.9

Sources: Reports of Account of the political parties and printed matter of Parliament, No. 11/ 4814 July 16, 1989, p. 4.

the CDU/CSU and the FDP paid roughly 1,000 DM per month to their parties while members of the SPD paid 1,400 DM per month.

By combining reimbursement for campaign costs, subsidies from the equal-protection scheme, and members' dues, the total sum of public money going to political parties may be calculated (see Table 3). This increased public financing does not take into account public subsidies for party foundations and parliamentary groups that other authors usually include in their calculations.[9] Since the activities of party foundations and parliamentary groups are not exclusively in the interests of parties, these subsidies are not included in the figures in this chapter.

Until 1988, there were no public subsidies for the operational costs of parties in West Germany, as is still the case with Austria, Italy, and Sweden.[10] This changed with the law of December 1988 (*Sockelbetrag*), which, in paragraph 18, introduced public subsidies for the operational costs of party organizations. Beginning in 1989, parties winning at least 2 percent of the votes in the prior election, received 6 percent of the total sum of their campaign costs. According to a 1988 survey, 64 percent of the voting population did not welcome this innovation.[11]

Along with a growing etatization of the income structure of political parties, capitalization also can be discerned. Legislators granted special privileges to big donors in both the 1984 and 1988 laws by expanding tax deductions for private donations to political parties, and by reducing the degree of disclosure required for private c ontributions. The 1984 law benefited big donors under Germany's progressive tax system. In 1986,

TABLE 3. Average Total Income, Membership Dues, and Public Subsidies to Political Parties
In Four Year Terms

	Total Income	Membership Dues and Donations up to 20,000 DM	Percentage of Total Income	Public Subsidies	Percentage of Total Income
1968-71	120	57	47	51	43
1972-75	236	127	55	88	37
1976-79	322	168	55	131	36
1980-83	407	202	53	175	40
1984-87	506	246	49	223	44
1988-91	658	360*	56	292	43

* For 1989, 1990, and 1994 this column includes membership dues and donations up to
40,000 DM because of new regulations concerning disclosure.

Source: Reports of Account of political parties.

the Federal Constitutional Court declared this regulation unconstitutional
because it violated the citizen's right to participate in political affairs on
equal terms. The court ruled instead that it was constitutional to deduct
donations of up to 100,000 DM. This solution, clearly, was no less a violation of the citizen's right to participate equally in politics than the law
that had been passed by Parliament.[12]

The party financing law was amended in 1988, making private donations to political parties tax-deductible up to 60,000 DM per year. Despite the equal-protection scheme, the regulation meant a windfall for big
donors and for those parties which attract people with high incomes or
corporations with high turnover. The public subsidies of the equal-protection scheme do not have the same effect as private donations, as a private donor has the possibility of influencing the political course of a party
through sizable donations.

Another way the process of capitalization is furthered is through inadequate disclosure of private donations to political parties. The 1967
law stated that donations to political parties in excess of 20,000 DM had
to be published (with the donor's name and amount) in their Reports of
Account. When the 1984 law gave new tax privileges to big donors, it
was assured that misuse of these privileges would be checked by extensive disclosure rules:

> Increased transparency and disclosure requirements will provide neces-
> sary safeguards against abuse as the German system of political finance

shifts away from reliance on government funding toward a greater role for the private sector.[13]

However, the Law of 1988 decreased disclosure requirements. Since 1988, only donations of more than 40,000 DM per year must be published in the parties' Reports of Account. Decreased transparency, in addition to increased tax deductions, meant a double-advantage for the large donors. The law of 1988 violated the right of political parties to equal opportunities, which could not be compensated for by the equal-protection scheme. In April 1992, the Constitutional Court revised its decision of 1986 and ruled unconstitutional the present state of disclosure of donations to political parties. The regulation that only donations of more than 40,000 DM per year have to be published will now have to be changed by Parliament. The Court also decided, again reversing itself, that tax-deductible donations to political parties of up to 60,000 DM per year violated the Constitution.[14]

By analyzing the period from 1968 until 1991, donations, as a percentage of the total income of political parties, have lost ground while membership dues have, for the most part, gained importance (see Table 4). The data show that donations have not played a dominant role in the income of political parties, with only the FDP receiving roughly a third of its total income from this source. This would seem to negate the claim that the income structure of political parties is marked by increasing capitalization.

Another test of this claim might come from a comparison of the influence of large donations (those in excess of 20,000 DM) in relation to the

TABLE 4. Membership Dues and Private Donations as a Percentage of the Total Income of Nationwide Political Parties

| | CDU | | SPD | | FDP | |
| | Membership | | Membership | | Membership | |
Terms	Dues	Donations	Dues	Donations	Dues	Donations
1968-71	32	27	48	11	21	35
1972-75	34	35	51	12	21	39
1976-79	44	24	58	9	25	36
1980-83	47	22	56	8	27	33
1984-87	45	15	52	9	25	34
1988-91	41	19	48	10	21	31

The CSU is not included in these calculations because it is present only in Bavaria.

Source: Reports of Account of Political Parties.

total sum of donations. If the sum of donations to a party were to consist primarily of large donations, capitalization would be apparent. In the period from 1984-1987, these donations reached 9.5 percent of the total donations to the CDU, 5 percent of donations to the CSU and SPD, and 17 percent of donations to the FDP. Clearly, this does not demonstrate the process of capitalization at work. In addition, no decisive increase in importance of big donations reveals itself between 1968 to 1991. The percentage of these donations in relation to all donations has grown since 1968 for the SPD and FDP, but has declined significantly for the CSU.[15] During the period 1984 to 1987, big donations to all political parties in Parliament increased only about 2 percent.[16]

However, the process of capitalization cannot be adequately estimated without taking into consideration the many illegal big donations made to political parties before the 1984 law introduced sanctions for underreporting of contributions. The uncovering of scandals by the courts and the Parliamentary Commissions provided evidence that the large donations published in the parties' Reports of Account did not reflect their real amount. The district court of Bonn found, in its research during the Flick trial, that, from 1969 to 1980, illegal big donations to the CDU, the CSU, and the FDP amounted to, roughly, 183 million DM.[17] This sum of illegal donations was three times higher than the sum of reported legal big donations made to these parties during the same period (66 million DM).[18]

The influence of a donation cannot be measured only by its amount. A donation given directly to a politician may be more influential than money given to that politician's party. From data put together by the courts in financial scandals, as well as from the reports of the Parliamentary Commissions, it appears that many donations were given directly to politicians. This is a characteristic of political finance that has been underestimated so far in Germany. Of the Flick Corporation donations to the CDU, CSU, SPD, and FDP during 1974 to 1980, 26 percent were given directly to politicians. Also, donations to a party or to a party foundation were often earmarked and cannot be considered on the same level as general donations to a party.[19] Thus even the so-called "official donations" to political parties and organizations are often donations to politicians. Quite often the politicians themselves told donors they should give directly to them and not to the political party.[20] These direct donations were not particular to the Flick Corporation but were general practice in the 1970s. As the Flick scandal showed, these direct donations made it possible for the donors to gain political concessions.[21]

Thus illegal big donations and those given directly to politicians have contributed to a capitalization of the income structure of political parties. While capitalization is not determined by looking solely at the official

Reports of Account and published donations, it is clearly discernible when other factors are taken into consideration. If we add the illegal donations to the total sum of legal donations to the CDU, CSU, and FDP, from 1969 to 1980, 60 percent consisted of donations of more than 20,000 DM.[22] This percentage shows that the process of capitalization has indeed taken place. In addition, direct donations have enabled donors to capitalize politically on their money. The danger of corruption is always possible with direct donations to a politician.[23] This is exacerbated by the fact that bribery of a Member of Parliament is not punishable in Germany as it is in the United States and other Western democracies, and disclosure rules are minimal. While in the United States every member of the House of Representatives and every senator must publish a detailed report of his or her income, a Member of Parliament only has to report donations of more than 10,000 DM, and that to the President of the Parliament, not to the general public.

Expenditure and Commercialization

To test the professionalizaton of campaigning in Germany, campaign expenditures must be analyzed. Such a pattern is easy to discern in the United States where campaign expenditures are not secret, but in Germany there is not comparable detail. Only since 1984 have German political parties had to publish their expenditures as well as their income. The total expenditure from 1984 until 1987 for the CDU increased from 196 to 208 million DM per year, and from 186 to 211 million DM per year for the SPD. The expenditure of the FDP decreased from 38 to 36 million DM. The two big parties are spending nearly half of their money on political activities. The Greens have the highest percentage of expenditure for political activities at 58 percent of the total amount. Costs for staff amount to roughly a third of the expenditure for both the CDU and the SPD. In administrative costs there is a difference between the two great political parties: the CDU spends approximately a fifth of their total expenditures on administration, while the SPD allocates a sixth of their expenditures.

Campaign costs are expressly identified in only two fields: "expenditure for publicity work and campaigning" and "expenditure for information and group work" which can be interpreted together as "political activities." Because of the missing data, research of campaign costs in Germany "...is a frustrating business."[24] One reason for this opaqueness may be that when parties receive public subsidies for reimbursement of campaign costs, they spend part of this money for operational costs. The Constitution (Article 21, No. 1GG) specifies that political parties should give information about their incomes and expenditures. But these expenditures are sometimes unclear, such as "costs related to campaigns." An arrangement between the treasurers of political parties specifies that as much as 50 percent of operational costs may be counted as costs related to campaigns. In a survey among the treasurers of länder political parties, the majority of treasurers were not certain which costs should be listed in which sections of the *Reports of Account*.[25]

To determine the direct costs of campaigns for Germany, one has to rely on estimates and incomplete data. For the election of 1987, a realistic estimate of direct campaign costs is 197 million DM for the CDU/CSU, SPD, and FDP together, or 4.50 DM per vote.[26] Comparisons with estimates of campaign costs for earlier elections, for example the election of 1965, show that campaign costs have doubled in the last twenty years, even though television time is not paid for by the parties.

There is also little information regarding what political parties and candidates spend money on in campaigns. Pollsters are hired only by party headquarters, not by the candidates themselves. The headquarters of the SPD, for example, spends roughly 600,000 DM for polling per year, which doubles in election years.[27] Politicians spend their money in campaigns largely on printed matter, advertisements, and posters. The author's 1988 survey among Members of Parliament concluded that the CDU/CSU candidates for Parliament spent 32 percent on printed matter; the SPD candidates, 28 percent; and the FPD candidates, 31 percent. Only the Greens spent much less in this area, at 5 percent. For advertisements, the CDU/CSU candidates spent 23 percent; SPD candidates, 21 percent; FDP candidates, 15 percent; and candidates of the Greens, 10 percent. Expenditure for political activities amounted to 11 percent of the total expenditure for the CDU/CSU candidates, 19 percent for SPD candidates, 13 percent for FDP candidates, and 50 percent for candidates of the Greens.[28] Data to compare these figures with the election year 1961 exists only for the CDU, and shows that little has changed in the structure of expenditures for a candidate for Parliament. One may criticize politicians for spending too much on printed matter and advertisements, and too little on political activities, but there are no indicators that campaign spending by politicians can be called commercialized. There is evidence that commercialization of campaigns in Germany has taken place, but it has taken place exclusively at party headquarters, not in election districts.

Proposals for Reform

The effect of public funding depends on its amount in relation to the total income of political parties and on its distribution among the different levels of party organizations. With the introduction of public funding of the parties' operational (administrative) costs in 1988, the process of etatization has reached a degree that should not be exceeded, especially since political parties in West Germany are no longer in financial jeopardy. The Presidential Commission on the Financing of Parties sought to measure the parties' financial state (using the cost-of-living as an indicator), the costs of staff, the number of members of political parties, and the number of persons entitled to vote, compared to the parties' income. The Commission discovered that political parties were, from 1973 until 1981, in financial straits.[29] However, the calculation performed on subsequent years showed that costs and income of political parties have been balanced since 1982.[30]

With respect to the distribution of public money at the different levels of party organization, public funding of national party headquarters should be reduced. More than 50 percent of all headquarters' incomes comes from the public purse, thereby permitting them a financial base independent of their membership. Part of the public money coming from the reimbursement of campaign costs should be redistributed to the lower levels of party organization, such as districts, while party headquarters should increase their share of membership dues (which has been the main source of income for the lower levels of party organizations). The party headquarters of the FDP, for example, only receives one DM per member of the membership dues. Such a redistribution of funding systems could improve communication between the political elites and party members.

German regulations on donations to political parties also are in need of reform. Theodor Eschenburg advocates a radical change abolishing private donations to political parties. He believes that donations always raise the danger of corruption, thus it would be better for political parties to receive their income from membership dues and public subsidies alone.[31] Yet this proposal has little chance of actually being realized. A possible solution would be to forbid donations by legal entities to political parties. This would address the problem of unfair advantage more effectively than the April 1992 Constitutional Court decision which ruled that donations of legal entities could no longer be tax-deductible. As legal entities are not entitled to vote, they should not be allowed to participate by giving money to a political party. In the author's survey among treasurers of political parties in 1988, eight treasurers were in favor of such a ban on donations of legal entities to parties while thirteen were opposed.

The danger that a donation to a party has been given in exchange for certain political concessions increases with the amount of money that is involved. Legal entities give especially large sums of money to political parties. The penalty for a violation of this regulation should be high enough to discourage potential offenders, such as the sanction the Presidential Commission proposed for illegal donations, a fine equal to ten times the donation.

Regulations pertaining to the tax deductibility of donations should strictly consider the right of citizens to equal participation in political affairs. According to a decision of the Constitutional Court in 1992, this right is violated if donations up to 60,000 DM to political parties are tax deductible, since there are very few people who can take advantage of such a regulation. To avoid an unconstitutional privilege and capitalization, tax-deductible donations should not exceed 5,000 DM. This limit would not put an unusual burden on the political parties as, according to the treasurers, the majority of donations are in amounts under 5,000 DM.[32]

Limiting tax deductions on political donations would make it possible to discontinue the unsuccessful equal-protection scheme. Considering the many problems connected with the equal-protection scheme,[33] it would be best to revoke the regulation. This would have the positive effect of diminishing the process of etatization, as the equal-protection scheme is paid with public money.

A weak point of the present system of political finance is insufficient disclosure of donations. Compared with the U. S., German regulations on the transparency of donations lag far behind. In the United States, every donation to a political party or politician of more than $200 has to be reported to the Federal Election Commission. In Germany, only donations of 40,000 DM or more must be published in the parties' Reports of Account. Donations to a politician that exceed 10,000 DM must be reported to the President of Parliament. While donations to political parties in Germany are published, donations to politicians are not. These regulations do not meet the demands of the Constitution that requires (Article 21, no. 1) that it be known who is financially supporting a political party and a politician (Article 38, no. 1). To meet the demands of the Constitution, donations to political parties in excess of 10,000 DM should be published. Donations to politicians should be reported and published in the Reports of Account of the political parties. These shortcomings may, in fact, soon be rectified as they have been held to be unconstitutional by the Federal Constitutional Court in the decision of April 9, 1992. Parliament will now need to pass a new law by 1994.

Lesser public subsidies for party headquarters, less influence of big donors, and greater disclosure of donations to parties and politicians would likely connect the political elite in an indirect way to party members and citizens. More direct ways to tie the political elites to citizens also have been proposed, such as the so called "citizen bonus,"[34] which Eschenburg advocated in 1957 and the Presidential Commission incorporated in its recommendations. This type of bonus would mean that every citizen in an election would have, besides his vote for Members of Parliament, a "financial vote," which would designate a certain amount of the public subsidy to the political party of his or her choice. A citizen could vote for party A and designate his or her financial vote to party B. Five out of six experts who were consulted by Parliament to prepare the Law of Financing Political Parties of 1988 were in favor of this bonus, but it was not supported by the majority of MPs. Only the Green Party voted for it.[35]

Besides these direct and indirect methods of reform aimed at promoting better communication between citizens and the political elite, one also must realize that problems of party financing are not exclusively problems for the experts. Citizens have an interest in these matters and the democratic decision-making process is advanced when citizens are able to make use of this interest in political finance.

Notes

1. See Klaus von Beyme, *Political Parties in Western Democracies* (New York: St. Martin's Press, 1985), chapter 3.

2. See the author's *Parteifinanzen und politische Macht* (Baden-Baden: Nomos, 1990), p. 15ff.

3. Renate Mayntz, "Funktionelle Teilsysteme in der Theorie Sozialer Differenzierung," in Renate Mayntz et al., *Differenzierung und Verselbstandigung: Zur Entwicklung gesellschaftlicher Teilsysteme* (Frankfurt: Campus, 1988), p. 41.

4. These figures are from the Reports of Account of political parties; published by Koln, Bundsanzeiger fur 1968-1982 and by Deutscher Bundestag, Bonn for 1983-1991.

5. Decision of the Federal Constitutional Court of July 14, 1986, BVerfGE, vol. 73, p. 40ff.

6. Hans-Peter Schneider holds the opinion that the compensatory payments from the equal-protection scheme are not a form of public funding. Cp., Hans-Peter Schneider, "The New German System of Party Funding: the Presidential Committee Report of 1983 and its Realization," in Herbert E. Alexander, ed., *Comparative Political Finance in the 1980s*, (Cambridge: Cambridge University Press, 1989), p. 227.

7. Bericht zur Neuordnung der Parteienfinanzierung, *Vorschlage der vom Bundesprsidenten berufenen Sachverstndigenkommission* (Kln: Bundesanzeiger, 1983), p. 188.

8. Landfried, *Parteifinanzen*, p. 98.

9. Hans Herbert von Arnim, *Parteienfinanzierung* (Wiesbaden: Karl-Brauer-Institut, 1982), p. 134, and Karl-Heinz Nassmacher, "Offentliche Parteienfinanzierung in Westeuropa: Implementationsstrategien und Problemstand in der Bundesrepublik Deutschland, Italien, Osterreich und Schweden," in *Politische Viertel-jahresschrift*, (Opladen: Westduetscher Verlag, 1987), p. 108.

10. Karl-Heinz Nassmacher, "Structure and Impact of Public Subsidies to Political Parties in Europe: The examples of Austria, Italy, Sweden and West Germany," in Alexander, ed., *Comparative Political Finance*, p. 245.

11. INFAS Survey of West Germany, August 1988.

12. The dissent of Justices Bckenfrde and Mahrenholz points to this as a violation of the citizen's right of equal participation in political affairs. *BVerfGE*, vol. 73, p. 103ff.

13. Schneider, "The German System of Party Funding," p. 233.

14. The decision of April 9, 1992, has been published in: *BVertGE*, vol. 85, p. 264 ff.

15. For data, see Landfried, *Parteifinanzen*, p. 333.

16. Printed matter of Parliament, no. 11/4814 of June 16, 1989, p. 6.

17. District Court of Bonn, decision of the Flick trial of February 16, 1987, p. 460.

18. For comparison, see table in Landfried, *Parteifinanzen*, p. 135.

19. District Court of Bonn, Decision of the Flick trial of February 16, 1987. For extensive material, see p. 399.

20. Ibid, p. 451ff.

21. Ibid, p. 403.

22. Landfried, *Parteifinanzen*, p. 134.

23 . Theodor Eschenburg, "Paragraphen gegen Parlamentarier?" in Theodor Eschenburg, *Zur politischen Praxis in der Bundesrepublik*, Vol. 1 (Mnchen: Piper, 1967), p. 124.

24. Gottrik Wewer, "Money, Media and Politics in Western Germany," paper prepared for the ECPR Workshop, Money and Politics, Rimini, April 5-10, 1988, p. 12.

25. Survey among treasurers of political parties conducted in 1988, in Landfried, *Parteifinanzen*, p. 255.

26. Ibid., p. 257.

27. Ibid., p. 263.

28. Survey among Members of Parliament conducted in 1988, in Landfried, *Parteifinanzen*, p. 264.

29. Bericht zur Neuordnung der Parteienfinanzierung, *Vorschlage der vom Bundesprsidenten*, berufenen Sachoetstandigen-kommission, p. 99.

30. Data in Landfried, *Parteifinanzen*, p. 318.

31. Theodor Eschenburg, " Kommission soll Diaten Vorschlagen," in *Rhein-Neckar Zeitung*, July 25, 1988, p. 2.

32. "Statement of the Treasurers of Political Parties Before the Federal Constitutional Court," in *Decisions of the Federal Constitutional Court*, vol. 73, p. 115.

33. The statement of Hans-Peter Schneider during a hearing of experts before the Committee of the Interior of Parliament, 36th Session, November 21, 1988, p. 55.

34. Theodor Eschenburg, *Rechtliche Ordnung des Parteiwesens. Probleme eines Parteiengesetzes* (Frankfort/Berlin: Metzner Verlag, 1957), p. 198.

35. Printed matter of Parliament, no. 11/3697 of December 8, 1988, p. 3.

11

Citizens' Cash in Canada and the United States

Karl-Heinz Nassmacher

As a form of mixed government, Western democracy operates under several different concepts at the same time. One person, one vote, is one; the legitimate use of money for political purposes is another. Political competitors vie for both. In addition, a government of the people, for the people, and by the people is, in actuality, a regime of political elites. Active and interested minorities manage the political process. They rely on the consent, or at least the tolerance, of the masses who remain generally passive.

Democratic systems and their subsystems, such as parties and pressure groups, depend on voluntary participation. To ensure participation, a democracy needs reasonable incentives, such as honor, rank, patronage, or money, to funnel individual activity into functions necessary to maintain the political system. Such participation in a public arena is characterized by a spectrum of intensity for specific resources, differing with respect to input and output, investment and impact. The different forms of democratic participation available to both the general public and its politically active members fall along a continuum that begins with voting. Further along the scale are those who prefer to contribute or solicit money for issues, parties, and candidates, followed by people writing letters to politicians or newspaper editors. Those who donate leisure time for voluntary campaign work for issues, candidates, and parties are at the other end of the continuum.

Those citizens who participate along this continuum[1] tend to belong to different elite groups, of which only the voting elite embraces the majority of the population in most liberal democracies. The minority of citizens who take part in political debate seem to constitute a larger constituency than the joining elite—citizens who actively join any political organization--or the contributing elite--people who donate money for political purposes.[2] Even so, the contributing elite is usually larger than the campaigning elite—citizens who actively work for a political candidate, party, or issue during a campaign.

If citizens decide to contribute their own money to politicians, a financial link of grassroots support for party politics is maintained. However, the claim that political action should be paid for by those who take a voluntary interest in ideologies, issues, and candidates, has led to "...an outdated individualistic ideology [which] tends to obscure the fact that the flow of funds into the party system reflects the economic and social structure of society."[3] In most Western democracies, despite the general economic well-being of their citizens, parties and candidates have found it increasingly difficult to raise the funds they consider necessary to support their routine, not to mention campaign, activities. Great Britain's Houghton Committee *Report* stated that parties were no longer able to raise sufficient income to meet increased costs.[4] In order to bridge the gap between donations and party needs, many countries now grant public subsidies.

As a result, citizens of democratic countries, by means of "pathological learning,"[5] have become accustomed to a political situation which demands opinions and occasional voting but not widespread personal money. If democracy is to survive, this trend will need to be reversed. To encourage this, some Western democracies have developed rules for the public funding of political parties and candidates that combine subsidies with devices to ensure participation. The national governments of Canada and the United States, as well as some of their respective provinces and states, provide tax add-ons and checkoffs, tax deductions and credits, matching funds, or partial reimbursement of campaign expenses.[6] A common feature of public subsidy programs applied to campaign finance in North America is a close link between private and public activity. Public and private actors work together to produce certain results; for example, insufficiency in raising money in the private sector results in the inability of government to provide matching funds.

Tax Add-On and Checkoff

The tax add-on option allows political competitors the opportunity to collect private donations voluntarily contributed by citizens by using a governmental sponsored collection mechanism: the income tax return.[7] Thus a type of service is provided by public agencies to raise additional funds from private sources.

The tax checkoff system offers citizens an option as to how a specific part of public revenue shall be spent. "[T]axpayers can earmark part of their normal tax liability to be set aside for use in election campaigns."[8] Delineating a dollar of the tax obligation implies consent to a diversion of public funds towards political purposes by means of an annual "referendum" of individual taxpayers in their capacity as citizens, a device to legitimize public funding schemes.

While all elements of campaign finance reform programs include the notion of citizen participation, an evaluation of programs demands reflection on the participation rate. Although voting in elections is the most general form of participation, there is no average or standard level of voter participation common to all Western democracies. Some countries in Europe expect 80 to 90 percent of the electorate to vote in every election, but Switzerland and the U.S. generally experience far less participation. If half of the people entitled to vote actually enter the polling booth in these two countries, the balloting is considered a success.

Bearing this in mind, the rate of tax checkoff participation at the national level in the U.S., as well as in the states of New Jersey and Michigan, initially can be considered satisfactory, but participation rates reveal different levels of state participation and a general decline over time.[9] For example, the tax checkoff rate in New Jersey declined from 38 percent in 1976 to approximately 28 percent in 1990. Minnesota, Wisconsin, Iowa, and Kentucky all experienced declines from 18 percent to approximately 12 percent. According to Ruth S. Jones, in the early 1980s, the situation seemed pretty clear:

> Although there have been occasional slight increases or decreases in the number of taxpayers participating in the public financing programs, the overall picture, state by state, is one of relatively constant percentages of taxpayers supporting these programs year after year.[10]

Jack L. Noragon proposed a hypothesis relating the participation rate to "the degree of competitiveness between the two major parties"; but reports "little explanatory value" after his analysis.[11] Jones believes that there are "several possible explanations for why participation in the checkoff systems differ so among states. The political culture and context of the state is probably a significant factor."[12] The biggest difference, in fact, seems to be caused by what appears to be a minor technicality: "... state programs that require taxpayers to increase their tax liability, [the add-on option]... are destined to low participation at the outset."[13] Data for Massachusetts and Virginia, which use the add-on option, as well as Montana (after a change from checkoff to add-on), strongly suggest this as the main factor.

Noragon also cites statistical evidence to support a causal relationship between the tax checkoff participation rate and the per capita personal income, as well as the rate of taxation ("tax effort"), for individual states. In his analysis he notes a close association between the checkoff rate and ranking based on per capita personal income (Spearman's Rho = .62) as well as per capita state taxes (Rho = .80). Seemingly, if the average level of personal income were a factor influencing the success of the checkoff option, the federal public funding program would have to be less successful than those of the high-ranking states. But this is not the case. New Jersey, Michigan, and the U.S. on the federal level belonged to the same bracket for about six years, despite disparities in the income tax burden.

For states that use the checkoff, specific provisions determine the participation rate. States, such as Iowa and Kentucky, which require people to declare a party preference on the tax form, rank lowest among the checkoff states. This point is supported by evidence from Utah, which "managed to frighten off a sizable number of potential contributors, many of whom possibly believed that their political beliefs were being scrutinized."[14] A medium level of participation is achieved by an arrangement that distributes small amounts of money for a variety of political races, such as Hawaii, Minnesota, and Wisconsin. However, the only tax checkoff option that initially produced a reasonable participation rate concentrated all the checkoff funds on one important political competition, either the presidential or the gubernatorial race. When ample funds can be concentrated on only a few campaigns or a few candidates, as in New Jersey or Michigan, public funding has a significant impact on the election campaign process.

There may yet be additional measures that can still improve the level of participation, as well as the long-term trend. One may involve improved communication: "The success of public financing policies in raising money may also vary according to the efforts that officials and party leaders make to familiarize taxpayers with the program."[15]

The political behavior of individual citizens seems inconsistent to many researchers. Opinion polls asking for citizens' preferences find respondents willing to provide additional tax dollars to substitute for campaign funding from private sources, but many are not using the tax checkoff or add-on option available in their state. Perhaps this inconsistency results from a belief "that too much money is being spent."[16]

One possible reason for the decline in checkoff programs in the late 1980s and into the 1990s might be that people are becoming increasingly cynical about politics and are unsatisfied with parties and candidates. A possibility is that after Watergate, public awareness of the ramification of campaign funding from private donors was very high, but this awareness has been declining since.

Also, using the add-on option for other political issues such as wild-life preservation, child abuse, or the Olympic games,[17] as some states do, runs the risk of dissipating taxpayer participation among various causes. These competing options may add to the taxpayers' confusion, although effects from this competition may be minor when compared with other explanations.[18] Also, empirical evidence supports the expectation "that the specific method of placing the checkoff system on the tax form influences the rate of participation.[19] To maximize awareness, the checkoff option must be placed on the front page of the tax form.

Systems such as competing checkoff options and actual placement on the tax form may improve the level of participation, but most likely do not influence the decline observed in participation rates in all the jurisdictions.[20] When participation decreases, legislators may try to save the public funding program by increasing the amount an individual may check off to the campaign fund. This may increase actual revenues, as in Minnesota, but it may endanger widespread democratic participation.

Tax Deduction and Tax Credit

The only participatory instrument of public funding programs equally familiar to North Americans and Western Europeans, is the tax incentive for political contributions.[21] Technically, these tax incentives may be provided either as tax deductions or tax credits. The tax deduction is applied to taxable income, the gross income before tax. The tax credit decreases the actual tax burden because it can be claimed against income tax due, not just taxable income. In practical terms, this results in a bonus provided from the public purse for political donations from selected private sources.

Completely different approaches were used by West Germany in 1954, and the state of Minnesota in 1955, when they first introduced tax deductions for political donations. West German "bagmen" went after the corporate donor, with a maximum of either 5 percent of gross income or 0.2 percent of total sales plus wages and salaries paid. On the other hand, Minnesota's legislation was aimed at the small donor with a maximum of $100 per individual per year.[22]

Today, in the U.S. only eight of the fifty states still operate this type of program: three (California, Minnesota, and Oregon) with a tax credit, and five (Arizona, Hawaii, Montana, North Carolina, and Oklahoma) with a tax deduction.[23] The federal tax deduction has fallen victim to President Reagan's deregulatory activities and was repealed in 1986.

Conversely, in Canada, tax credits have become an important element in the fund-raising process. Residents in the Canadian province of Alberta may claim tax credits for a maximum donation of Cdn. $2,875 per year, if they split their total contributions between federal parties, provincial parties, and candidates.[24] The total income of federal parties and candidates has increased considerably since its political finance regulation became effective in 1974,[25] substantially due to individual donations. While the share of individual donations has increased for the Progressive Conservatives (PCs), corporate giving by the major industrial, commercial, and financial institutions (a traditional source of money for that party)[26] has decreased at an equal pace. Although the Liberals introduced reform legislation, the PCs (then in opposition) have been able to change impressively from a party of "big money" to a party of "small donations."[27]

The tax credit for political donations and the provision that allows the issuing of tax receipts have proven to be very important for the federal parties in Canada, especially in supporting their efforts to solicit small donations from individual citizens. "Big money in little sums"[28] has become a political reality due to an innovative combination of public regulation and organizational effort by the Canadian parties.

Customarily the New Democratic Party (NDP) and the Parti Quebecois, due to their different party structures (as mass membership parties), stage annual membership drives which perform different functions.[29] Party activists call on their neighbors, renewing formal memberships and collecting additional donations, in a door-to-door activity that keeps the local organizations funded. A considerable part of the money thus collected is then transferred to provincial and federal headquarters through assessments imposed on the local associations.

The three national parties in Canada experienced different patterns of individual donations during the years 1976 to 1988. There appears to be no significant increase among the number of donors to the Liberal cause, holding steady around 25,000. But, the donor base for the NDP has more than doubled, rising from 62,500 to more than 115,000. While the average donation to the NDP has stagnated somewhat over time, averaging around $50, the Liberal Party of Canada has fared quite well in most election years, averaging $120 in 1980; $180 in 1984; and $155 in 1988. The Liberals have been slow to adapt their fund-raising procedures to new regulations and technological standards, and this is probably why they have failed to keep pace with their competitors in expanding their pool of donors. The PC experience with political contributions from individual citizens approached by direct mail has been an almost steady increase in the average donation, together with fluctuations in the number of donors.[30]

Nevertheless, the recent history of Canadian fund-raising reveals the limitations of the direct-mail effort. A European-style party which sends its activists to knock on doors, such as the NDP west of Quebec and the Parti Quebecois, can be more effective than any party headquarter's efforts that depend solely on direct-mail. Fund-raising by mail through the PC Canada Fund reached its peak just before the 1984 election returned a PC majority to the House of Commons. A comparison between the long-term number of donors in the PC and the NDP indicates that an opposition party may find it easier to collect funds from among its supporters.

For supporters of democratic principles, direct-mail soliciting places a new role and responsibility on the upper-middle class, such as affluent white-collar workers and professionals who are sensitive to targeted fund raising. A problem with direct-mail is that different levels of the same party (such as the PC Canada Fund, the provincial PCs, and two different sets of PC riding associations) may ask for donations without coordination, and the money pool can become "over-fished." Yet another effect is the risk this introduces into political financing. When the Mulroney government lost the support of the general public, the federal PC also lost fund-raising potential. Earlier, the PQ and the PLQ in Quebec went through similar experiences.

Tax data in Canada reiterate the theme of rising donations (and tax credit totals), an increasing numbers of donors, and a growing average of tax credits claimed per tax return.[31] Differences arise when individual provinces across the country are compared. On average, when the results are adjusted for year, province size, and administration level, 1 to 2 percent of all Canadian taxpayers claimed an accumulated tax credit of $100-$180 on their federal and provincial income tax forms for the years 1974 to 1988. In most provinces, deviation from these averages is marginal. Disregarding the province of Prince Edward Island (the last province to introduce a provincial tax credit in 1986), two areas stand out significantly from the average: Saskatchewan and Quebec. In Saskatchewan, the average federal tax credit of $72 basically matches that of the other provinces (except Atlantic Canada), but the 2.3 percent participation rate is almost three times higher than the federal average of .8 percent. In Quebec, the participation rate of .2 percent for the federal tax credit is extremely low, while participation in the provincial tax credit, 1.3 percent, scores about normal. The average amount of tax credit claimed at $30 provincially and $85 federally, reverses this.

Because neither Saskatchewan nor Newfoundland provides a provincial tax credit, the difference in participation rates is worth considering. Donors in Saskatchewan rely on the federal tax credit because a provincial tax credit is not available. For Newfoundland, two explanations for the participation rate of .2 percent seem applicable: either politics in this province is not yet ready to accept this procedure, or else the population of the province is low income when compared with other Canadians.

Among the eight provinces where an additional tax credit can be claimed against provincial income tax, the French province of Quebec ranks lowest on the participation rate in the federal tax credit and average on the tax credit claimed against provincial tax. This may be due in part to the extremely low maximum amount ($140) permitted for provincial tax credits in Quebec.

Matching Funds and Reimbursement

Devices such as tax benefits or matching provisions guarantee a system of mixed funding from private and public sources for political activities. The ratio may vary, but the principle remains the same. In matching funds, a certain amount of private money collected or spent for political purposes (especially campaign activity) is matched by a specific amount of public money granted as a subsidy for the same purpose.[32] In the U.S., matching funds from the public purse contribute to many campaign chests after certain types of private contributions have been collected. In Canada, a different approach is taken for the reimbursement of election expenses. Here public funds cover one part of "documented" campaign expenses, provided that the rest have been funded by private donations.

The regulation systems providing matching funds (the federal level of the United States, and the states of Hawaii, Massachusetts, Michigan, and New Jersey) seem far from perfect. In part, this is due to the matching principle: some amount has to be specified as a matchable maximum. The determination of that maximum is always arbitrary and the amount may be adjusted over time, as in New Jersey, due to increases in inflation.

The basic idea of matching funds is to provide some public control over campaign financing with an institutionalized guarantee of mixed funding. Only candidates who have already collected a reasonable amount of private donations qualify for matching funds from the public purse. The limit set for matchable donations differs widely between jurisdictions. Among the examples studied, Hawaii and Michigan match donations up to $100, Massachusetts and the United States (federal level) match donations up to $250, and New Jersey matches donations up to $1,500.[33]

Whereas tax benefits provide an incentive for the individual taxpayer to become a donor, matching funds are aimed at candidates, campaign workers, party activists, and "bagmen," who must collect a specified amount of private money in order for the candidate to apply for public matching funds. Moreover, the matching funds program (more precisely than the tax credit) is addressed to contributions of a specific size. Matching funds encourage the political competitor to seek small donations within the specific limit set by the applicable regulation. As a result, matching funds encourage fund-raising efforts aimed primarily at the broad mass of affluent, middle class voters. If Aristotle's judgment that a large middle class makes a contribution towards an optimum political system is correct, this matching funds strategy may lead to a stable middle-of-the-road type of democratic politics.

A feature of the matching funds programs defined differently by individual jurisdictions is the matching rate. A 1:1 match, as applied in Hawaii, Massachusetts, and the United States federal level, seems simple and reasonable. Nevertheless, a generous 2:1 match has been implemented successfully in Michigan and New Jersey, where every dollar from individual donors is matched by two dollars from state funds.[34]

As far as the impact of matching funds can be assessed from the few examples studied, the system is partially successful. In New Jersey, Michigan, and the U.S. primaries, matching funds have opened up the campaign process for numerous candidates. In Hawaii and Massachusetts, however, due to specifications not related to the matching provisions, the rules for political finance remain more or less symbolic. In these states, the reform program as implemented seems like a facade to maintain the basic features of the status quo.

For Michigan, New Jersey, and the U.S. as a whole, matching funds have had an important impact on PAC money. With fund raising for gubernatorial and presidential races focused on small individual donations, PAC money has not been so much reduced as diverted into the unregulated legislative races. Because the PAC phenomenon has not been equally important in Canada, its matching-fund arrangement, consisting of reimbursing election expenses already incurred by parliamentary candidates, seems to have been more successful.

There seems to be no connection between the U.S. matching funds and Canadian reimbursement programs, but in review, striking similarities appear. Both devices, for example, institutionalize a guarantee of mixed funding. The public purse and private donors jointly cover the cost of specific candidate campaigns. Whereas matching funds are tied to specific income, the reimbursement covers part of the expenses only if the candidate stays within statutory limits. However, there is one basic difference between the provisions. Matching funds provide an incentive for collecting a specific kind of donation while the reimbursement method is tied only to the candidate's ability to prove that he or she spent the matchable amount from the campaign chest for campaign purposes.

To receive matching funds, a candidate need be successful at fund raising; there are no other qualifications, such as collecting signatures or receiving a certain percentage of the vote. But Canadian candidates expecting reimbursement for their campaign expenses must prove the relevance of their participation in the race by mobilizing a minimum of support among voters, in most cases 15 percent of the votes cast in their constituency. As far as the search for small donations is concerned, it is not relevant for a parliamentary candidate who aims for reimbursement. The similarity between matching funds and reimbursements is striking. On average, candidates of different parties in different elections (federal and provincial) get a 1:1 match of private funds spent on campaign expenses.

The impact of the campaign expense reimbursement for Canadian parliamentary candidates seems to be very similar to the effect of matching funds on American primaries. In both public money has opened up competition for individual races. In Canadian federal elections over the last two decades, only two provinces seemed to have had a one-party system at the riding level: Quebec in 1979-1980 and Alberta in 1984. By 1988, even these provinces were highly competitive. In all other Canadian regions, at least two candidates received more than 15 percent of the votes cast. In general, the number of one-party-dominated ridings has considerably decreased, from fifty-one to four. From 1979 to 1988, the number of constituencies with three relevant candidates has even increased slightly, from 137 to 152, which is more than half of the total number of federal ridings in Canada. Many changes occurred in the 1993 elections, but none in this respect.

Conclusion

Although political momentum has been "passing from reformers to powerbrokers," many North American jurisdictions have proven their potential as "laboratories for reform."[35] Summing up the overall impact of tax provisions and matching rules, it seems obvious that the tax add-on, a voluntary donation collected by tax authorities, is a misconstructed instrument and a political failure. The minimal impact that this concept has had in a few U.S. states strongly suggests that lawmakers neither wanted a legitimizing device nor widespread participation of taxpayers in the political process. Since the politicians could not avoid legislating some instrument for the regulation of money in politics, they chose the one that did the least harm to the status quo.[36]

On the other hand, intelligently designed public funding does work better than a flat grant. The tax checkoff (the 100 percent tax credit[37] being a subcategory of this instrument) offers an effective device for political participation. A program based on tax checkoff funds introduces a legitimizing plebiscite for providing public money for political activity.

In this way, an "enlightened minority" of taxpayers voluntarily declares support for a program substituting for a system wherein lawmakers legislate for their own benefit and in their own interest. Also, to protect the political preferences of individual citizens, privacy can be maintained. Funds gathered anonymously from taxpayers are distributed according to procedures established by legislated regulation.

The other provisions operate on a principle quite different from that of the tax checkoff. A person may contribute a certain amount of his or her money to an issue, a candidate, or a party of his or her preference. The individual motivation for this act of political participation, with regard to private money, can be increased or improved, but not replaced, by public policy incentives. The incentive provided by public regulation, and funded by the public purse, may aim at the solicitor or the donor. Reimbursements and matching funds are particularly directed toward the solicitor because they are intended to trigger fund-raising efforts of political activists. Tax benefits of any kind (tax deductions or tax credits) primarily aim at the taxpayer in his or her capacity as a potential political donor.

As a collective commodity for public good, modern democracy does not show a price tag; it is available free of charge to all citizens. But because there is no "free lunch," either the voluntary contributor or the taxpayer has to pay for political campaigns. Established Western democracies are relatively affluent societies that often seek to raise funds for "worthy causes." Those affluent members of the democratic mass public, who are not in need economically, can afford to pay for their privileged form of government. Success depends on details of the public-private mix thus implemented. Experience from North America proves that most of the devices discussed in this chapter are useful as elements of training programs, helping to educate parties, candidates and citizens for responsible action in the field of political finance.

Notes

1. See Robert A. Dahl, *Who Governs? Democracy and Power in an American City* (New Haven, Conn: Yale University Press, 1961), p. 226; and Herbert E. Alexander, "Money and Politics: Rethinking a Conceptual Framework," in Herbert E. Alexander, ed., *Comparative Political Finance in the 1980s* (Cambridge, UK: Cambridge University Press, 1989), pp. 11-12.

2. See Ruth S. Jones, "State Public Financing and the State Parties," in Michael J. Malbin, ed., *Parties, Interest Groups and Campaign Finance Laws* (Washington, D.C.: American Enterprise Institute, 1980), pp. 27, 29. She analyzed the situation but did not coin the term.

3. Khayyam Z. Paltiel, "Campaign Finance: Contrasting Practices and Reforms," in David Butler, Howard R. Penniman, and Austin Ranney, eds., *Democracy at the Polls: A Comparative Study of Competitive National Elections* (Washington, D.C. and London: American Enterprise Institute, 1981), p. 171.

4. *Report of the Committee on Financial Aid to Political Parties* (Houghton Report), Cmd. 6601 (London: H.M.S.O., 1976), p. 48.

5. Karl W. Deutsch, *The Nerves of Government: Models of Political Communication and Control* (New York: The Free Press, 1966), pp. 170, 248.

6. Even a few municipalities in the U.S. have followed suit. For details, see Herbert E. Alexander, *Reform and Reality: The Financing of State and Local Campaigns* (New York: Twentieth Century Fund Press, 1991), pp. 46–48; and Herbert E. Alexander and Michael C. Walker, *Public Financing of Local Elections: A Data Book on Public Funding in Four Cities and Two Counties* (Los Angeles: Citizens' Research Foundation, 1990); and Herbert E. Alexander, Eugene R. Goss and Jeffrey A. Schwartz, *Public Financing of State Elections: A Data Book on Tax-Assisted Funding of Political Parties and Candidates in Twenty-Four States* (Los Angeles: Citizens' Research Foundation, 1992).

7. For available information concerning the different types of contributing elites, see Ruth S. Jones, "Contributing as Participation," in Margaret L. Nugent and John R. Johannes, eds., *Money, Elections, and Democracy: Reforming Congressional Campaign Finance* (Boulder, Colo: Westview Press, 1990), pp. 30-37; and Thomas U. Wawzik, *Grosses Geld in kleiner Muenze: Amerikanische Erfahrungen mit der Finanzstimme zur Wahlkampf-und Parteienfinanzierung* (Oldenburg: BIS, 1991), pp. 82-93.

8. Jones, "State Public Financing and the State Parties," p. 287.

9. Alexander, Goss and Schwartz, *Public Financing of State Elections*, p. 7; for other details, see Alexander, *Reform and Reality: The Financing of State and Local Campaigns*, p. 44.

10. Ruth S. Jones, "Financing State Elections," in Michael J. Malbin, ed., *Money and Politics in the United States: Financing Elections in the 1980s* (Washington, D.C.: American Enterprise Institute, 1984), p. 198.

11. Jack L. Noragon, "Political Finance and Political Reform: The Experience With State Income Tax Checkoffs," *American Political Science Review*, Vol. 75, No. 3, Sept. 1981, p. 674.

12. Jones, "State Public Financing and the State Parties," p. 288.

13. Noragon, "Political Finance and Political Reform" p. 672.

14. Ibid, p. 672.

15. Jones, "State Public Financing and the State Parties," p. 288.

16 Alexander, *Reform and Reality*, p. 49.

17. Robert Gunnison, "Salamanders Over Politicians in State's Income-Tax Checkoff," *California Journal*, February 1985, pp. 78-79.

18. Alexander, in "Public Financing of State Elections," a paper prepared for the Eagleton Institute of Politics, Rutgers University, 1989, p. 21; and *Reform and Reality*, pp. 89-90 seems to think otherwise.

19. Jones, "State Public Financing and the State Parties," p. 288.

20. Hawaii remains the only exception here. See Alexander, Goss and Schwartz, *Public Financing of State Elections*, p. 43, and note 11 above.

21. *Rapport van de Commissie subsidiering politieke partijen: Waarborg van Kwaliteit (The Hague: Ministerie van Binnenlandse Zaken*, 1991), pp. 44-46, 153 and 157.

22. Alexander Heard, *The Costs of Democracy* (Chapel Hill: University of North Carolina Press, 1960), pp. 445-448.

23. Alexander, *Reform and Reality*, pp. 110-111.

24. *A Comparative Survey of Election Financing Legislation, 1988.* (Toronto: Ontario Commission on Election Finance, 1988).

25. Waltraud Kreutz-Gers, *Die Reform der Wahlkampf und Parteienfinanzierung in Kanada: Problemlage, Programmgestaltung, Implementation und Wirkungen* (Oldenburg: BIS, 1988), p. 171; and Karl-Heinz Nassmacher, "The Costs of Party Democracy in Canada: Preliminary Findings for a Federal System," in *Corruption and Reform*, Vol. 4, No. 3, 1989, p. 225.

26. For details, Khayyam Z. Paltiel, *Political Party Financing in Canada* (Toronto: McGraw-Hill, 1970), pp. 31 and 40.

27.   W. T. Stansbury, "The Mother's Milk of Politics: Political Contributions to Federal Parties in Canada, 1974-1984," in *Canadian Journal of Political Science*, Vol. 19, No. 4, December 1986, p. 803.

28.   As Heard, in *The Costs of Democracy*, p. 249, has put it.

29.   Harold M. Angell, "Duverger, Epstein and the Problem of the Mass Party: The Case of the Parti Quebecois," in *Canadian Journal of Political Science* (Vol. 20, No. 2, June 1987), pp. 365-368.

30.   See Khayyam Z. Paltiel, "The 1984 Federal General Election and Development in Canadian Party Finance," in Howard Penniman, ed., *Canada at the Polls, 1984: A Study of the Federal General Elections* (Durham, N.C.: Duke University Press, 1988), p. 139.

31.   See Leslie F. Seidle and Khayyam Z. Paltiel, "Party Finance, the Election Expenses Act, and Campaign Spending in 1979 and 1980," in Howard R. Penniman, ed., *Canada at the Polls, 1979 and 1980: A Study of the General Elections* (Washington, D.C.: American Enterprise Institute, 1981), p. 276.

32.   Herbert E. Alexander, *Financing Politics: Money Elections and Political Reform*, 4th ed. (Washington, D.C.: CQ Press, 1992) pp. 142-146; and Alexander, *Reform and Reality*, p. 31.

33.   Alexander, "Public Financing of State Elections," p. 15; and Alexander, *Reform and Reality*, p. 31.

34.   Alexander, "Public Financing of State Elections," pp. 12-15, 23.

35.   For quotes refer to headlines by Alexander (and Fling respectively) in Herbert E. Alexander, ed., *Political Finance* (Beverly Hills, Calif.: Sage Publications, 1979), pp. 75, 245.

36.   This fits in with more general considerations on election reform by Alexander, *Political Finance*, pp. 93-96.

37.   As proposed by the California Commission on Campaign Financing, *The New Gold Rush*, p. 274.

12

The Reform Efforts in India

R. B. Jain

The successful management of a modern election in a country with over 500 million electors is a complex administrative undertaking, which must be carefully planned and supervised. Though the election machinery in India should be credited for conducting elections of such magnitude at very short notice in a "free," "fair," and peaceful manner, there are still certain aspects of the system that need streamlining.

The Election Commission

The writers of the Indian constitution recognized the need for a vast apparatus to conduct the periodic elections to the central legislature, state assemblies, and other representative bodies of the Union Territory. The Fundamental Rights Subcommittee of the Constituent Assembly had unanimously agreed that independent elections which avoided executive interference should be a fundamental right. It recommended, therefore, the inclusion of the following clause in the list of Fundamental Rights:

> The superintendence, direction, and control of all elections to the legislature, whether of the Union, or the Unit including the appointment of Election Tribunals, shall be vested in the Election Commission for the Union or of a Unit as the case may be, appointed in all cases in accordance with the law of the Union.[1]

The drafting committee of the constitution decided to have the chief election commissioner permanently set in office to organize and conduct by-elections, arrange for general elections to the legislatures (in case of premature dissolution), and prepare electoral rolls for the prospective general election. The skeletal staff in the chief election commissioner's office was to be augmented by large reinforcements, deputed from other work during general elections to the union and state legislatures, including the appointment of regional commissioners.

The Constitution of India, accordingly, prescribes that the Election Commission shall consist of the chief election commissioner and such number of other election commissioners that the president may determine, that these commissions shall be appointed by the president and subject to the provisions of any Parliamentary law, and that the chief election commissioner shall act as the chairman of the Election Commission. The Congress-I government of Rajiv Gandhi increased the strength of the commission, making it a multi-member body of three persons, including the chief election commissioner.[2] However, the National Front Government led by Janta Dal leader V. P. Singh, which came into power in 1989, abolished the multi-member status of the commission, returning it to a single election commissioner.[3] On October 1, 1993, the Narasimha Rao Government once again converted it into a three-member body.[4]

The Election Commission enjoys all powers and functions needed for the supervision, direction, and control of elections to Parliament, every state legislature, and the offices of the president and the vice president. The Election Commission also is assigned certain quasi-judicial functions, particularly regarding the governors and the president under Articles 102 and 103 of the constitution, respectively. The commission is responsible for ensuring the integrity and efficiency of the entire electoral process.

However, despite the commission's primary role in Indian elections, it is almost powerless in regulating election financing. The commission has not been able to curb the rising expenditure because it has no authority to make any laws regarding financing. The commission may only enforce the prevailing regulations and recommend modifications to the system of election financing, which may or may not be accepted by the government.

Financing Elections in India

The increasing costs of periodic elections and the huge sums of money spent by vote-seekers have become serious concerns in the Indian polity. If the misuse of money power, muscle power, and state power in the electoral process could be minimized through reform, it would be a great step towards breaking the stranglehold of corruption that has so completely enveloped Indian society. Laws limiting election expenditure do exist, but are blatantly abused, making such legal provisions meaningless.

Candidate's Election Expenses: Ceilings and Regulations

In 1950, the Representation of the Peoples Act fixed the ceiling on a candidate's election expenses. In 1956, however, the law was liberalized through amendment and ceilings were varied from state to state, ranging from Rs. 20,000 to 1,50,000 for candidates to the Lok Sabha, and from Rs. 5,000 to 50,000 for candidates to the State Assembly.

Other changes introduced in 1956 were as follows: (1) the period for maintaining the accounts was limited to the interval between the dates of notification of the poll and declaration of the results; (2) the period of disqualification for a false declaration was reduced from five to six years; and (3) a candidate was required to declare by oath before a magistrate as to the correctness of the election expenditure returns. After 1956, the ceiling on election expenditure has been virtually disregarded, as most MPs and members of the Legislative Assembly make false statements regarding election expenses before taking the oath of office.

In 1974, an amendment of the act further diluted the effectiveness of the ceilings by stating that any expenditure connected with the election of a candidate by a political party, by an association or body of persons, or by an individual (other than the candidate or his election agent), would not be considered to be an expenditure of the candidate.[5] Later several loopholes appeared in the implementation of the act, which allowed the display and use of money without fear of punishment, making the enforcement of the ceiling a worthless exercise. Such liberalization may have been justified in the early stages of India's government, but four decades of democracy should provide the maturity necessary to abide by the more stringent rules followed in other established democracies. As contributions are curbed by such rules, they cannot be used to organize lavish campaigns, or to indulge in an assortment of malpractices.[6]

Reforms Proposed for Correcting Abuses

In 1982, the Election Commission recommended a package of corrective proposals: (1) the inclusion of all election expenses incurred under the ceiling, whether made before, during, or after the election; (2) the reinstatement of the declaration about the correctness of the returns; (3) the prohibition of incurring election expenses by any person or by any club, association, society, etc., other than the candidate or his election agent; (4) an increase in the period of disqualification on a proven, false declaration from three to four years; and (5) the granting of power to the commission to scrutinize the returns, and, if necessary, to disqualify. The package also permitted the political parties to spend money on a candidate provided that the expenditure was incurred by the candidate.[7] The government disregarded these proposals.

The Election Commission issued another report for 1986 and 1987, which conveyed to the Parliament its "serious concern" over the use of money during elections. The commission noted that "even though the electorate has not been, by and large, swayed by such display and use of money power, so long as there is no fear of punishment, those having money power will persist in using it."[8] Since the government still refused to include election expenditures paid by organizations and individuals, the commission's proposal to increase the candidate's limit from Rs. 1,50,000 to Rs. 2,20,000 for the Lok Sabha, and from Rs. 50,000 to Rs. 70,000 for the Assembly, would have become an exercise in futility.[9]

Contributions to Party Funds

In the beginning of the Indian republic, under the first prime minister, Jawaharlal Nehru, companies were permitted to donate funds to political parties. Predictably, industrial houses and shrewd businessmen took out "political insurance coverage" with all the parties. However, when big business houses began donating to the rightist Swatantra Party, which strongly supported free enterprise, Indira Gandhi's centrist government and the ruling party socialists became concerned. The socialists proposed an unofficial bill in the Lok Sabha demanding a ban on company donations. Mrs. Gandhi's government responded by banning company donations and blocking the flow of funds to the opposition. Under the new law, only the ruling party received company donations, though this was done under the table.

This decision, "played...hell with the system and also with business ethics and morality."[10] Funds were still needed to win elections, but since they could not be gotten lawfully, other methods of raising money were discovered. The late Lalit Narain Mishra, A. R. Antulay, and others showed Mrs. Gandhi some of these methods and became her fund raisers. Licenses and permits were unabashedly hawked. Dubious foundations and organizations were created with a view to raising and soliciting funds. Leading industrial houses, known for their impeccable business morality initially refused to join the new cult, but eventually buckled under in the race for survival. Several ministers made big money in the process, and the electoral system itself was debased.

The party in power, by virtue of its control over permits, licenses, and import controls, has access to enormous slush funds not available to others. In place of donations made by businessmen to the ruling party in the 1970s, there are now kickbacks to commissions for foreign trade, and on orders for equipment, machinery, and essential supplies. Enormous amounts are kept in secret accounts abroad for both personal and party interests. Although the ban on company donations was removed by Prime Minister Rajiv Gandhi, the damage done to political life in the last decade, with repeated allegations and counter-allegations of bribery and kickbacks (as in the Bofors affair), has been irreparable.

Distortions of the Electoral System

Scholars have identified four "M"s of power responsible for distorting India's electoral system over the last four decades: money power (wooing or bribing voters), muscle power (booth capturing and stuffing ballot boxes with bogus ballot papers), ministerial power (using official machinery and resources by government candidates), and media power (persistently using state-owned audiovisual media for a pro-government news "tilt" and subtly using images by the ruling party leaders). Remedial steps suggested to reduce or eliminate these problems include state funding of elections, using electronic voting machines, issuing identity cards to voters, expanding the size and staff of the Election Commission, statutory auditing of party accounts, and freeing the media from government control.[11]

However, the worst malady affecting the electoral system since 1967 fits into none of these categories: the politics of defection. Despite various pronouncements by the parties, and subsequent introductions of related bills in the Parliament, nothing was accomplished in this area until 1974. The veteran socialist leader Jayaprakash Narayan, on behalf of Citizens for Democracy and with the cooperation of the Gandhi Peace Foundation, appointed a committee headed by V. M. Tarkunde to explore various aspects of electoral reforms. The report focused on three main issues: (1) the use and misuse of administrative machinery in elections, (2) the role of money in elections, and (3) alternative systems of representation. Even so, no real reforms were made by the promising Janafa Party, brought to power after the 1977 post-emergency elections, because of internal squabbles.

After Indira Gandhi's return to power in 1980, the country witnessed the most blatant operation to date of defections in Haryana, where the entire government, led by then Chief Minister Bhajan Lal, defected to the ruling party, and in Andhra Pradesh, where the MLAs were openly sold and purchased as commodities by contending parties. The phenomenon was arrested somewhat by the enactment of the Anti-Defection Law in February 1985, which required a candidate to resign his seat in the legislature if he defects to another party after election.

The 1985 reform effort fell short of the basic need to minimize the role of money, particularly use of "dirty money" in the election process. The Tarkunde committee had earlier recommended that

> All recognized political parties should be required by law to keep full and accurate accounts, including their sources and details of expenditure. The accounts should be audited by Chartered Accountants nominated by the Election Commission and would be open to public inspection to moderate charges.[12]

Even simple and straightforward suggestions like this have not been enacted into law by the central or state governments in India.

State Funding of Elections

No reform effort to curb the use of money in elections can be effective unless means are devised to block the undisclosed sources of funds to which some parties or groups have easy access. In addition to compulsory accounting and audit of all receipts and donations by recognized agencies, state funding of elections, based on the Federal Republic of Germany's system, has often been suggested as a means of reform. State funding would provide assistance to political parties proportionate to their percentage of votes polled in the preceding election. Many public figures, even some chief election commissioners, have recommended this strategy. The short-lived Charan Singh government at the center during 1979-80 was almost ready to implement this proposal when it was vetoed by President Sanjiva Reddy.[13]

L. P. Singh, former Home Secretary of the government of India and former member of the Indian Civil Service (ICS), said that state funding of elections was essential for wider economic and social considerations and equality of opportunity among political parties in elections.[14] According to a paper prepared in 1977 at the request of then Prime Minister Moraji Desai, the Center for Policy Research in New Delhi endorsed state funding and recommended the following provisions:

1. The state should have the exclusive responsibility of financing elections. The financing of Parliament elections should come under the central government's purview while the state governments should see to the financing of the state assemblies and lower bodies.
2. An election fund should be created, based of one rupee per voter (at 1977 prices) according to the numbered votes polled in the pre-

vious elections (200 million persons voted in the 1977 Lok Sabha election, resulting in a total fund of Rs. 200 million).

3. A special funding agency should be created to administer the funds or, alternatively, the Election Commission should fulfill this role;

4. The parties should be apportioned money from the fund based on the following ratio: 50 percent (except in the case of a new party) based on their performance in the preceding election and the rest on their performance in the current one.

5. There should be a ceiling on the amount given to a party based on the ceiling applicable to candidates (a party receiving 42 percent of the 200 million votes polled will be eligible for a maximum support of Rs. 54.2 million of the Rs. 1,00,000 ceiling per candidate).

6. The amount should be released to individual candidates, not to the political parties, based on nominations made by the party.

7. Every candidate should be required to maintain detailed accounts, subject to audit by the Election Commission.

8. The cost of political party campaigning activities should be included under the ceiling of election expenses.

9. Independent candidates, also subject to applicable ceilings, should be provided funds after the election, provided that they secure at least 10 percent of the vote.

10. These provisions should, with appropriate modifications, be applied to elections to State Assemblies.[15]

11. Eligibility as a national or major party should entail receipt of 20 percent of the national votes cast in parliamentary elections. A minor or new party should be designated by receiving 10 percent of the national vote cast in parliamentary elections, and non-party candidacy based on drawing one-eighth or one-tenth of the votes cast in the parliamentary constituencies.[16]

Difficulties in State Funding

State funding of elections in India requires the government to raise adequate resources and involves a number of prerequisites. Such funding proposals also must assume a level of integrity which may not be attainable by present party leaders and members. Public funding may only supplement the resources now being deployed in elections and in party work. A report of West Germany's experience noted that "state funding of elections has neither rid political parties of their financial burdens nor cleaned public life."[17] Party managers find various methods of raising additional money for their campaigns and candidates.

Many electoral reform efforts in India have not supported the state-funding proposal, but have suggested instead that certain facilities, like printing, postage, and telephone, be provided free of charge to all candidates. In 1988, the Congress Working Committee's panel on electoral reform did not favor state funding, but proposed some government assistance, such as company vehicle provisions, financial support to print posters and organize meetings, and free postal services and advertising in newspapers and on television. This assistance would provide about Rs. 5,80,000 to each candidate sponsored by recognized political parties.[18] The 544 Lok Sabha candidates would receive a total of Rs. 980 million. The legitimate expenses of party-sponsored candidates could be met by the government, but it would not be possible to provide such assistance to independents.

There are a number of precedents, in countries such as Austria, Finland, France, Italy, the Netherlands, Norway, Sweden, the United States, and West Germany, for granting assistance in cash and kind to political parties or their candidates. However, in India, this type of subsidization is highly complicated by the enormous electorates of Assembly and Parliamentary constituencies, the multiplicity of parties, the inchoate nature of their organization and financial management, and the competing demands on the scarce government resources. As a result, the government has been dismissive of a public funding proposal, arguing that it would aggravate the problem. Thus, the proposals did not find acceptance by the Gadgil Committee on Electoral Reforms in 1988 and, subsequently, were not taken up for consideration by the government. While the opposition parties felt that state funding would end the dependence on the rich and the corrupt, the ruling Congress-I party argued that it would not prevent parties from collecting money from other sources, putting an extra burden on the state, and increasing the number of independent candidates in the field.[19]

The Reform Package of December 1988

In October 1988, the All India Congress-I Committee (AICC-I) core group on electoral reforms, headed by its general secretary, V. N. Gadgil, proposed a package of electoral reform which was adopted as amendment to the Representation of the People Bill and the Constitution Bill enacted by the Parliament in December 1988. The major provisions were as follows: (1) lowering the voting age, (2) introducing electronic voting machines in 150 sensitive constituencies, (3) raising the penalty for booth capturing from Rs. 250 to Rs. 1,000, with possible imprisonment for up to three months, (4) if government servants were involved, requiring political parties to register with the Election Commission and, in doing so, make the pledge of allegiance to the Constitution, and (5) providing the Election Commission with more power to take administrative action against election staff.[20]

Although these reforms were welcome, they fell short of taking the radical steps needed for reforming the electoral process. As former Chief Election Commissioner S. L. Shakdher said,

> [T]hese bills could have included provisions for partial state funding of elections, accountability by political parties for receiving donations from business houses, an increase of the security deposit (to Rs. 20,000) to discourage non-serious candidates from filing nomination, and the introduction of multipurpose identity cards to prevent impersonation. The government did not look to curb electoral corruption; it completely shied away from the issue of the use of money in electioneering. It was an opportunity for this party that has been under a cloud of corruption charges, to prove that it was sincere in its attempt to eliminate electoral corruption; unfortunately, it threw away that opportunity.[21]

In addition, no provision was made for a multi-member Election Commission, one of the reforms recommended by the Gadgil Committee.

Post-1989 Elections Reform Proposals

The Ninth general elections in India, held in November 1989, correctly advertised as the "greatest show on earth," once again demonstrated the free verdict of an "illiterate" electorate for a change of government. The elections were testimony to the vast Indian electorate who refuses to be taken for granted and demands that a party holding office be judged by its performance record and its response to complaints or criticisms. This clear verdict against the establishment, deposing the almost uninterrupted forty-year rule of the Congress-I at the center and toppling the so-called "dynastic rule," was made despite the most violent election campaign to date. Apart from poll violence, in which more than 110 people lost their lives in three days, there were instances of capturing booths, stuffing ballot boxes, burning jeeps, mishandling election staff, and free use of arms.

The Ninth general elections have also earned the dubious distinction of being the most expensive elections in India's history, estimated at Rs. 100 billion.[22] This does not include the expense of administering the elections, which could amount to another billion.

The ceilings placed on the candidates' election expenditures became a farce, compelling every elected MP to sign an almost unbelievable declaration that he or she spent less than Rs. 20,000 or Rs. 1,50,000 on the election campaign, depending upon the size of the constituency. Even taking into account the loophole that money spent by the candidates' parties and friends was not to be included, there can be little doubt the candidates all spent more than was permitted.

It was in this context that, immediately after the new government (led by the National Front leader V. P. Singh) assumed office, the chief election commissioner, R. V. Peri Sastri, made a strong plea for more stringent punishments, including imprisonment and disqualification, for booth-capturing during elections. Because poll reforms were a priority of the Singh government, a comprehensive reform package, providing for limited state funding of elections, eliminating non-serious candidates, and strengthening the Election Commission to make it "truly independent," seemed possible.[23] Public funding was seriously regarded as a key method to reduce the role money plays in politics. Regular audits of party funds and assurances by political parties to comply with the rules framed by their respective constitutions also were contemplated.

The package also was expected to incorporate certain other important measures suggested by the commission but not favored by the previous government, such as the delimitation of constituencies. With many of the urban constituencies becoming unwieldy because of a steady influx of people, the Election Commission has suggested redrawing the constituency boundaries so that they are uniformly representative. Similarly, the continued reservation of certain constituencies for certain communities (some for thirty years) has given rise to discontent among candidates belonging to other communities, who have to look for some outside constituency to contest. The commission also favors rotation of the reserved seats from time to time.

Finally, the new package was expected to give legal sanction to the model code of conduct, expedite disposal of election petitions, and see to the installation of electronic voting machines. Despite the earlier unanimity on the advantage of these machines, they were not deployed in the just-concluded polls because a number of non-Congress-I parties suddenly revised their opinion and voiced apprehension that the machines could facilitate the rigging of elections.[24]

The new package of reforms was debated by the high-powered Committee on Electoral Reforms headed by then Law Minister, Dinesh Goswami. Based on the committee recommendations, three bills on electoral reforms were introduced in the Rajya Sabba (the upper house of the Union Legislature) by the law minister himself on May 30, 1990.[25] Two of these bills were aimed at amending the Constitution to lay down the procedure for the appointment of the chief election commissioner and to delimit the constituencies based on the 1981 census. The third bill sought to amend the Representation of the Peoples Act of 1950 and 1951. Among the other provisions of the bill, one important item was to put electoral expense back to its pre-1974 position, so that the total expenditure by parties or candidates would be required to remain within the ceiling. The bill also proposed a modest beginning toward the state funding of elections including copies of the electoral rolls, a certain amount of fuel for a certain number of vehicles, and payment to the candidates of recognized political parties for rental charges or microphones.

The bills could not get through Parliament as the V. P. Singh government fell and went out of office in November 1990. But even if the bills had passed, they did not vest the Election Commission with the power to scrutinize the accounts of election expenses filed by the candidates. In the absence of that, the ceilings remain meaningless. Also, the provision for assistance to candidates proposed constitutes only a fraction of the money which candidates and political parties usually spend in elections. Nominal assistance to candidates could hardly be considered a major electoral reform.

Arrangements to reduce the influence of big money in elections have yet to receive real government attention. The root of the problem is the huge amount of unaccounted money at the disposal of political parties. This can be checked only with compulsory auditing, a step the Singh government failed to take. The successor Chandra Sekhar government hardly had any time to move in this direction before it also fell, paving the way for the Tenth general elections in May 1991. Although it has increased the Election Commission to three members, it remains to be seen to what extent the January 1992 government of P. V. Narasimba Rao is able to make any concrete reforms.

Conclusions

Most of the reforms proposed, made and adopted in the Indian electoral systems to date have been half-hearted. They lack the will to curb the power of money which, along with muscle power, breeds a growing nexus between politicians and criminals. The outcomes of the July 1989 elections in the municipal corporations of Lucknow and Allahabad, in the state of Uttar Pradesh, were more an indication of the connection between criminals and politicians than of the respective strength of the various political parties. It is evident that some independents who have won elections have close links with the underworld—one who was jailed for criminal offenses has been elected to the Allahabad municipal corporation. In addition, two dozen individuals of criminal background will be members of the corporations in Lucknow and Allahabad. In Lucknow, of the fifty candidates with a criminal history, twelve have been voted to office. The nation cannot afford to look at these trends with indifference.[26]

A recent report prepared by the Home Department has disclosed that several legislators, representatives of local bodies, and politicians, are involved either in criminal activities or in providing protection to lawbreakers. One leader is reported to have links with several criminals, one of whom was his main campaigner in the Assembly elections. A history-sheeter (a repeat offender) is secretary of a district party committee. In several other states besides Uttar Pradesh, criminals play a major role in politics and most parties actually seek their support. In Bihar, the coal mafia has a hold on politicians. In many parts of Andhra Pradash, criminals dictate to political leaders.[27]

The importance of criminals in politics arises mainly because politicians want the easy money and muscle power. When a politician seeks a criminal's support at election time, that person is looked upon as a vote gatherer, not as a criminal. The crime leader, in exchange, receives respectability when he enters politics, and may even be offered a political post.

It is imperative that electoral reform efforts in India concentrate on checking the role of money and the influence of "musclemen" or criminals in the election process. Unfortunately, to date, neither the government nor the political parties, nor even the Election Commission, have come out with any package of reforms to this end. With mandatory elections on village Panchayats and local urban bodies soon to come, Indian politics is likely to remain a game that parties and party leaders will play with the money and muscle power at their command. No legislation can keep criminals away from politics. Only a change in attitude by the political parties and candidates who stand for elections can do that. It is high time that political parties realized that seeking the help of criminal organizations can only result in their enslavement to them.[28]

Notes

1. B. Shiva Rao, *The Framing of India's Constitution: A Study* (New Delhi: Indian Institute of Public Administration, 1960), Vol. IV, p. 538.

2. See "A Multi-member EC Planned," *The Hindustan Times*, October 5, 1989.

3. See *The Times of India* (New Delhi), December 2, 1989, p. 1.

4. See the Notification of Government of India, *The Hindustan Times*, October 2, 1993, pp. 1 and 12.

5. See the *Representation of the People (Amendment) Act*, 1974, No. 58 of 1974, December 21, 1974, Clause 77, Explanation 1.

6. "EC Move on Expenditure Rejected," *The Times of India* (New Delhi), July 3, 1989, p. 1.

7. See Inder Jit, "Poll Expense Ceiling Now a Farce," *Economic Times* (New Delhi), July 11, 1989, p. 8.

8. "EC Move on Expenditure Rejected," p. 1.

9. Ibid, p. 1.

10 Inder Jit, *Economic Times*.

11. See S. C. Gangal, "Not by Law Alone," *The Hindustan Times*, August 8, 1988, p. 9.

12. *Report of the Committee on Electoral Reforms* (popularly known as the Taekunde Committee), (New Delhi: Citizens for Democracy, 1975), p. 14.

13. Gangal, *The Hindustan Times*.

14. L. P. Singh, *Electoral Reform: Problems and Suggested Solutions* (New Delhi, Uppal Publishing House, 1986), p. 108.

15. See V. A. Pai Panandiker and Ramashray Roy, *Financing of Elections* (New Delhi: Centre for Policy Research, 1977), mimeographed report, pp. 18-21.

16. Ibid, p. 18.

17. As reported in Gangal, *The Hindustan Times*.

18. "State Funding of Poll Opposed," *The Hindustan Times*, October 18, 1988, p. 1.

19. "Electoral Reform Belie Expectations," *The Hindu* (New Delhi), July 9, 1989, p. 8.

20. The Report of the All India Congress-I Committee (AICC-I) Core Group on Election Reforms, headed by its General Secretary, V. N. Gadgil, was not published as such. But its proposals were reported in "Bills for Election Reform Proposed," *The Hindustan Times*, December 16, 1988, pp. 1 and 16.

21. As reported in *India Today*, January 15, 1989, p. 77.

22. See "The Price of Power," *Sunday* (Calcutta), November 26/December 2, 1989, p. 59.

23. See the statement of Dinesh Goswami, law minister in the National Front Government, in *The Hindustan Times*, December 17, 1989, p. 1. See also "Panel on Electoral Reforms Soon," *The Hindustan Times*, January 10, 1990, pp. 1 and 10.

24. *The Times of India* (New Delhi), January 5, 1992, p. 1.

25. For details of the recommendations of the committee, see *The Statesman* (New Delhi), May 10, 1990, p. 1; and *The Hindustan Times* (New Delhi), May 8, 1990. Also see S. P. Singh, "Need for Poll Reform," *The Hindustan Times*, May 9, 1990, p. 11.

26. For a detailed account of the election results, see "Criminals Among UP Corporators," *The Hindustan Times*, August 4, 1989, pp. 1 and 12.

27. See Editorial, "Crime and Politics," *The Hindustan Times*, August 5, 1989, p. 9. Also see "A Symbiotic Tie Vitiates Politics," *The Times of India*, August 20, 1989, pp. 1 and 8.

28. "Crime and Politics," *The Hindustan Times*, August 5, 1989, p. 9.

13

Financing Political Parties in South Korea: 1988-1991

Chan Wook Park

South Korea has endured a turbulent political history since the end of World War II. President Sygnman Rhee's authoritarian regime of the First Republic was toppled by a student uprising in 1960. The Second Republic lasted only nine months before it was overthrown by General Chung Hee Park's military coup d'etat in 1961. Two years later General Park was elected president of the Third Republic, but his desire to perpetuate arbitrary rule culminated in the adoption of the undemocratic constitution of the Fourth Republic in 1972. The regime collapsed when President Park was assassinated in 1979, and in the maelstrom of uncertainty, General Doo Hwan Chun took over the government. The junta leader closely followed the steps taken by his predecessor two decades before.

In June 1987, President Chun had to concede to the opposition forces who demanded a revision of the constitution of the Fifth Republic to allow for direct popular election of the president. A three-way presidential election followed in December 1987; two prominent civilian leaders split the opposition vote resulting in the ruling party's Roh Tae Woo's electoral victory. President Roh's government of the Sixth Republic was inaugurated in February 1988.

In the 13th National Assembly election of 1988, the ruling Democratic Justice Party (DJP) obtained 125 seats, 25 seats short of an overall majority in the legislature. The opposition, divided into three parties, secured

a combined majority. The Party for Peace and Democracy (PPD), organized by Kim Dae Jung and others who had left the Reunification Democratic Party (RDP) immediately before the 1987 presidential election, won
70 seats; the RDP, under the leadership of Kim Young Sam, took 59 seats;
and the New Democratic Republic Party (NDRP), headed by Kim Jong
Pil, former prime minister under President Park, secured 35 seats. Without a single majority party, each party became significant competitors for
power, although they did not show any marked ideological or program-
matic differences as they were all conservative or centrist parties.[1] Even
the PPD, claiming that it represented the interests of the lower middle-
classes, industrial workers, and poor farmers, upheld the principles of
liberal democracy and a free market economy.

During the earlier period of the 13th Assembly (May 1988-January 1990),
Korean legislative politics could be characterized as coalition-building.
In order to pass their legislative proposals, the DJP had to secure the
support of at least one opposition party. Amid the checks and balances
provided by the multiple parties, some party leaders gradually became
uneasy about the inherent fluidity of partisan alignments and cleavages
in the legislature. The governing party soon found it both time-consuming and difficult to build working majorities and demonstrate adaptive
capacity.

On January 22, 1990, the top leaders of the DJP, RDP, and NDRP made
a surprise announcement to merge the three parties. The governing Democratic Liberal Party (DLP) now could command over a two-thirds majority, opposed by only the PPD and the Democratic Party (DP), which was
organized by about a half-dozen former RDP legislators who refused to
join the DLP.

In April 1991, the major opposition party changed its name from the
PPD to the New Democratic Union (NDU) in an effort to broaden its appeal beyond the area that formed its support base, the Honam region.
The opposition parties finally merged in the fall of 1991. Kim Dae Jung
remains the most prominent opposition leader, although the unified opposition has chosen the label of the previous splinter PPD party. In view
of the predominance of the ruling DLP, the partisan configuration can
now be aptly dubbed a one-and-a-half party system.

These interparty mergers in the Sixth Republic suggest that Korean
parties lack organizational stability. Due to frequent regime changes and
fluid partisan politics, most citizens have not yet developed psychologi-
cal attachments to political parties. Inside the party, there is a great deal
of centralization in decision making, despite the fact that the party is
potentially fractious because of factional rivalry. The national headquarters effectively controls its local units, and major decisions lie in the hands

of central party leaders. Additionally, the power within the party head-quarters or the parliamentary group is concentrated in a handful of bosses.

In terms of grassroots membership, the governing party appears to be a mass-based party, while the opposition resembles a cadre party. Owing to ample resources and well-established formal networks, the governing party can secure numerous followers, while the opposition party commands a relatively small number of rank-and-file members. This difference in numerical strength should not challenge the fact that the parties are not substantially divergent in terms of ideologies. Party organization in Korea does not follow ideological divisions, class lines, or general policy views. Instead, it is grounded on particulars, such as regionalism, personal acquaintance, and clan or family ties. Ordinary members of a party do not have much input regarding partisan matters. Rather the grassroots organization is used as the personal political instrument of a particular politician.

Legal Rules for Political Funding

The Political Funds Law was initially enacted in 1965 to foster democratic development by providing public funding and publicizing parties' incomes and expenditures. The law was revised in 1969, 1973, 1980, 1989, and 1991. The emphasis in these revisions was on party sponsorship and the state subsidy system.

The major sources of funds for legislators, parties, and other political organizations can be divided into the following categories: (1) party dues, (2) contributions through a Sponsors' Association (SA), (3) donations entrusted to the Central Election Management Committee (CEMC), a constitutional organ, (4) subsidies from the state coffer, and (5) parties' business incomes.

Members of a party subscribe to it as prescribed by its constitution or charter. Party dues vary in amount, depending upon a member's intraparty status. For example, in 1987 the DJP decided that monthly dues for ordinary members were to be at least 300 won; the legislator of the party, 150,000 won; and the party's executive chairman, 500,000 won (approximately $.40 US, $227, and $676, at 1984 prices).[2] A similar differential schedule also can be found within the opposition party.

Individuals or corporations with no party affiliation are prohibited from donating directly to a party or politician, but can donate indirectly through the SA (*huwonhoe*) linked to a politician or to one of three levels of the party (district, provincial, or central). SAs are conveyor organizations formed to channel funds from individuals and corporations to specific politicians or parties. SAs must be registered with the CEMC or its local contingents. SAs collect political funds by levying fees on their members or by raising money from nonmembers under the Funds Law's regulations.

The size of the SA tied to the central headquarters of a party cannot surpass 1,000 persons, including individuals and corporations. The provincial SA can retain no more than 300 members, and a district's or politician's SA is limited to 200 members. Individuals may contribute up to 10 million won a year to a politician's and district's SAs taken together, and up to 50 million won a year to provincial and central SAs altogether. An individual donor's total contributions to all types of SAs in a calendar year may not exceed 60 million won. A corporation may contribute no more than 30 million won a year to the politician's and district's SAs together, and no more than 100 million won to provincial and central SAs, for a maximum of 130 million won each year.

SAs also are limited in the amount of their contributions. The SA formed to support a legislator or legislative candidate may contribute a total of 100 million won each year; the same amount is allowed to the district SA. The provincial SA may financially aid its connected party up to 1,000 million won a year, and the central SA is held to 5,000 million won each year. These limits on SA contributions may be increased by 100 percent in the year when the presidential or Assembly election takes place.

There is another way in which individuals and corporations contribute to political parties. Funds (*kit'akkum*) can be entrusted to the CEMC, which serves as a conduit to allocate the funds to parties. The rationale for institutionalizing this method of financing is that opportunities for scandals and corrupt practices can be reduced by discouraging direct transactions between donors and receivers.

When the CEMC is entrusted with funds, the consigner's name must be registered. The consigner may or may not designate the recipient for which the consignment is intended. In case the consignee is not specified, the funds are distributed in accordance with the predetermined manner of apportioning state subsidies. In a year, each individual may entrust 100 million won or 5 percent of his income earned during the previous year, whichever is larger. A corporation may donate to the CEMC 500 million won or 2 percent of their capitalization at the end of the previous business year.

The state budget includes provisions for lump sum payments to political parties. Public subsidies, administered by the CEMC, are expected to provide for equal opportunities in party competition. Since public financing was carried out for the first time in 1981, there have been changes concerning the scale and method of funding. From 1981 through 1990, the annual amount for state subsidies was arbitrarily set by the government, but the 1989 revision of the Funds Law fixed the subsidy level at

400 won a year for each voter. In 1990 and 1991, state subsidies were allotted on the basis of this rule. In December 1991, parties agreed that the basic subsidy would be increased to 600 won per voter with an additional 300 won for each "nationwide partisan" election, such as those for the president, the National Assembly, and province-level governments.

From 1981 to 1989, the allocation rule was as follows: 20 percent of the total subsidy was divided among the four parties with the most legislative seats; 40 percent was distributed in proportion to each party's seat share; and the remaining 40 percent was disbursed according to each party's vote share in the recent Assembly election. In late 1989, the NDRP, the fourth largest party (actually the smallest) in the legislature, demanded that the evenly divided portion be enlarged from 20 percent to 40 percent of the total annual subsidy. This proposal was accepted by the other parties, with the remaining parts divided at 30 percent each.

In December 1991, more changes were made that were to go into effect in 1992. The Funds Law, with its revisions, now states that a party with at least twenty seats in the national legislature is eligible to form a negotiation group and is assured an equal share from the first 40 percent of the annual sum (5 percent goes to each party that does not form a negotiation group but numbers five or more seats). Each remaining party which fulfills either of the following qualifications is entitled to 2 percent: receiving at least 2 percent of the votes cast in the recent National Assembly election, or receiving at least one-half of 1 percent of the votes in the recent election for the province-level governments. One-half of the remaining money is distributed in proportion to the share of legislative seats; the other half is in proportion to the vote share in the recent National Assembly election.

The Funds Law also prescribes how state subsidies should be spent by the receiving parties. The use is restricted to expenses of office rent and maintenance, costs for office equipment and supplies, payment of salaries and utility charges, and funds for membership training, policy research, and development. Only the additional subsidy at each election time may be spent on election expenses.

Other features of the law address deductions contributors may take on personal and corporate income taxes, limitations on the eligibility of contributors, and openness of party revenues and expenditures. By February 15 of each year, the treasurers of parties and SAs are required to report to the CEMC their incomes and expenses for the previous year. Individuals and organizations prohibited from contributing include foreign individuals and corporations, public or semi-public corporations, the media, labor unions, educational and religious institutions, and business firms incurring losses in the previous three business years.

Besides the Political Funds Law, the legal codes concerning political parties and elections regulate political finance, especially election campaign spending. There is no separate regulation on the sources of campaign funds in particular, but spending is limited. Prior to the campaign, the expenditure ceiling is set by the CEMC, which varies from district to district, for the legislative election. The ceiling is based on the CEMC's estimates of administrative expenses, the costs of renting and running offices and vehicles, and displaying placards and printing handbills. The campaign manager of a district party must report campaign expenses within fifteen days following an election.

Financing Parties: Officially Reported Income and Expenditures

As prescribed by the Funds Law, political parties annually report their income and expenditure to the CEMC. Close observers of Korean politics contend that the official reports constitute a small portion of actual funds received from all sources, including clandestine, illegal contributions. Despite prevalent skepticism of accuracy, this analysis starts out with officially disclosed information on party finance, and the data available from the CEMC can be useful for finding clues to general patterns or trends in the funding practices (see Table 1).

From 1988 through 1990, the government party has relied most heavily on contributions through the CEMC, while the opposition has received virtually none. The data also indicate the SAs are a useful source only for the government party. In 1990, SAs provided about 22 percent of the party's total revenue. Contributions through the CEMC and SAs may reinforce the inequitable distribution of political funds between the op-

TABLE 1 Party Revenues, 1988-1990 (in millions of won)

Party	1988*	1989	1990
Democratic Justice Party	32,370	23,606	--
Reunification Democratic Party	14,240	5,737	--
New Democratic Republican Party	12,583	6,209	--
Party for Peace and Democracy	15,481	6,243	8,775
Democratic Liberal Party	--	--	39,895
Democratic Party	--	--	2,199

*For the 13th Assembly election in 1988, every party had to lay out election expenses. This is the reason for a higher level of income in 1988 than in 1989.

Source: Central Election Management Committee (CEMC).

posing groups. State subsidies, meanwhile, seem to be playing an increasingly significant role in financing parties, particularly the opposition. The proportion of state subsidy for the PPD increased remarkably from 2 percent in 1988 to 31 percent in 1990.

Table 2 shows the total amount of party headquarters' expenditure and a breakdown of the main categories of spending in 1990. Comparing the official figures in Tables 1 and 2, each of the Korean parties appears to have recorded a surplus. The DLP expended approximately 90 percent of its income in 1990; the PPD, 99 percent; and the DP, 93 percent. There seems to be no sign of a shaky financial state for any party.

The system of political contribution through the CEMC was introduced at the inception of the Funds Law in 1965. The CEMC is not legally required to disclose information on the sources and amounts of the consigned funds, but the agency usually supplies the relevant data if requested. Almost 100 percent of the resources consigned to the CEMC from 1965 through 1986 originated from big businessmen and their organizations,

TABLE 2 Party Expenditures, 1990 (in millions of won, and percent)

Expenditures	Democratic Liberal Party	Party for Peace and Democracy	Democratic Party
Rent, Salaries & Administration	19,639 (55%)	5,240 (60%)	1,347 (66%)
Organizational Maintenance (Aid to Local Units, etc.)	8,951 (25)	1,495 (18)	273 (13)
Election Campaigning	310 (1)	189 (2)	0 (0)
Publications and Propaganda	2,900 (8)	1,052 (12)	234 (11)
Policy Research and Development	1,647 (5)	188 (2)	75 (4)
Others	2,296 (6)	539 (6)	114 (6)
Total	35,743 (100)	8,667 (100)	2,043 (100)

Source: Central Election Management Committee (CEMC).

such as the Federation of Korean Industries, the Korean Chamber of Commerce and Industry, and the Korean Foreign Trade Association.[4] Generally, donations were not designated for specific parties during the period, thus they were allocated according to the formula applied to the allocation of state subsidies.

From the year 1987 on, designated, rather than non-designated, contributions have become dominant. In the Sixth Republic, a total of 81,649 million won (an average of 20,412 million per year) were entrusted and channeled to political parties. Of this amount, 71,649 million won was designated to the governing party. In the first three years (1988 through 1990), undesignated contributions were nil. In 1991, Kim Dae Jung of the PPD took issue with the heavy tilt of this financing system toward the government party in talks with President Tae Woo Roh. Afterward, 10,000 million won in undesignated funds were entrusted to the CEMC, and the opposition party benefited from the system for the first time in the Sixth Republic.

Opposition leaders frequently challenge the notion of designated consignments, for they are always directed toward the government party. The complaint turns readily into criticism of the close ties between the government and big business. The CEMC, intended to be neutral, runs errands for large conglomerates (chaebol) by receiving, laundering, and finally sending the money over to the ruling party.

For the opposition, the system of financing parties through the use of registered SAs is even worse than contributions through the CEMC . In the Fifth Republic (1981 through 1987), money raised by SAs for the parties totaled 17,830 million won. The ruling DJP's SA accounted for about 90 percent of this amount. In 1990, the DJP received 8,598 million won from its SA, while opposition parties reported nothing received from SAs. Pivotal members of the government party's SA are leaders of the financial circle, and this indicates again the strong alliance between the government and big business.

The 1989 revision of the Funds Law enabled parties to form SAs for their national headquarters and local units. Independents also are allowed to organize their personal SAs. As of December 5, 1991, the ruling DLP had an overwhelmingly higher rate of registration than the opposition DP. The DLP had a total of 248 registered SA's while the DP held two. In December 1991, the Korean National Assembly consisted of 298 legislators (223 district seats and 75 at-large seats) with one district seat vacant. In principle, legislators elected from single- member districts may retain one SA for the district party as well as another personal SA. In practice, a government party legislator is instructed by the national center to form either the district or the personal SA. There are 214 government party legislators and 233 SAs, suggesting that almost every government party legislator is linked to at least one SA.

In contrast, registered SAs are rare for opposition legislators. Yet one should not conclude that financial sponsorships are not available to them. In fact, they deliberately maintain informal support groups because people are still concerned that the government may unfairly sanction those who contribute to opposition legislators' finances. As long as this kind of situation exists, opposition politicians cannot successfully rely on open channels to raise funds.

The state subsidy was introduced in 1980 to curtail political corruption and to establish fair access to political resources among political parties. During the first seven years of the subsidy system (1981-1987), the CEMC distributed an average of 971 million won per year to all parties. The funding level increased more than twice to 2,500 million won in 1989 and rose up again to 10,479 million won in 1990. The latter increase was made possible by the parties' agreement on the 1989 revision of the Funds Law. The 1991 revision further increased the amount of subsidy: 600 won per voter with an additional 300 won per voter at election time. Three nationwide partisan elections were to be held in 1992, with an electorate of about 25 million won each. The 1992 total was roughly 37,500 million won, further increasing the role of the state subsidy in the financing of Korean political parties.

Opposition parties are not discriminated against in the state subsidy system. From 1981 through 1987, they received 57 percent of the total subsidy with a combined seat share of 46 percent in the national legislature. Similarly, they commanded a legislative majority of 58 percent in 1988 and 1989, and benefited from 63 percent of the total subsidy. Since the merger of three parties into the DLP in 1990, the opposition has been reduced to a minority of 26 percent and receives roughly 35 percent of the subsidy. Furthermore, the 1991 revision of the Funds Law increased state aid to minor opposition parties inside and outside of the national legislature.

The election laws require every candidate's campaign manager to report all campaign costs to the CEMC after the election. In instances of spending above the ceiling and dishonest reporting, the candidate's electoral victory can be nullified. In the 13th Assembly election, the CEMC set the upper limit immediately before the campaign, which ranged from about 56 million yen in Tonghae to 164 million yen in Haenam. The average limit was 85 million won. The post-election reports claimed that the campaign costs for every candidate stayed within the legal limits. In theory, campaign expenses are well controlled in Korea. However, in practice, it is widely known that the official reports account for only a small portion of actual total expenses. An insider estimated that in the

13th Assembly election, candidates spent on average 700-800 million won
(US $ 0.98 million to $1.08 million), about nine times as much as the average limit, and that several candidates spent no less than 1,000 million
won.[4] In Korea, it is accepted that an election cannot be won without
spending much more than the legal ceiling.

Realities of Extravagant Politics: Korean Style

The parties' reports on their expenses for routine operation and election campaigning expose only the tip of the iceberg. The costs of Korean
political life are high and put great pressure on political aspirants and
politicians. Contrary to what is suggested by a surplus of funds in Tables
1 and 2, no party claims that its needs are appropriately met. According
to journalistic sources, routine administration alone led to a monthly deficit
of 150 million won for the PPD in 1990.[5]

Legislators from single-member districts occasionally release the estimated costs of managing the district party and their own political life.
According to one source, an average government party legislator spends
no less than 15 million won a month in an off-election year. The comparable figure for an average opposition legislator is 8 million won.[6] Most
of this money goes to cover district level maintenance since public funds
are allocated to cover administrative and other expenses associated with
the legislator's main office space in the Assemblymen's Building. For most
legislators, 20 to 30 percent of their total expenditure is spent for constituents on ceremonial occasions, such as gifts, wreaths, money, and other
favors, to congratulate constituents and to offer condolences.

The Korean district party is a political machine based on patron-client
ties. The organization is consolidated by factors such as personal acquaintance, school connections, and, most importantly, the provision of tangible benefits and favors by the legislator in return for political support.
The ruling party's district unit has a more extensive and better-organized
mass following than that of the opposition party. This difference is due to
the inequalities in the amount of resources available to a legislator for
nursing the district. Every legislator maintains informal vote-gathering
machines along with the district party organization. Common examples
are various friendship societies, and alumni and recreation groups.
Legislators perform an all-encompassing role as guardians of constituents' welfare, and are always in need of ample funds.[7] Extravagance in
politics reaches its peak at election times. Candidates spend lavishly,
completely ignoring the laws regulating campaign money.

A former director of the Korean Central Intelligence Agency, who led
the ad hoc special task team for re-electing President Park in 1971, re-

cently revealed just how far this extravagance has, on occasion, gone.[8] In the 1971 presidential election, in which President Park was victorious over Kim Dae Jung of the New Democratic Party, the ruling Democratic Republic Party spent about 60 billion won, an amount equivalent to more than 10 percent of the overall government budget for fiscal 1971.

Legislative races also invoke high spending. In Korea, mass advertising is not a factor accounting for the high costs, because television and radio are not used for legislative election campaigns. Instead, huge sums of money go to the nurturing of district parties and other vote-gathering machines, and to the provision of services, food, spa trips, and "goodies" for voters. New entrants into a party are often provided "gratitude fees" to reward them for their participation. Large sums are expended to mobilize and convey voters to campaign speech rallies. As a last resort, cash is distributed in exchange for votes. On the eve of the 13th Assembly election, one ruling party candidate apparently tried to mail more than 3,000 envelopes, each containing 20,000 won.

The acute need to raise large war chests makes elected officeholders much more accessible to those with great personal wealth, discouraging otherwise qualified candidates. Furthermore, a sudden, large surge in the flow of political funds exerts a negative impact on the economy, including unbridled expansion of the total money supply, inflationary spirals, and a drain of manpower from manufacturing industries to campaign work. Four elections were scheduled for 1992: the president, the national legislature, and two local government elections. Economic research institutes predicted more than 5 trillion won would be spent in these elections.[9] Legal sources play their part in the funding game, but they are not sufficient to meet the rising demands from political parties.

For the government party, the president and his aides at the Chong Wa Dae (presidential office and residence), together with leaders of the party, are responsible for making up the difference between funds required and those raised through formal channels. Because the Funds Law makes other forms of fund raising illegal, this aspect of resource mobilization usually remains a veiled area. But behind-the-scenes transactions between top leaders and big business groups are sometimes revealed much later. In the 1960s and 1970s, under President Park, big businesses provided kickbacks or bribes in return for items such as large-scale government contracts, and huge domestic and foreign loans. Multi-national corporations active on Korean soil were not exempted from filling the financial pipeline for the ruling circle. In 1971, for example, Caltex, Mitsubishi, and other foreign firms contributed a total of US$ 8.5 million to the ruling party for President Park's re-election campaign purposes.[10] In the Fifth Republic, President Chun allegedly received donations directly from big business owners at Chong Wa Dae. It was said that "prior inside approval" was required of businesses to interact with the jurisdictional government agencies. President Chun, at any rate, was well-known for his juggling of political donations toward the end of consolidating his power base.[11]

The opposition leaders do not have as much leverage for securing covert funds as those in the ruling camp, but they still manage to retain their loyal followers. Their sponsors include religious leaders, Koreans residing abroad, and owners of small-to-medium size businesses, none of whom are highly visible.[12] In financially difficult times, opposition leaders have resorted to desperate methods for funding their parties. In the 13th Assembly election, the PPD collected 7 billion won by selling to wealthy political aspirants the top ten positions on the party's list for nationwide proportional representation seats. The contributions were labeled "special party dues" and were used to support 160 candidates for district seats.[13]

Legislators also may seek compensation from clientele groups or constituents in exchange for their activities within the legislative chamber or elsewhere. This may then lead to public condemnation as the lawmakers are accused of being more aptly entitled "lawbreakers."[14] During the period of the 13th Assembly, 13 legislators were arrested in a string of corruption scandals. In early 1991 two major bribery scandals were disclosed. One case implicated three government and opposition legislators who illegally obtained financial support from a business association for luxurious overseas travel. In the other, a construction company bribed five legislators to ensure that government administrative agencies would distribute housing lots in favor of the company. In the wake of the scandals, an ethics code and committee have been established in an attempt to keep the legislature honest. In spite of these efforts, however, bribery scandals involving legislators are not likely to disappear as long as political extravagance persists.

Conclusion

The rival parties are all aware of the problems involved in South Korean political financing, and in principle do not disagree on the necessity of solving them. But the opposing groups differ significantly in their proposed solutions to the prevailing patterns of political funding.

In the 1991 regular session of the 13th National Assembly, the DLP and DP negotiated a revision in the Funds Law. Because the two parties regarded the strengthening of the state subsidy system as a key to securing fairness and equal opportunity, they moved to increase the subsidy level. As mentioned earlier, the parties reached a compromise position of 600 won a year for each voter with a supplement of 300 won at each nation-wide partisan election. Accommodation of the subsidy issue was rela-tively easy to achieve since the attentive public, especially reform-oriented intellectuals, backed a substantial hike in order to curb political corrup-tion and ease the burden of raising money.

Apart from the subsidy issue, however, the parties were unable to reach agreement. The opposition DP wanted to abolish designated entrustment to the CEMC because it always favored the government party and forti-fied the nexus between the government and big business. The DP called instead for the introduction of coupons to raise funds in small amounts from as many anonymous donors as possible. Under this system, con-tributors would buy CEMC-issued coupons to give to their favorite par-ties who would then redeem them. The government party refused to re-place designated contributions with the coupon system. The DP also sug-gested eliminating the clause prohibiting the give-and-take of funds in the process of party nomination. This proposal, tantamount to legally selling public offices, evoked more public criticism than sympathy and was later withdrawn. Another point of contention was the opposition party's assertion that, for reasons of equity and freedom of expression, newspaper and broadcasting corporations, labor unions, and religious institutions should be allowed to make political contributions. The gov-ernment party's objections overrode this argument.

With the exception of the subsidy hike, the parties failed to reconcile their conflicting interests, and the funding bill was passed with the DP dissenting. The unresolved issues will certainly come to the surface again whenever the opposition next finds an appropriate time to raise them.

Linked to the negotiation over the Funds Law was discussion of the National Assembly Election Law. The rival parties, after twists and turns, eventually passed the election bill by a unanimous vote. The new elec-tion law includes some provisions designed to reduce election costs and has tightened prohibitions on candidates' receiving financial donations and dispensing favors. Also, under the law, voters who have received money or gifts from candidates would be exempted from legal punish-ment if they turned themselves in. It is hoped that such may discourage lavish spending during the campaign.

Still, the election law leaves many problems unsolved. For one thing, meaningful steps must still be taken to meet candidates' needs by provid-ing specific grants and services, such as printing and distributing cam-paign leaflets and handbills. More importantly, great care needs to be taken to generate legal rules that will shift the focus of campaigns from personalized appeals and offered tangible benefits, to policy programs and universal principles.

Notes

1. See the author's, "The 1988 National Assembly Election in South Korea, *Journal of Northeast Asian Studies*, Vol. 7 (1988), pp. 59- 76.

2. Byong Man Ahn, *Han'gukchongburon* [On Korean Government] (Seoul: Dasanch'ulp'ansa, 1989), p. 340; Young Rae Kim, "Chongch'i'ja gumbiriwa chongch'imunhwajonghwa [Political Corrupt Practices and Clean Politics]," *Sasanggwa Chongchaek* (Fall 1988), p. 123.

3. The party rule concerning membership dues is virtually unenforceable and very few ordinary members are willing to pay even a nominal amount of dues. Party dues largely refers to regular and special contributions made by party leaders, the party's legislators, and party cadres.

4. Park, "The 1988 National Assembly Election," pp. 64-65.

5. *Sisa Jonol*, June 7, 1990, pp. 42-45.

6. Young Ki Kwon, "Shipsamdae Kukoeui pup'aekucho [The Patterns of Corruption in the 13th National Assembly]," *Wolgan Choson*, March 1991, pp. 145-147.

7. See the author's, "Legislators and Their Constituents in South Korea," *Asian Survey*, Vol. 28, 1988, pp. 1049-1065.

8. See the articles on the KCIA directors, which were published in *Dong-A Ilbo*, May 10, 1991, and May 17, 1991.

9. *Chung'ang Ilbo*, December 24, 1991, pp. 1, 3.

10. Ahn, *Han'gukchongburon*, pp. 344-346.

11. Kap Je Cho, "Chonduhwanui inmaekkwa gummaekk [President Chun's Personal Networks and Financial Sources]," *Wolgan Choson* (May 1988), p. 218.

12. *Sisa Jonol*, June 7, 1990, p. 46.

13. Ibid.

14. Su-Ik Hwang, "Chogch'ijagumgwa pujongbup'ae [Political Funds and Corruption]," *Sasang*, (Winter 1991), pp. 270-272.

14

Political Finance and Scandal in Japan

Rei Shiratori

More than 120 million people live in the four small mountainous islands of Japan where habitable areas are quite limited. Due to high population density, formal and informal systems and customs are highly developed to prevent social frictions. For example, the Japanese have a respect of *wa* or harmony. They also tend not to blame others when they fail, and they tend to be permissive toward others' mistakes.

With the recent scandals involving politicians, including the Lockheed and the Recruit Cosmos stock transaction scandals, the Japanese are finding it unnecessary to apply such generous "cultural merits" to politicians, so long as they are consciously taking advantage of the public's permissiveness.

The Lockheed Scandal

On February 4, 1976, the United States' Subcommittee on Multinational Corporations of the Senate Foreign Relations Committee revealed that the Lockheed Aircraft Corporation had handed over $10 million U.S. to the Marubeni Corporation--Lockheed's agent in Japan--and to Yoshio Kodama --a right-wing fixer in Japanese politics and Lockheed's secret representative in Japan.[1] The subcommittee claimed that Lockheed was attempting to acquire political influence in the sale of Tristars to All Nippon Airways (ANA). Many people believed, however, that the real objective of

Lockheed's "payment" was to push the sale of Orion antisubmarine patrol planes to the Japanese Self Defense Force.

Two days later, A. C. Kotchian, former president of Lockheed , testified before the subcommittee that $2 million had been handed over to Japanese high officials through Marubeni. The incumbent prime minister, Takeo Miki, requested transmittal of information about the scandal from U.S. President Gerald Ford. The Tokyo District Public Prosecutor's Office sent its staff to the United States and granted immunity to Kotchian in exchange for his deposition. On June 22, 1977, Tosheharu Okubo, Marubeni's managing director, was arrested for bribery. The next month, Hiroshi Itoh, another managing director of Marubeni, H. Hiyama, chairman of Marubeni, and T. Wakasa, president of All Nippon Airways, were arrested.

On July 27, former prime minister Kakuei Tanaka also was arrested for bribery. Tanaka was charged with accepting a bribe of 500 million yen from Lockheed through Okubo and Itoh between August 1973 and March 1974 while he was prime minister. This bribe was accepted in exchange for influence on ANA' selection of Lockheed Tristar airbuses, after being approached by Marubeni President Hiro Hiyama in 1972.

On August 20, K. Satoh, former Vice Minister of Transportation, was arrested for accepting a bribe of two million yen. On August 21, Tomisaburo Hashimoto, former Minister of Transportation, was arrested for accepting a bribe of five million yen. At the end of the year, the names of four more politicians were published in connection with bribery. These four were regarded as "gray high officials" not because they were indicted but because they received money.

The Lockheed scandal was simple bribery, and made an enormous impact upon Japanese politics and society. The former prime minister's involvement in the scandal caught the public's attention because it was caused by a foreign multinational company in Japan. During the development of Japan's economy in the 1970s, it was a serious concern that a Japanese company might be the cause of bribery in foreign countries in the future, as Lockheed had done in Japan.

The author wrote in 1976:

> In the case of the Lockheed payoff scandal, I consider the fact that the Japanese political world was placed in the position of what might be described as a victim of the "black" sales methods practiced on a global scale by the Lockheed Aircraft Corporation is one consolation in a woeful tale. If, on the contrary, a Japanese corporation had corrupted politicians of another country, I think that I would have felt that situation was irredeemable.[2]

On October 12, 1983, the Tokyo District Court ruled in the Lockheed scandal and sentenced former Prime Minister Tanaka to four years in prison. On July 29, 1987, the Tokyo High Court upheld the 1983 ruling against Tanaka and found him guilty of bribery and violating the Foreign Exchange and Foreign Trade Control Law. Presiding Judge Takeo Naito said in the ruling that "Tanaka used his authority for personal gain by accepting a large reward from a private company, and in so doing shook the very foundations of democracy."[3]

The high court sentenced Tanaka to four years in prison without a stay of execution and a forfeit of 500 million yen, the same verdict as the lower court ruling. The court also upheld the lower court decisions sentencing Hiyama to two-and-one-half years in prison, and Okubo and Itoh to two years in prison but suspended for four years.

The Recruit Gate Scandal

Almost twenty years after the Lockheed scandal, a stocks-related scandal occurred. While the Lockheed affair was a large scale simple bribery case, the Recruit Gate scandal was a more sophisticated and subtle affair. As Lockheed was called "a scandal of the era of production growth," this new scandal could be called "a scandal of the era of money games."

The scandal occurred over the stock of Recruit Cosmos Company (a subsidy of Recruit Company) a rapidly growing information conglomerate which had its origin in the employment information business. Recruit chairman Hiromasa Ezoe granted a special favor to politicians, a local official, and journalists, by allowing them to buy Recruit Cosmos stock before it was listed. When it was listed as an over-the-counter issue, its value skyrocketed, resulting in gigantic profits for those on the inside track. In December 1984, bureaucrats and journalists bought Recruit Cosmos stocks at 1,200 yen per share. When listed in October 1986, the stock was quoted at more than 5,000 yen per share, and rose to in excess of 7,000 yen per share.

The scandal was revealed in June 1988 when Kawasaki City Deputy Mayor Hideki Komatsu was found to have bought 3,000 Recruit Cosmos shares in 1984, before the listing, and sold them in 1986, making more than 100 million yen.[4] Komatsu was in charge of the redevelopment of the Kawasaki Station area where the Recruit company's office building was located. Two days after the news was reported, Komatsu was dismissed.

So far, seventy-six persons are known to be involved in the case. Although the names are not all known, among those that are were former Education Minister Yoshiro Mori, former Agriculture, Forestry, and Fisheries Minister Mutsuki Kato, former Defense Agency Director General Koichi Kato, Liberal Democratic Party (LDP) Policy Affairs Research Council Chairman Michio Watanabe, Democratic Socialist Party (DSP) Chairman Saburo Tsukamoto, and secretaries to former Prime Minister Yasuhiro Nakasone, Prime Minister Noboru Takeshita, LDP Secretary General Shintaro Abe, and Finance Minister Kiichi Miyazawa. Among the journalists involved were Ko Morita, President of Nihon Keizai Shimbun (Nikkei), and Reizo Utagawa, former Managing Editor of the Mainichi Shimbun.[5] Nikkei President Morita resigned after his name was revealed.

Mori purchased 3,000 Recruit Cosmos shares in 1984 and sold them in early 1987, making a profit of more than 100 million yen. A private secretary to former Prime Minister Nakasone made 120 million yen by handling 2,300 shares. Yoshihiko Kamiwada, official secretary to Prime Minister Nakasone, sold 3,000 shares in November 1986 and made a profit of 16 million yen. Secretaries to Nakasone and Miyazawa, who earned 88 million yen, said that they conducted the transactions on their own initiative.

Coinciding with the Recruit Cosmos scandal, the Supreme Court ruled that presenting stocks to public officeholders is bribery and found a Tokyo Stock Exchange executive guilty. Even so, these stock transactions did not violate any laws. Prime Minister Takeshita discussed the issue at the Diet in his reply to a question from Japan Socialist Party Chairman Takako Doi:

> Generally speaking it is known from our experience that in the process where family businesses and small enterprises grow and become public by putting their stocks on sale, the makeup of shareholders will change from relatives to friends and acquaintances and that in many cases, a great amount of profit will be expected after the stocks are listed on the stock exchanges.[6]

It was surprising that Prime Minister Takeshita equated the Recruit Cosmos scandal with a family-operated town inn which had grown, and in which friends and acquaintances had bought their company's stocks. Those who purchased Recruit Cosmos stocks as a special favor to then Recruit Chairman Hiromasa Ezoe were not simply friends or acquaintances. They were legislators who could decide the state budget and tax system, and their secretaries. They were journalists and noted scholars who could exert influence on society. They were specially chosen to be recipients of Recruit Cosmos stocks.

It was apparent that Recruit Cosmos expected some return for the special favor. The seventy-six people who purchased the stocks at bargain prices had to be aware of the intentions of Recruit. They knew what Recruit and Ezoe expected. That is why they had appointed Ezoe as a special member of the Government Tax System Research Council, the Educational Curriculum Council, and the University Council of the Education Ministry.

On August 4, 1988, Michio Watanabe, Chairman of the LDP Policy Affairs Research Council, emphasized at the Diet, that prices of stocks might go up or down after their listings, although it was not proper that ordinary people were kept from a comparable opportunity to purchase Recruit Cosmos stocks. However, it was certain that those seventy-six people knew they were selected purchasers of Recruit Cosmos shares. Almost all of them received financing from a Recruit financing firm and in turn sold the shares immediately after the stock was put on public sale. This is illegal insider trading.[7]

At the same time, Recruit Cosmos expected a return for such special favors. The purchasers, knowing the intention of the seller, took this special money-making opportunity, which amounts to bribery.

The recent political corruption in Japan is more subtle than vote buying and tyrannical bosses. Usually, such corruption is carefully planned and woven into the political and social system. It is not illegal, but is considered unethical. The political scandal over Recruit Cosmos shares was typical of this new type of Japanese political corruption, as well as a new way of political funding.

If one examines the electorate's attitude toward both scandals and politicians involved in scandals, it can be concluded that the electorate's attitude is severe in its judgment. For example, in the results of elections held immediately after large political scandals since the end of World War II, the parties which were involved invariably decreased their seats in the elections, as shown in Table 1.

In the case of the Showadenko scandal in 1949, when Showadenko Electric Company scattered bribes to more than sixty politicians to get financial assistance from semi-governmental banks, the three coalition government parties involved in the scandal decreased their seats in the Lower House from 230 to 131, while the opposition Democratic Liberal Party (DLP) increased its seats from 152 to 264.[8]

In the case of a shipbuilding scandal which occurred in 1954, when the shipbuilding industry gave bribes to the Secretary General of the Liberal Party and other politicians to control the contracts of government subsidized shipbuilding, the Liberal Party seats were decreased from 180 to 112. In both cases, the opposition parties won power from the ruling parties.[9]

The same severe attitude of the electorate was shown in the case of the Lockheed scandal in 1976. Although the LDP's government remained in power, the party decreased its seats from 264 to 249 and lost the absolute

TABLE 1 Scandals and the Results of Elections

Case 1: Showadenko Scandal (September 1948-December 1948)
      General election: January 23, 1949

Parties	At the time of Dissolution	Result
Democratic	90	69
Socialist	111	48
National Cooperative	29	14
Democratic Liberal	152	264
Communist	4	35

Case 2: Shipbuilding Scandal (February 1954-April 1954)
      General election: February 27, 1955

Parties	At the time of Dissolution	Result
Liberal	180	112
Democratic	124	185
Right Wing Socialist	61	67
Left Wing Socialist	74	89
Communist	1	2

Case 3: Lockheed Scandal (February 1976-September 1976)
      General election: December 5, 1976

Parties	At the time of Dissolution	Result
Liberal Democratic	265	249
Socialist	112	123
Communist	39	17
Komei	30	55
Democratic Socialist	19	29
New Liberal Club	5	17

Source: Tetsuro Murobushi, "Seiji Shikin, Oshoku, Senkyo" in *The Ushio,* October 1976, p. 79.

majority in the Lower House for the first time since its formation. Even in the December 1983 election of the House of Representatives, two months after the first ruling on the Lockheed affair, the LDP's seats decreased from 286 to 250. Although Prime Minister Nakasone remained after the

1983 election, he had to form a coalition government with the New Liberal Club because the LDP had lost its majority.[10] While the electorate has always severely judged political scandals, the inclination has been to show tolerance toward other people's failures, on the ground that Japanese democracy is sound and must be supported. At the same time, legal action against the defendants will not solve the problem by itself. Even though the major players in the Lockheed scandal were punished, the social system which spawned the incident has remained unchanged.

The Lockheed payoff scandal occurred when four elements came together: (1) the primary goal of profits in the free-market system, (2) the lack of a sense of morals and of mission by the businessmen concerned, (3) the low level of ethics among politicians, and (4) the lack of effective and legal control of money in politics.

In order to maintain a sound free-market system, we have to admit its structural defects and strengthen an Anti-Trust Law to facilitate fair trade dealings and provide regulations to prevent anti-social actions by private companies, such as land speculators or heavy buyers of consumer products. In addition, it is necessary to improve the sense of morality in the business world. Unfortunately, compared with businessmen in the United States or Great Britain, Japanese businessmen seem to be less aware of their responsibility as leaders.

One problem remains to be solved. While the majority of Japanese citizens consider that the politicians who were involved in political scandals should resign their membership in the Diet, there is no way to force them to do so since they are elected by their constituencies. Former Prime Minister Tanaka has been elected five times since the Lockheed scandal.

Regulation and Reality

The organizations that are permitted to collect political funds are classified into four categories: (1) political parties, (2) fund-raising organizations that collect money on behalf of political parties, (3) persons who occupy public offices (politicians), and (4) other political organizations. Among these organizations, those that are active nationwide are required to make financial reports to the Central Election Administration Committee.

On September 4, 1987, the Ministry of Home Affairs announced the account of political funds reported to the ministry during calendar year 1986.[11] According to the report, the money collected for political activities and elections by these organizations amounted to a record-breaking

TABLE 2　Quantitative Limits on Political Donations in the Political Fund Control Law

Donors/Recipient	Individuals	
	Total Sum	Toward a particular recipient
Parties and parties' fundraising organizations	20 million yen per annum	No limit except the total sum per annum
Politicians	20 million yen per annum	1.5 million yen per annum
Other political organizations	10 million yen per annum	1.5 million yen per annum

Donors/Recipient	Companies, Trade Unions	
	Total Sum	Toward a particular recipient
Parties and parties' fundraising	7.5 million yen sum per annum	No limit except the total
Politicians	100 million yen per annum	1.5 million yen per annum
Other political organizations	3.75 million yen 500 million yen per annum	1.5 million yen per annum

Donors/Recipient	Political organizations	
	Total Sum	Toward a particular recipient
Parties and parties' fundraising	No limit	No limit
Politicians	No limit	No limit
Other political organizations	No limit	No limit

Source: *Seiji Shikin Kisei Ho* (Political Fund Control Law), Chapter 5.

167.5 billion yen, a 15.1 percent increase from the previous year. The total amount of political funds amassed in Japan, including those collected by local organizations, reached 342 billion yen.

The political funds collected in 1986 reached such a high amount because there were "double" national elections for both houses of the Diet in

July 1985 and unified local elections in April 1986. Also, the presidential election for the Liberal-Democratic Party was to have been held in October, but was called off because the incumbent President Nakasone was given an exceptional one-year third term.

Since the three "new leaders," N. Takeshita, S. Abe and K. Miyazawa, DLP presidential hopefuls in 1986, collected a large amount of money for the party presidential election, the sum of political funds received by the LDP factions and political organizations supporting particular politicians exceeded that amassed by the political parties and their political organizations for the first time since 1976, when the Political Fund Control Law was enacted.

The political funds collected by these organizations have been increasing continuously during the past ten years, from 69.3 billion yen in 1976 to 167.6 billion in 1986. Considering that the gross domestic product jumped three-fold in these ten years, however, the increase is not unusual. The amount of political funds has invariably recorded a big increase in the years when national or local elections were held, simply because it takes a lot of money to run Japanese elections (see Table 3).

Calculations based on the sums reported reveal that at the time of the "double" elections for both houses in 1986, the Abe faction spent on average 2.3 million yen for each neophyte candidate belonging to the faction, while the figures for the Maize faction and the Takeshita faction were 1.5 million and 1.3 million respectively. Kiyoko Ono, a female Olympic gymnastics champion who ran successfully for the upper house in the Tokyo

TABLE 3 Increase of Political Funds

Year	Political Fund (100 billion yen)	Elections
1976	693	House of Representatives
1977	739	House of Councillors
1978	781	
1979	966	Local, House of Rep.
1980	1,128	Double (both houses)
1981	1,000	
1982	1,094	
1983	1,472	Local, Double
1984	1,167	
1985	1,456	
1986	1,676	Double

Source: *Mainichi Shimbun,* September 4, 1987.

local constituency, received a remarkable 49.2 million yen from the Nakasone faction to finance her election campaign.

By party, the Japan Communist Party (JCP) collected the largest amount of money, followed by the LDP, Komeito, the Japan Socialist Party (JSP), the Democratic Socialist Party (DSP), the New Liberal Club (NLC), and the Democratic Socialist Union (DSU). The order has remained the same since 1976. Komeito accumulated about half of the funds collected by the JCP, while the JSP took in about one third as much (see Table 4).

Since business income, such as the sale of the JCP's official paper, "Akahata," accounted for 91.8 percent of their money collected, the party's net income was much smaller than the sum it reported.

In terms of net income for each party, the LDP leads other parties with 19.02 billion yen, followed by JSP with income of 5.77 billion. The JCP had a net income of 57.69 billion yen; Komeito, 5.53 billion; the DSP, 3.19 billion; and the New Liberal Club, 430 million yen.[12]

Those contributions of more than 20 million yen from companies, which have always been the target of criticism, amounted to 5.62 billion yen, accounting for 3.4 percent of the total political funds, about half the percentage of ten years earlier (6.5 percent). This decrease occurred because large companies increasingly make donations through their affiliates, or by buying tickets in mass quantities for fund-raising parties held by politicians.[13]

The largest share, or 22.3 percent of contributions to the LDP, was made by banks and other financial companies. The construction and real estate business ranked second, accounting for 12.2 percent, followed by insurance companies with 7.5 percent. Steel and metals, a regular contender for the top ranking, slipped from one of the top three contributors to fourth with 6.8 percent, due to the recession caused by the strong yen.[14]

TABLE 4 Political Fund by Parties (1986)

Party	Income (10 thousand yen)	Growth Rate (%)
Japan Communist Party	2,336,430	9.2
Liberal Democratic Party	2,055,478	8.4
Komeito Party	1,279,997	30.5
Japan Socialist Party	854,816	28.6
Democratic Socialist Party	361,576	97.6
New Liberal Club	45,733	2.7
Democratic Socialist Union	6,891	121.0

Source: *Kampo* (Government Official Report), September 4, 1987.

Among the three new leaders, Abe led by collecting 1.5 billion yen, followed by Takeshita with 930 million; Miyazawa, 810 million; and Nikaido, 450 million. Michio Watanabe, former chief of the Ministry of International Trade and Industry (MITI), who aimed at succeeding Nakasone as the head of the Nakasone faction, has drawn much attention by amassing 1.71 billion yen, 2.7 times as much as the previous year.[15]

As the debate over the proposed sales tax became a focal issue in 1986, the members of the LDP Taxation System Research Council, including pro-sales tax Chairman Sadanori Yamanaka, Deputy Chairman Tatsuy Murayama, and anti-sales tax Vice Chairman Kabun Muto, doubled the funds they collected.

Fund-raising parties held by politicians to avoid the Political Fund Control Law, which limits donations by corporations, have become quite popular. The profit rate increased from 78 percent in 1985 to 82 percent in 1986. The share of money collected through these parties, as part of the total political funds, increased from 0.7 percent in 1976 to 5.2 percent in 1986.[16]

The new Political Fund Control Law was enacted in 1976 after the Lockheed Scandal was revealed.[17] This law ordered political parties and other political organizations to register their official names, their representatives, and their locations. Without this registration, no organization can accept donations or spend money for political activities. The law also placed both quantitative and qualitative limits on political fund raising carried out by political organizations, and politicians were obliged to report their financial activities (income and expenditures) every year to Central or Local Election Administration Committees. These reports are kept for inspection by the public.

Concerning the qualitative limit of political funds with respect to the characteristics of the donors, the Political Fund Control Law prohibited donations by the following: (1) private enterprises which receive subsidies from the national government, local governments, or public corporations; (2) foreigners or foreign organizations; (3) anonymous persons; and (4) deficit-ridden companies.

Quantitatively, individual citizens were permitted to donate up to 20 million yen per year to political parties, their fund-raising organizations, and candidates for public offices. Companies or labor unions were permitted to contribute annual maximum sums ranging from 7.5 million yen to 100 million yen in accordance with the sum of capital issued by companies, in terms of its face value, or the number of union members. In addition, individual citizens were permitted to donate up to 10 million yen to other political organizations while companies or labor unions were permitted to donate annual maximum sums ranging from 3.75 million yen to

50 million yen in accordance with the size of the aforementioned capital or membership.[18]

The law also stated that one person, or one organization, was permitted to donate the maximum annual sum of 1.5 million yen to a politician, a political organization (not a political party), or a party's fundraising organization. To political parties or parties' fund-raising organizations, individual citizens or companies can contribute more than 1.5 million yen, up to the respective aggregate total per year.[19]

Concerning financial reports, the law required politicians and political organizations annually to report donations of more than 10,000 yen per head for political parties and their fund-raising organizations, and donations of more than 1 million yen per head for other political organizations and politicians. The names and the annual sums of these donations reported to the election administration committees are available for inspection by the public.

Many politicians try to circumvent the regulations set forth by the Political Fund Control Law. They hold fund-raising parties frequently and ask companies and industrial federations to buy large numbers of tickets since this money is not considered a political donation. Politicians set up as many political support organizations as possible since these organizations function as channels through which political funds can be introduced.

One interesting method to avoid the regulations was disclosed when K. Shirakawa, a LDP member of the House of Representatives, received political funds of 6 million yen from Isao Nakaseko, the owner of the Meidenko Company, Ltd., in the Meidenko scandal. This scandal became a political issue in June 1988 when tax evasion by the owner of Meidenko, was uncovered. He evaded some 1.8 million yen in taxes on income of 2.5 billion yen between 1984 and 1986.[20]

Meidenko manufactures a device claimed to save electricity based on an unfair electricity fee system, and was therefore a threat to the utility companies. The companies questioned the safety of Meidenko's device, as well as the legitimacy and effectiveness of the system. To counter the claims of the powerful utilities companies, Meidenko tried to involve politicians.

It was revealed that Meidenko's owner, Nakaseko, had made political donations of at least 30 million yen. His targets were not only legislators of the ruling LDP but also JSP lawmakers and a high-ranking official of the MITI. Among the revealed amounts, Meidenko donated 10 million yen to the political organization of former Prime Minister Yasuhiro Nakasone, who claimed that his organization returned the money to Meidenko. It also was discovered that a high-ranking MITI official received a similar amount from Nakaseko when he retired to run in the 1986 House of Representatives election.[21]

The Political Fund Control Law limits political contributions to an organization by an individual to 1.5 million yen. Shirakawa had two political organizations, one in Tokyo and another in Niigata, registered at the Ministry of Home Affairs. Therefore, he alone was eligible to receive 3 million yen from the same individual per year.[22]

Therefore, a secretary to Shirakawa asked secretaries of LDP lawmakers Takujiro Hamada and Seiichi Ota to accept 1.5 million yen each from Nakaseko on Shirakawa's behalf. The secretaries to Hamada and Ota received the money and transferred it to Shirakawa's bank account. Both secretaries told investigators that they issued receipts for the money on their own due to friendship. The secretary to Shirakawa also told investigators that the political donations had nothing to do with Nakaseko's tax evasion and it was his own idea.

Recent Developments

On August 27, 1992, it was disclosed that Shin Kanemaru, vice president of the ruling LDP and chairman of its largest Takeshita Faction, had illegally received political contributions of 500 million yen from Hiroyasu Watanabe, president of Sagawa Transportation Co. Ltd.[23] As noted, the Japanese Political Fund Control Law prohibited a politician from receiving political funds of more than 1.5 million yen per year from a business enterprise or from a private person. The law also required any politician receiving more than 1 million yen per year from a business enterprise or from a person to report that fact to the appropriate election committee.

Kanemaru admitted receiving money and resigned as vice president of the LDP on August 28. The Tokyo District Court fined him 200,000 yen on October 14, 1992. Kanemaru resigned his membership in the House of Representatives as well as his chairmanship of the Takeshita Faction on the same day.[24] This resignation coupled with the vacuum in its central leadership led to the split of the Takeshita Faction in the ruling LDP into the Obuchi and Hata Factions.

The fragmentation was characterized by a generational split. Those members of the House of Representatives in the Takeshita faction who had been elected more than three times and belonged to the older generation (fifty years and older) gathered under the leadership of Keizo Obuchi, former secretary general of the LDP. A majority of those members of the House who were elected less than three times and were considered to belong to the younger generation, formed a new faction under the leadership of Tsotomu Hata, former Minister of Finance, and Ichiro Ozawa, an immediate follower of Kanemaru and former Secretary General of the LDP. Most members of the House of Councillors belonged to the Obuchi Faction. Hata was a strong advocate of the single-member constituency system with a single ballot and simple majority system.

After receiving illegal contributions, the small fine imposed on Kanemaru caused the electorate to respond by calling for a change in the Political Fund Control Law, in order to strengthen the regulation of political fund raising. Politicians moved to exploit this occasion by introducing public financing of political party activities so that the heavy burden on individual politicians to collect political funds might diminish.

The LDP campaigned on the platform that political corruption was due to the uniquely Japanese middle-sized constituency system of the House of Representatives. In this system, each constituency elects three to five members of the Lower House.

The ruling LDP acquired more than 40 percent of the votes in almost all constituencies, and consequently, the LDP runs more than one candidate in every constituency. Multiple candidates of the LDP campaign with the same party affiliation and with the same policy program. The main factor creating the difference in the number of acquired votes in the election among the multiple LDP candidates came to be the volume of campaign money. LDP candidates told the electorate that this mechanism was creating corruption within the ruling majority LDP. They claimed that it was necessary to introduce, therefore, the smaller single-member constituency system in which any party could support only one candidate in one constituency. By introducing the single-member constituency system, corruption and factionalization in politics in Japan could be terminated or minimized. In March 1993, the Miyazawa Cabinet of the LDP put forward a proposal in the national Diet to change the electoral system from 131 middle-sized constituencies to 500 smaller constituencies.[25]

The repetitive disclosures of the political scandals committed by leaders of the ruling LDP also increased the electorate's dissatisfaction with its long lived one-party rule and the absence of other styles of democratic government. Makoto Tanabe, president of the Japan Socialist Democratic Party (SDP), the major opposition party, publicly admitted his close association with Kanemaru and also resigned his presidency. This popular dissatisfaction with the LDP's one-party rule transformed itself into a total rejection of the conventional "one-and-one-half party system" of the LDP and the SDP since 1955.[26]

The younger generation of the Takeshita Faction, which had split and formed the Hata Faction, also decided to utilize the popular dissatisfaction with the LDP's one party rule. The members voted against the bill, which introduced the small constituency system, in spite of their approval of this change. Members of the Hata Faction also voted against the prime minister when the no-confidence motion came to a vote on June 18, 1993. After the collapse of the Miyazawa LDP cabinet on June 23, 1993, members of the Hata Faction left the LDP and formed the Japan Renewal Party (*Shinseito*) with Hata as president and Ozawa as secretary general.

Prime Minister Kiichi Miyazawa dissolved the House of Representatives and the general election was held on July 18, 1993. The main issues in the election were "the end of long-lived one-party rule of the LDP" and "political reform," which were meant more to change the electoral system than to strengthen the regulation of political funds. While the LDP increased the number of its seats by one in this election, the party could not acquire an absolute majority because 36 LDP members left and formed Shinseito. All opposition parties except the Japan Communist Party established a coalition government with Morlhiro Hosokawa of the Japan New Party as prime minister. The LDP government, which was considered to be the most stable one-party government in the world, suddenly ended its 38 years reign due to the series of political scandals, its adherence to the small constituency system, and its intra-party factional struggles (see Table 5).[27]

The Hosokawa coalition cabinet proposed political reform bills in October 1993, which contained changes in the election system for the House of Representatives, stronger regulations of political funding, and public financing of party activities.[28]

According to the new proposals, the total number of seats in the House of Representatives would be 500, with 250 seats elected in single-member districts, and the other 250 seats elected by proportional representation. Voters would cast two votes, one for the individual candidate in the single-member constituency, and the other for the party lists of candidates. Those parties winning less than 3 percent of the total votes would not be allocated any seat, nor receive any public financing for their party activities.

Concerning political fund raising, the bill would prohibit any kind of political donation to individual politicians given by business enterprises or private persons. Only parties and party branches would be allowed to receive political donations. Quantitative limits on these political donations were the same amount as in the present law. Politicians and politicians' funding organizations could receive funds from parties and from party branches. The names of donors who give political funds of more than 50,000 yen to parties and party branches would be reported to either national or local election committees. The bill also required the disclosure of the names of those purchasing tickets of more than 50,000 yen for fundraising parties held by parties or politicians. In order to accelerate ordinary citizens' contributions to parties, the bill proposed that 30 percent of political donations to parties or party branches should be deducted directly from income taxes. The bill would increase the amount of fines by up to three times. The bill also defines that those who are sentenced to imprisonment shall have their civil rights suspended for up to five years

TABLE 5 Results of General Election of the House of Representatives: July 18, 1993

Party	Seats Won	Pre-Election Strength	Candidates
Liberal Democratic	223	227	285
Socialist Democratic	70	135	142
Japan Renewal	55	36	69
Komei Religious	51	45	54
Japan New Party	35	0	57
Japan Communist Party	15	16	129
Democratic Socialist	15	13	28
Sakigake New Party	13	10	16
United Socialist Democratic	4	4	4
Others	0	2	62
Independents	30	9	102
Total	511	497	955

Source: *Mainichi Daily News*, July 20, 1993.

after their release. This suspension of the civil rights would be implemented even if it is their secretaries who are sentenced to imprisonment.

The bill introduced direct public financing of a party's activities by providing them with public money in accordance with the number of votes won in the election. Those parties which have more than five members of the national Diet, in either the Upper or Lower House, and those parties which have at least one member of the National Diet and acquire more than 3 percent of the total votes in the last election, can enjoy public financing of party activities. The total amount of public financing would reach 41.4 million yen a year, equaling 335 yen per citizen.

On November 18, 1993, the bill was passed by the House of Representatives with some modifications, such as the allocation of seats in the single-member constituency system (274 seats) and in the proportional representation system (226 seats).[29]

Politicians seem more enthusiastic in discussing changes to the electoral system while the electorate seems more interested in strengthening regulations on political fund raising. Yet while the bill seems to tighten these regulations, it has many loopholes. A close examination of the bill, for example, reveals that politicians can freely accept political donations from private enterprises by utilizing party branches as reception windows. Even if the total amount of the donation from a private enterprise to a party branch is limited to 1.5 million yen per year, a party can receive almost limitless amounts of donations by establishing branches of various kinds, such as a Youth Branch, or a Womens' Branch. As the size of constituencies become smaller, the introduction of the single-member constituency system may worsen the funding situation, because the effect of money in acquiring votes in the smaller constituencies may increase. Only improved education of the Japanese public and a highly developed mass media in Japan can be expected to improve Japanese politics.

Conclusion

On January 29, 1994, Political Reform Bills which had occupied the Japanese political arena for the past six years were finally passed through both Houses of the National Diet on the basis of the last minute agreement achieved one day before the end of the session between Kono, president of the Liberal Democratic Party, and Prime Minister Morihior Hosokawa, the leader of the eight parties' coalition government, in the presence of Ichiro Ozawa, Secretary General of Japan Renewal Party (the group split from the LDP) as an observer.

Kono and the Liberal Democratic Party believe that they can recover the ruling position by introducing a single member constituency system because they have the highest ratio of the party support almost all over Japan; Ozawa, the real initiator of the coalition government, believe that he and his party can grasp the hegemony of Japanese politics in the future by introducing a single member constituency system and by establishing a new two-party system of the LDP and the Japan Renewal Party. Prime Minister Hosokawa might consider whether he will be able to retain unity of the coalition government solely by introducing a single member constituency system.

According to the Political Reform Bills, the total number of seats in the House of Representatives is fixed at 500. Three hundred seats will be elected out of single member constituencies with a single ballot and simple majority. The other 200 seats will be elected by a proportional representation system using eleven large constituencies. The electorate can cast two votes, one for the individual candidate by checking the candidate's name in his local single member constituency, the other for a political party by checking the party name in the proportional representation system. The bill defines political parties as organizations: (1) which run more than thirty candidates in the election; (2) which gained more than two percent of the vote in the previous national election; or (3) which have more than five incumbent members in the National Diet.

Concerning political fund raising, the original bill tried to confine political fund raising to political parties only. The final bills, however, allow one political fund-raising organization for each member of the National Diet, which can accept political funds from one business enterprise up to 500,000 yen a year for five years starting from 1994. The upper limit of the total contribution of political funds by business enterprises remains as it was: 10 million yen per annum. Politicians have to disclose the names of individuals and companies giving more than 50,000 yen a year although the amount was 1 million yen in the old system. In the case of political parties, however, the parties have to disclose the names of the individuals and companies who give more than 50,000 yen a year, although the amount was 10,000 yen in the old system.

Concerning public financing toward parties, the upper limit of the amount of public financial help for party activities is fixed at 40 percent of the amount of the expenditure of the respective party in the previous year. The total amount of pubic financing of party activities will be about 30.9 billion yen, which is 250 yen per citizen. Parties are expected to disclose expenditure that are in excess of 50,000 yen to the Election Committees.

Notes

1. This news was first published in the evening newspaper on February 5, 1976, but was published on the second page; apparently it was not considered to be very important. The news was published at the top of the front page in the evening edition on the same day. See *Asahi Shimbun*, February 5, 1976.

Several books written in Japanese analyze the Lockheed scandal: Tokyo Shimbun Tokubetsu Hodobu, ed., "Sabakareru Shusho No Hanzai," 10 vols., November 1977-November 1981; Tetsuya Chikushi, "Sori Daijin No Hanzai, 1976, published by the Simul Press, Inc.; *"Nihon Wo Shinkan Saseta 200 Nichi,"* August 1976, published by Mainichi Shimbun.

Several books on political money are written in Japanese: Michisada Hirose, "Seiji to Kane, October 1989, published by Iwanami Pubishing Company; Tomiaka Iwai, "Seiji Shikin No Kenkyu, April 1990, published by Nihon Keizai Shimbun; Kenichi Miyamoto, ed., "Hojyokin No Seiji Keizai Gaku, September 1990, published by Asahi Shimbun; Rei Shiratori, ed., "Seiji No Keizai Gaku," May 1982, published by Diamond Publishing Company.

Concerning political scandals in Japan since the end of World War II, see Tetsuro Murobushi, "Sengo Gigoku, February 1968, published by the Ushio Publishing Company; Yomiuri Shimbun, ed., "Gigoku (Political Scandals)," August 1976, published by Mikasa Publishing Company.

2. *Japan Echo*, Vol. III, no. 2, 1976, p. 30.

3. Sentence declared by Judge Takdo Naito at Tokyo High Court on July 29, 1987. See *Yomiuri Shimbun*, July 29, 1987.

4. See *Asahi Shimbun*, June 18, 1988.

5. See *Asahi Shimbun*, July 7, 1988, and *Mainichi Shimbun*, July 6, 1988. A list of the politicians who were involved in Recruit Scandal was published by *Asahi Shimbun*, July 11, 1988.

6. Answer by Prime Minister Noburo Takeshita to Chairman Takoko Doi of Shakaito (Social Democratic Party) on August 1, 1988, in the House of Representatives.

7. See *Mainichi Shimbun*, February 15, 1989.

8. See Tetsuro Morobushi, "Sengo Gigoku (Political Scandal Since the end of World War II)," February 1968, published by Ushio Publishing Company, pp. 105-132.

9. Ibid, pp. 133-174. See also Rei Shiratori, ed., "Nihon No Naikaku (History of Japanese Cabinets)," vol. 2, June 1981, and vol. 3, July 1981, published by Shin Hyoron Publishing Company.

10. See the author's "Tanaka Sosenkyo Kara Ran Renritsu He (From Tanaka Election to Confused Coalition)," in Rei Shiratori, ed., *Ran Renritsu No Jidai* (The Age of Confused Coalition), April 1984, published by Ashi Shobo Publishing Company, pp. 9-34.

11. See *Kampo*, September 4, 1987.

12. Ibid.

13. See *Mainichi Shimbun*, September 4, 1987.

14. See *Asahi Shimbun*, September 4, 1987.

15. See *Mainichi Shimbun*, September 4, 1987.

16. Ibid.

17. Seijo Shikin Kisei Ho (Political Fund Control Law) was first published and enacted on July 29, 1948. It was revised, however, after the Lockheed Scandal. The new Law was enacted January 1, 1976.

18. Ibid, Chapter 5, Article 22.

19. Ibid, Chapter 5, Article 22-2.

20. See *Nihon Keizai Shimbun*, June 10, 1988. Also see *Maicichi Shimbun*, June 29, 1988.

21. See *Tokyo Shimbun*, June 11, 1988, and June 28, 1988. Also see *Nihon Deizai Shimbun*, June 12, 1988.

22. See *Seiji Shikin Kisei Ho*, Chapter 5, Article 22-2.

23. See *Mainichi Shimbun*, June 29, 1988.

24. See *Yomiuri Shimbun*, August 28. The whole text of Shin Kanemaru's press conference was published in *Tokyo Shimbun*, August 28, 1992.

25. The contents of the Liberal Democratic Party's "Political Reform Bills" was published in *Yomiuri Shimbun*, April 1, 1993. Shakaito (Social Democratic Party), Komeito (Komei Religious Party) and Minshato (Democratic Socialist Party) proposed a proportional representation system with single membered constituencies, which is similar to the German system.

26. See *Nihon Keizai Shimbun*, December 25, 1992. Also see Rei Shiratori, "Japan: in *Political Data Yearbook*, in *European Journal of Political Research*, vol. 24, no. 4, December 1993.

27. See the author's "Politicians Put Power Ahead of Ideology," in *The Nikki Weekly*, July 26, 1993.

28. Concerning the contents of the Political Reform Bills, see *Tokyo Shimbun*, October 14, 1993. The Political Reform Bills consist of four bills: (1) Revision of Public Office Election Law; (2) Revision of Political Fund Control Law; (3) New bill of Financial Assistance of Political Parties; and (4) Bill of the Establishment of the Demarcation Committee of the House of Representatives.

29. See *Tokyo Shimbun*, November 19, 1993.

Index